Following Norberg-Schulz

An Architectural History through the Essay Film

ANNA ULRIKKE ANDERSEN

BLOOMSBURY VISUAL ARTS
LONDON • NEW YORK • OXFORD • NEW DELHI • SYDNEY

BLOOMSBURY VISUAL ARTS
Bloomsbury Publishing Plc
50 Bedford Square, London, WC1B 3DP, UK
1385 Broadway, New York, NY 10018, USA
29 Earlsfort Terrace, Dublin 2, Ireland

BLOOMSBURY, BLOOMSBURY VISUAL ARTS and the Diana logo are trademarks of
Bloomsbury Publishing Plc

First published in Great Britain 2022
Paperback edition published 2023

Copyright © Anna Ulrikke Andersen, 2023

Anna Ulrikke Andersen has asserted her right under the Copyright, Designs and Patents Act, 1988,
to be identified as Author of this work.

For legal purposes the Acknowledgements on p. xiii constitute an extension of this copyright page.

Cover design by Eleanor Rose
Cover photograph is a still from 'Livet finner sted' directed by Sven-Erik Helgesen © NRK 1992.

All rights reserved. No part of this publication may be reproduced or transmitted in any form or by any
means, electronic or mechanical, including photocopying, recording, or any information storage or
retrieval system, without prior permission in writing from the publishers.

Bloomsbury Publishing Plc does not have any control over, or responsibility for, any third-party websites
referred to or in this book. All internet addresses given in this book were correct at the time of going
to press. The author and publisher regret any inconvenience caused if addresses have changed or sites
have ceased to exist, but can accept no responsibility for any such changes.

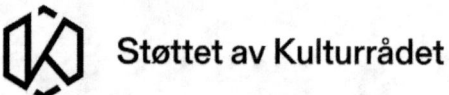

A catalogue record for this book is available from the British Library.

Library of Congress Cataloging-in-Publication Data
Names: Andersen, Anna Ulrikke, author.
Title: Following Norberg-Schulz: an architectural history through the essay film /
Anna Ulrikke Andersen.
Identifiers: LCCN 2021036114 (print) | LCCN 2021036115 (ebook) | ISBN 9781350248366 (hardback) |
ISBN 9781350248403 (paperback) | ISBN 9781350248373 (pdf) | ISBN 9781350248380 (epub) |
ISBN 9781350248397
Subjects: LCSH: Norberg-Schulz, Christian. | Architectural historians–Norway–Biography. |
Architecture–Historiography. | Experimental films–History and criticism. | Documentary films–
History and criticism.
Classification: LCC NA2599.8.N67 A53 2021 (print) | LCC NA2599.8.N67 (ebook) |
DDC 720.92 [B]–dc23
LC record available at https://lccn.loc.gov/2021036114
LC ebook record available at https://lccn.loc.gov/2021036115

ISBN: HB: 978-1-3502-4836-6
PB: 978-1-3502-4840-3
ePDF: 978-1-3502-4837-3
eBook: 978-1-3502-4838-0

Typeset by Deanta Global Publishing Services, Chennai, India

To find out more about our authors and books visit www.bloomsbury.com and
sign up for our newsletters.

Following Norberg-Schulz

til min pappa

CONTENTS

List of illustrations ix
Acknowledgements xiii
Map xvi

Framework 1
    Christian Norberg-Schulz (1926–2000) 1
    The essay form in film and writing 6
    Itinerary 9

Window 1 | Trondheim 17
    Place 17
    Practice 17
    Essay: *The sound of a windowpane shattering* 18

Window 2 | Oslo 31
    Place 31
    Practice 31
    Essay: *By the window* 31

Window 3 | Journey 49
    Place 49
    Practice 49
    Essay: *At the window of a train* 50

Window 4 | Hamburg to Basel 67
    Place 67
    Practice 67
    Essay: *Three windows on Europe, 1945* 68

Window 5 | Rome 81
    Place 81
    Practice 81
    Essay: *Fill in that window! Move into that frame!* 82

Window 6 | Piazza Navona 95
Place 95
Practice 95
Essay: *A Campari-moment by the water fountain* 96

Window 7 | Calcata 109
Place 109
Practice 109
Essay: *Are we not here to say . . . window* 110

Window 8 | Sierre 123
Place 123
Practice 123
Essay: *Les Fenêtres – en norvégien* 124

Window 9 | Oslo 137
Place 137
Practice 137
Essay: *Returned, X-rayed and exposed* 138

Window 10 | Trondheim 155
Place 155
Practice 155
Essay: *Reflections* 156

Appendix 163
Notes 170
Index 200

ILLUSTRATIONS

Map

1   Map of Europe, 2018. Designed by Essi Viitanen xvi

Figures

0.1 *Livet finner sted*, 1992. Sven-Erik Helgesen, NRK. All rights reserved 2
1.1 *The Death of the Chemist*, 2016. Anna Ulrikke Andersen 18
1.2 Plan for loftsetasjen [Plan for the attic], 12 November 1908, signed 20 May 1909. Box: PBE, Gløshaugen NTH, Tegninger fra 1905–20, 12. Trondheim Byarkiv 20
1.3 Still from *Le Baiser/The Kiss*, by Iñigo Manglano-Ovalle, 2000. 12 min 30 sec. Courtesy of the artist and Galerie Thomas Schulte, Berlin. © Iñigo Manglano-Ovalle 22
2.1 *Windows: 'My Shack of Cinema'*, 2015. Anna Ulrikke Andersen 32
2.2 Christian Norberg-Schulz's former office at Ris in Oslo, 2014. Anna Ulrikke Andersen 33
2.3 Helen Keller, typing at her desk by the window, 1929. Photograph by Alfred Tennyson Beals. Courtesy of the American Foundation for the Blind, Helen Keller Archive 35
2.4 Heidegger writing by the window in his hut in Todnautberg, 1968. By Digne Meller-Marcovisz. Courtesy of BPK Bildagentur. © bpk / Digne Meller-Marcovisz 37
2.5 The water well at Todnautberg, the windows from Heidegger's workstation in the back, 1968. By Digne Meller-Marcovisz. Courtesy of BPK Bildagentur 38
2.6 Rilke by his desk at Villa Strohl-Fern, Rome, 1903–4. Courtesy of AKG images/NTB 41
2.7 *Daguerréotypes*, 1976. Courtesy of Agnès Varda and Cine Tamaris. All rights reserved 43
2.8 *My Shack of Cinema*, 1968–2013. Photograph of installation by Agnès Varda. © 2021. Digital Image Museum Associates/LACMA/Art Resource NY/Scala, Florence 44

2.9 Twenty-two DVDs, postcards and film stock, Toute Varda – L'integrale Agnès Varda. ARTE, 2012. Photography by Anna Ulrikke Andersen, 2018. Courtesy of Agnès Varda and Cine Tamaris 45
2.10 Agnès Varda peeping through her shack of cinema, 2013. By Gary Freidman. Courtesy of Getty Images, Agnès Varda and Cine Tamaris, Los Angeles Times 45
2.11 Blackmagic Design Cinema Camera, Agnès Varda's shack of cinema and my box, 2021. Anna Ulrikke Andersen 46
2.12 'My Shack of Cinema', 2015. Anna Ulrikke Andersen 47
3.1 *Journey to Italy*, 2016. Anna Ulrikke Andersen 50
3.2 *Livet finner sted*, 1992. Sven-Erik Helgesen and NRK. All rights reserved 53
3.3 MRI scan of head, 11 April 1994. Anna Ulrikke Andersen 63
3.4 *RAPT I*, 1998. Courtesy of Justine Cooper 64
3.5 *RAPT II*, in *Probe: Explorations into Australian Computational Space*, at the Australian Embassy, Beijing, China, 1998. Courtesy of Justine Cooper 64
4.1 *Three Windows on Europe, September 1945*, 2018, by Anna Ulrikke Andersen. Archival source and date unknown. Broadcast by NRK, 1992 68
4.2 Ludwig Mies van der Rohe, The German Pavilion. Barcelona, International Exhibition, 1928–9, digital image, ©1928–9 The Museum of Modern Art/Scala, Florence. © 2021. Digital image, The Museum of Modern Art, New York/Scala, Florence 71
4.3 Hamburg, 2014. Anna Ulrikke Andersen 72
4.4 Hamburg, 2014. Anna Ulrikke Andersen 73
4.5 Unidentified woman, perhaps Edith Farnsworth, at Farnsworth House, undated, photograph. Unknown photographer. Courtesy of Newberry Library, Chicago, Illinois 74
5.1 *The Norwegian Institute in Rome*, 2016. Anna Ulrikke Andersen 82
5.2 Map of Valle Giulia, with the proposed Norwegian plot, undated, hand-drawn map. Box: 1959–2002, 003.4. Diverse, Avisklipp, Opprettelse. Istituto di Norvegia in Roma. Courtesy of the Norwegian Institute in Rome, University of Oslo 83
5.3 The Norwegian Institute in Rome, facade, 1958, architectural drawing. By Christian Norberg-Schulz. Box: 1959–2002, 003.4. Diverse, Avisklipp, Opprettelse. Istituto di Norvegia in Roma. Courtesy of the Norwegian Institute in Rome, University of Oslo 84
5.4 *The Norwegian Institute in Rome*, 2016. Anna Ulrikke Andersen 87
5.5 Socrates and Plato, thirteenth-century manuscript, by Matthew Paris (1217–59). The Bodleian Library in Oxford, MS Ashmole 304, 31v. Courtesy of the Bodleian Libraries, University of Oxford. Courtesy of Digital Bodleian, University of Oxford via Creative Commons. CC-BY-NC 4.0 89

ILLUSTRATIONS

5.6 In the archive, 2016. Anna Ulrikke Andersen 90
5.7 *The Gleaners and I*, 2000. Agnès Varda and Cine Tamaris. All rights reserved 91
6.1 *II: Campari-Moment*, 2016. Anna Ulrikke Andersen 96
6.2 Piazza Navona, 2016. Anna Ulrikke Andersen 98
6.3 Campari moment, 2014–16. Anna Ulrikke Andersen 102
6.4 *The Miracle Worker*, 1962. Arthur Penn and Playfilm Productions. All rights reserved 104
6.5 *The Miracle Worker*, 1962. Arthur Penn and Playfilm Productions. All rights reserved 105
6.6 Helen Keller, typing at her desk by the window, 1929. Photograph by Alfred Tennyson Beals. Courtesy of the American Foundation for the Blind, Helen Keller Archive 106
7.1 *Calcata*, 2017. Anna Ulrikke Andersen 110
7.2 Paolo Portoghesi suggests to leave his office, *Calcata*, 2017. Anna Ulrikke Andersen 111
7.3 Portoghesi and Norberg-Schulz eating the polenta, undated. Courtesy of Paolo Portoghesi 112
7.4 The critic's section, 1980. Venice Architecture Biennale. Courtesy of Archivio Storico della Biennale di Venezia, the Historical Archives of Contemporary Arts (ASAC), Venice 113
8.1 *Vinduene*, translation of Rainer Maria Rilke's *Les Fenêtres IV* (1927), 2017. Anna Ulrikke Andersen 124
8.2 Paolo Portoghesi and Giovanna in their garden in Calcata, undated. Courtesy of Paolo Portoghesi 125
8.3 Rainer Maria Rilke in his garden at Muzot, in Sierre, 1924. Unknown photographer. Courtesy of AKG/NTB 126
8.4 Muzot, Sierre, 2016, Anna Ulrikke Andersen 127
8.5 Paolo Portoghesi and Christian Norberg-Schulz eating polenta, undated. Courtesy of Paolo Portoghesi 135
9.1 *The Window and I*, 2015. Anna Ulrikke Andersen 138
9.2 *Livet finner sted*, 1992. Sven-Erik Helgesen and NRK. All rights reserved 140
9.3 The Farnsworth House at dusk, designed by Ludwig Mies van der Rohe, 1945–51, undated. Courtesy of The Farnsworth House, a sight of The National Trust for Historic Preservation 141
9.4 Planetveien 14, interior, still from film, 2016. Anna Ulrikke Andersen 143
9.5 'Hand mit Ringen' [Hand with Rings], Bertha Röntgen's hand, one of the first X-rays by Wilhelm Röntgen printed, 22 December 1895, printed X-ray. H MS c1 [Hawes Collection] Courtesy of Countway Medical Library, Harvard University 145
9.6 My hands X-rayed, 2014. Anna Ulrikke Andersen 146
9.7 *The Window and I*, 2015. Anna Ulrikke Andersen 146
9.8 *The Window and I*, 2015. Anna Ulrikke Andersen 147

9.9 *The Gleaners and I*, 2000. Agnes Varda and Cine Tamaris 148
9.10 Helen Keller, typing at her desk by the window, 1929. Photograph by Alfred Tennyson Beals. Courtesy of the American Foundation for the Blind, Helen Keller Archive 149
9.11 Ludwig Mies van der Rohe, 1969. Courtesy of HB-35283-Z, Chicago History Museum, Hedrich-Blessing Collection 150
9.12 *Livet finner sted*, 1992. Sven-Erik Helgesen and NRK. All rights reserved 153
10.1 Exhibition, *The Death of the Chemist*, Gamle Kjemi, 23–26 May 2016. Anna Ulrikke Andersen 156
10.2 Lecture, Kunstarken, Trondheim Academy of Fine Arts/NTNU. 2016. Ellen Martine Andersen 158
10.3 Leaflet, *The Death of the Chemist*, 2016. Anna Ulrikke Andersen 159
10.4 Passport, 1998. Anna Ulrikke Andersen 160

ACKNOWLEDGEMENTS

This book was developed, researched and written with the incredible support provided by a great number of people, who in their own special way contributed to the realization of the project. Thanks to the editor James Thompson and editorial assistant Alex Highfield for believing in the project, and the peer-reviewers for invaluable comments and suggestions. The project could not have been realized without funding from the Norwegian Arts Council, Kulturrådet.

As the book derives from my PhD research, I wish to thank my PhD supervisors Jane Rendell and Claire Thomson for their incredible support throughout the process, thoughtful comments and insightful questions. Thanks to my examiners Mari Hvattum and Elettra Carbone, who had read my thesis carefully and critically; my viva was a fruitful and thought-provoking experience, leading to vital improvement of the thesis and further reflection.

Sections of this book have been published in journals and magazines, including *Screenworks*, *InForma Journal*, *Oxford Journal of Artistic Research* and *LOBBY* magazine. The feedback I received from reviewers and editors was pivotal in shaping the book. I benefitted from presenting my work on a wide range of conferences and institutions including Oslo School of Architecture and Design, Trondheim Academy of Fine Arts/NTNU, University of Oxford, University of Gothenburg, Piloto University Colombia, Harvard BioRobotics Lab and University of Puerto Rico. A selection of my films were screened as part of the event Following Thinkers at Kunstnernes Hus, Oslo, with Ina Blom, Ingrid Dobloug Roede and d.n.rodowick, and later in 2020 at Arctic Moving Image and Film Festival, Harstad. The material formed the basis for the 'Windows', the fiftieth episode of the BBC Boring Talks, edited by Luke Doran and published 7 April 2020.

A special thanks to the Bartlett, where I thrived in the interdisciplinary, open and encouraging environment. As the founder of the Bartlett Film+Place+Architecture Doctoral network, I was able to gather a group of people with similar interest. Discussions and collaborations with Thi Phuong-Trâm Nguyen, Sander Hölsgens, Bihter Almaç, Henrietta Williams, Hannah Paveck, Anna Viola Sborgi, Clara Jo, Rebecca Loewen, Henry Miller and Mark Breeze were fruitful. Thanks to Jordan Rowe at UCL Urban Laboratory for great input and for initiating fruitful collaborations. Eva Sopeoglou and Quynh Vantu helped me design and make *Windows:*

'My Shack of Cinema' (2015), a box made in plywood. Thanks to the incredible cohort of PhD students at the Bartlett, who have shared their experiences and incredible work from start to finish: Amy, Ollie, Danielle, David, Stelios, Regner, Berni, Felipe, Polly, Katie, Quynh, Roo, Thandi, Claire, Huda, Claudio, Natalia, Sol, Judit, Merijn, Yota and Colin.

I also wish to thank Adrian Forty, Barbara Penner and Penelope Haralambidou for providing me with vital input at different stages of the project, D. N. Rodowick and Kari Hoel for championing my work, and Léa-Catherine Szacka and Mari Lending for advice and help. Thank you Hannah Kanter for invaluable support in the process. As a 2018/2019 Fellow at Harvard Film Study Center, I particularly benefitted from discussions with Alen Agaronov, Kathryn Abarbanel, Katarina Burin, Lucien Castaing-Taylor, Peter Gallison and Christian Struck, and the 2018/2019 Harvard Film Study Center and Critical Media Practice cohort. The manuscript was completed during a visiting scholarship at the Department of German, Russian and East European Studies at Vanderbilt University, Nashville. Discussing the project with Lutz Koepnick, Meike Werner, Christoph Zeller, Wout Cornelissen, Alexander Lambrow, Hanno Berger and Heidi Grek was both invaluable and refreshing.

Thanks to Per Stenseth and Markus Linge at SG arkitekter for believing in my project and offering their kind support; the Norwegian Institute in Rome for offering me funding and support, and the Danish Cultural Fund for a residency at Can Lis, Majorca.

Thanks to Manuela Michelloni and Mona Johansen at the Norwegian Institute in Rome, Ole Gaudernack and Bente Solbakken at the Architectural Collections, the National Museum of Art, Architecture and Design, Egil Rasmussen at Trondheim City Archive and the Norwegian National Library in Oslo and Mo i Rana.

Thanks to Thi Puong-Trâm Nguyen, Claire Tunacliffe, Davide Spina, Kimon Krenz, Christian Struck, Claudio Leoni, Gregorio Astengo and Ian Giles for help and advice with translation.

I wish to thank Anna Maria Norberg-Schulz, Else L'Orange, Jan Digerund, Paolo Portoghesi, Thomas Thiis-Evensen, Einar Petterson and Kari Greve for interviews, Sven-Erik Helgesen for answering my multiple phone calls with enthusiasm and Maria Ercadi with the help along the way. Thanks to Stig Pallesen and Raymond Sterten for allowing me access to the buildings at Gløshaugen Trondheim, Morten Bryde at Oslo by Steinerskole for access and Anna Fryxelius, Kristin K. Urrang from NRF and Harald Johan Halvorsen at Reuma-Sol. Thanks to Hilde and Lars Mortvedt, Sven Weidemann, Vegard Sundsbø Brynildsen, Hilde Kristin Mundheim, Anna Maija and Øyvind Isachsen for letting me into their homes: all designed or inhabited by Norberg-Schulz.

I wish to thank Arnt Edvin Andersen (1957–2021) and MEDvin Ultralyd for allowing me to experiment with medical imaging technologies: MRI, X-ray and ultrasound. Jostein Gleiditch at Sykehuset Østfold offered important feedback at the final stage of the thesis.

Thanks to my wonderful friends Robert, Åshild, Andrea, Lars Ole, Ingeborg, Lars Ole, Jørgen and Julie, who have followed the project from start to finish. Thanks to Helga, Tomm, Siggi, Jon, Anne, Christian, Anne-Silje, Mikkel, Magnus, Morten, Helga, Marius, John-Arild, Andreas and Håvard for valuable distractions.

I wish to thank my family for always showing their support and enthusiasm for my projects: Arnt, Marianne, Hedvig, Gaute, Martine, Tilde and Maja. Thanks are due to Edmund Günter Pechtel (1930–2016) for being my harshest critic, for keeping me on my toes and for introducing me to the German language and culture. And finally, and above all, thank you, Mikkel, for your support and for standing patiently by my side from the initial stage of proposal writing through fieldwork, writing and publishing.

MAP 1 Map of Europe, 2018. Designed by Essi Viitanen.

Framework

Christian Norberg-Schulz (1926–2000)

Christian Norberg-Schulz is standing by the window of a train moving quickly through a densely forested landscape. Looking out of the window, the architectural theorist recalls a moment many years prior when he returned to Norway after a year spent in Italy. Suddenly, he is hit by a familiar feeling: 'This, I know! This is part of me!',[1] he exclaims (Figure 0.1).

Described here is the opening scene of the film *Livet finner sted* (1992), a film concerned with the life and work of the Norwegian architectural theorist Thorvald Christian Norberg-Schulz. The film was directed by Sven-Erik Helgesen, co-written with the architect and architectural historian Ulf Grønvold and produced by the NRK (the Norwegian Broadcasting Corporation). Norberg-Schulz himself contributed to the production and appeared before the camera. The film was broadcast on TV once, on 7 October 1992, before being stored in the NRK archive, where it remained and became undiscussed by scholars to date.

I first encountered this film in 2013, having been made aware of its existence in a bibliography from 1996.[2] I had wanted to watch the film for some time, and I eventually found the film in the NRK archive and booked a session to watch it in one of the viewing rooms at the National Library in Oslo. At that point, I had already been following Norberg-Schulz for years, studying his books, articles, archive, designs and biography. But I had never met the theorist in person. When he died in the year 2000, my research into his life and work had not yet begun. My encounters with him had taken place in archives and library reading rooms. Then, in 2013, I could, for the very first time, see him move and hear the sound of his voice. Upon my request the film was made available on the NRK's online player in early 2014, now available for all to watch in its original Norwegian language.[3]

And it was particularly the opening scene of *Livet finner sted* that intrigued me. Framed by the camera, the theorist re-enacts a journey from Italy he took many years prior, pinpointing the window of a train as the precise location where his thinking took place. I made a note of this, and these

FIGURE 0.1 *Livet finner sted*, 1992. Sven-Erik Helgesen, NRK. All rights reserved.

observations from the National Library in 2013 eventually determined the approach of this book. It defined how I came to ask what role the window played in the life and work of Norberg-Schulz, why I became interested in looking more closely at his extensive travelling and how I saw the potential of film-making and re-enactment as tools for architectural history. In this book, I use these tools to engage with the window of Norberg-Schulz's life and work, and consider my own position as a follower, as someone who is coming after and watching him on film years after his death. I see these key themes as epitomized in the opening scene of *Livet finner sted*.

I come after Norberg-Schulz in a literal sense. He was born in 1926, and when he died in 2000, I was about to turn twelve years old and had no understanding of architecture or its history. A couple of generations separate the reality of my childhood from his. He grew up with his mother Lalla in Munchs gate, central Oslo. As a young man, Norberg-Schulz contemplated pursuing a career in music, and he was a talented pianist, but eventually decided on architecture as a career path. In 1945, he became part of a programme that educated architects in Zürich, where he graduated in 1949. After this, he worked as an architect in Oslo and designed a few buildings in Italy, but he is above all known for his architectural theory.

From his first article published in 1951,[4] Norberg-Schulz's oeuvre of books and articles is extensive. His breakthrough as a theorist came with

Intentions in Architecture (1963). Originally his PhD thesis, written at the Norges Tekniske Høiskole (the Norwegian Technical University) in Trondheim, the book offers a theory of architecture which involves a human aspect, looking at 'the relationship between buildings and those who use them, that is the prerequisites and effects of architecture'.[5] To address this theme, Norberg-Schulz turns to the field of Gestalt psychology, urging the architect to 'learn to see, [which] above all means to acquire schemata which allow an adequate intentional depth'.[6]

Norberg-Schulz builds this theory of architecture on the Gestalt psychologists Jean Piaget and Rudolf Arnheim, whose work is concerned with how 'schemata', or patterns, create a meaningful whole in our psyche. The general similarities between objects form in the child's mind and create meaning. Such schemata could be proximity, enclosure and continuity.[7] Piaget sees schemata to form in early childhood and not as a result of intellectual abstractions. Arnheim argues that specific lines and shapes respond to specific emotional states.[8] To Norberg-Schulz, understanding the way these shapes relate to emotions could be a tool for architects. He writes: 'The Gestalt psychologists were the first to stress that we experience the environment as consisting of objects or "wholes"',[9] which he suggests is what the architect should do in their design process. We must understand the intentions in architecture, and how architecture fits into a whole, in order to create a meaningful built environment.

From this initial theoretical work, Norberg-Schulz continued his quest to understand how architecture becomes meaningful, how design fits into a whole and how our built environment affects human beings, in order to form a theory of architecture, discussed in books such as *Existence, Space, Architecture* (1971).[10] But it is with his landmark treatise *Genius Loci: Towards a Phenomenology of Architecture* (1980) that he infamously turns to the philosophy of Martin Heidegger for a theoretical framework. In this book, initially published in Italian the year before,[11] Norberg-Schulz builds upon Heidegger's understanding of *Dasein*, *being-in-the-world*, to explain how our being is formed in relation to a surrounding world. Here, he discusses the phenomenon of place, which he defines through its character, structure and spirit, and argues that the architect should take the *genius loci* into the design process. Vital to his thesis is the concept of dwelling: that certain architecture allows for meaningful dwelling and other buildings do not. 'The place is a concrete manifestation of man's dwelling, and his identity depends on his belonging to places.'[12] Thus, it is vital for the architect to design in a way that manifests dwelling, and Norberg-Schulz makes his argument with three case studies: Prague, Karthoum and Rome. Here, he outlines how each place and their architecture express a *genius loci*, a spirit of the place. The character, structure and spirit of these cities are specific to the place in question and offer examples of architecture which allow for dwelling.

Norberg-Schulz was concerned about what he saw as a loss of place in contemporary society. He writes: 'The qualities which traditionally distinguished human settlements have been corrupted or have got irreparably lost. Reconstructed or new towns also look very different from the places of the past.'[13] To avoid this problem of place being lost, Norberg-Schulz urges the architect to recover place. The recovery of place can be accomplished through an understanding of what place is, where Norberg-Schulz's theory of place – following Heidegger – proposes a 'comprehensive conception of the relationship between man and his environment'.[14] Such a comprehensive conception can be accomplished by experiencing place. As he proposes: 'this direction is not dictated by politics or science, but is existentially rooted in our everyday lifeworld. Its aim is to free us from abstractions and alienation, and bring us back to things.'[15] To bring us back to things, Norberg-Schulz advocates for art and experience to be brought into education and for students to understand how place gives us identity.[16] A shorter and more accessible version of *Genius Loci* was published in Norwegian two years prior. *Mellom jord og himmel: en bok om steder og hus* (1978) links Norberg-Schulz's theory of place and phenomenology of architecture to a Norwegian reality, using local examples.[17] The books Norberg-Schulz published after *Genius Loci* continue addressing the importance of dwelling and place when designing architecture, such as *The Concept of Dwelling: On the Way to Figurative Architecture* (1985) or *Stedskunst* (1996).[18] He also applied his theory to studies of the architectural history of specific regions, such as *Modern Norwegian Architecture* (1986) and *Nightlands: Nordic Building* (1997).[19] Two collections of essays, *Øye og hånd* (1997) and *Et sted å være* (1986), contain more personal accounts and experiences of architecture, place and dwelling.[20]

A substantial focus of existing research on Norberg-Schulz's theoretical work revolves around his concept of place, the relation of his ideas to the phenomenology of Heidegger and the latter's importance for architecture.[21] The 2009 publication *An Eye for Place: Christian Norberg-Schulz: Architect, Historian and Editor* evolved from a conference and stands as the most comprehensive publication presenting the variety of international research on Norberg-Schulz.[22] This conference included a paper by Jorge Otero-Pailos, who with his book *Architecture's Historical Turn: Phenomenology and the Rise of the Postmodern* (2010) secured Norberg-Schulz a pivotal place within postmodern architectural culture.[23] Recent publications show his relevance to architects and historians today, bringing his work into the twenty-first century. Hendrik Auret's *Christian Norberg-Schulz's Interpretation of Heidegger's Philosophy: Care, Place and Architecture* (2018) brings the notion of care into the debate, whereas Gro Lauvland's (ed.) *Fellesskapets Arkitektur – opprør! Christian Norberg-Schulz som arkitekt og stedstenker* (2020) invites contemporary architects to reflect on their own practice in light of Norberg-Schulz's theoretical oeuvre.[24] A few scholars have delved into Norberg-Schulz's biography, linking the theorist's thinking of 'life taking place' with the life of the scholar himself. But these accounts are often short and/or not available in English.[25] This book makes some of this information available in English for the first time, where interviews, archival research and a close look at the film *Livet finner sted* bring new aspects of Norberg-Schulz's life and work into the light.

But while Norberg-Schulz is considered to be one of the most influential architectural thinkers of the 1960s and 1970s,[26] and still today is being taught at many architecture schools around the globe, his authorship has also suffered harsh critique. He is described as a 'traditionalist'[27] and a theorist worthy of question due to his emphasis on rootedness over rootlessness.[28] Scholars have been critical of the close connection Norberg-Schulz has made between identity and place, linking this *blut und boden* rhetoric to that of Nazi ideology.[29] For instance, Alberto Pérez-Gómez outlines generalization of experience in Norberg-Schulz's thinking, advocating a more nuanced conception of place. Drawing attention to the way, '*Genius loci* cannot be objectified through descriptive texts and photography',[30] Pérez-Gómez argues. Also, Norberg-Schulz's use of photography and other historical evidence has been critiqued as being ahistorical, alongside the theorist's use of prose and tone contributing to his writings being dismissed as romantic nostalgia.[31]

Others have been concerned with his interpretation – or misinterpretation – of Heidegger, where terms and concepts in philosophy have been taken out of its context to further an architectural agenda.[32] Eli Haddad offers a critical evaluation of Norberg-Schulz's phenomenology of architecture and his take on modernity.[33] Haddad provides an overview of Norberg-Schulz's theoretical authorship and argues how 'Norberg-Schulz did not propose anything beyond a synthesis of these various concepts from structuralism to phenomenology into yet another work that attempts to give a "comprehensive" account of architecture from all periods and regions'.[34] As such, Haddad is critical to Norberg-Schulz's theoretical project and sees it as a naïve misreading of Heidegger's phenomenology, where certain key terms from Heidegger is brought into architectural contexts unsuccessfully.

According to Rowan Wilken, the criticisms Norberg-Schulz has received have been quite persistent since the 1980s. Wilken describes Norberg-Schulz's authorship as a 'cautionary tale concerning the difficulties and potential pitfalls associated with the incorporation of theory into architecture'.[35] Wilken is critical of Norberg-Schulz's work but simultaneously underscores how the persistent critique aimed towards Norberg-Schulz signals not only the theorist's faults but also his relevance. If Norberg-Schulz's ideas were irrelevant to architectural culture, Wilken argues that critics would not have bothered addressing his work again and again, decade after decade. He acknowledges that there are critical aspects of Norberg-Schulz's work but remains enthusiastic about the phenomenological project, urging scholars to find 'alternative paths',[36] using new digital technologies. An interesting contribution to this discourse comes from Auret, who in his book rethinks Norberg-Schulz's theory of place by focusing on the concept of care. While acknowledging the potential pitfalls of Norberg-Schulz's thinking, Auret delves right into these potentially problematic aspects of Norberg-Schulz's work, arguing that the notion of care solves many of the issues brought forth by critics.[37]

I share Wilken's take of Norberg-Schulz's persistent critics and embrace his argument that critique is a sign of relevance. As Wilken, I refuse to dismiss Norberg-Schulz completely but instead following his encouragement to engage with the theorist's thinking in new ways. Through my earlier work, I have used different approaches and methods to rethink Norberg-Schulz. In the films *The Spirit of the [Natural] Place* (2013) and *The Spirit of the [Natural] Place: Commentary* (2013), I address the problematic aspects of Norberg-Schulz's notion of natural place through film-making and modelmaking, where I explore the framing features of a window and those involved in film-making as a tool for critical inquiry.[38] In the article 'Translation in the Architectural Phenomenology of Christian Norberg-Schulz' (2018), I adopt a theoretical framework from translation studies, which opens up for a more complex and mobile understanding of Norberg-Schulz's notion of place.[39] In my current work, I adopt these interdisciplinary and practice-led approaches as I continue my critical investigation of Norberg-Schulz's life and work, with a specific focus on windows. What remains a pivotal question in my work is how I position myself within the existing discourse on Norberg-Schulz's oeuvre, among Wilken, Auret and others. Fuelled by a genuine interest and admiration for the theorist, I am simultaneously drawn towards the critics. How, and where, should I encounter his work?

According to architectural theorist Jane Rendell, the spaces where encounters with works take place, and the way we talk about them, are of critical potential. Coining the term 'critical spatial practice' in 2003,[40] she explores how theory tends to involve spatial concepts and explores how spatial practices negotiate theory in return. At the same time, she looks at the way critical theory offers a way to be self-reflexive and critically exposing different forms of power relations. Rendell coins the term 'critical spatial practice' to describe these projects that are both spatial and critical in the way they are made and experienced.[41] To Rendell, the way that the 'critic encounters the work influences the process of criticism'.[42] Critical spatial practices also offer a way to discuss the self and its position in the world and in relation to others. For Rendell, such practices can 'challenge criticism as a static point of view, located in the here and now'.[43] In my approach to Norberg-Schulz, I create a body of work that is a form of critical spatial practice. I write myself into the texture of this book, continually referring to feminist practices and theoretical frameworks.

The essay form in film and writing

In my choosing of using the essay form, in both film and writing, it was also the genre's critical potential and possibility to include and reflect upon the author's position that I found promising. The essay form started with the French philosopher Michel de Montaigne (1533–92), who used himself as the starting point of the inquiries of the world around him. His method of thinking about the world started with his own experience, beginning always with what he knew. Leslie Feidler describes his writing as tentative and exploratory, 'whose essential subject is always the self'[44] evident in essays such as 'On Presumptions' (1580). Here, Montaigne begins by discussing his own opinion of his self as he states: 'I think it would be very difficult to find a man who has a smaller opinion than I have of myself.'[45] But from this self-absorbed first discussion, he commonly refers to historical past and references. As a train of thought, as if thinking out loud, Montaigne goes from outlining his weaknesses to describing his strengths, before eventually making a point about the poor quality of what he describes as 'the absurd educational system'.[46] Montaigne's personal traits, experiences and anecdotes form a subtle argument that the educational system should be changed. But beyond using the self and subjective experience to discuss a larger societal issue of the educational system, the essay also functions as a way to develop the self and one's thinking about the world.

Brian Dillon argues that essayism itself is a trait of the essay. He writes: 'Not on the practice merely of the form, but an attitude to the form – to its spirit of adventure and its unfinished nature – and towards much else.'[47] As such essayism in its elusiveness is tentative and hypothetical, lacks shape and gives emphasis to the passing and ephemeral.[48] The essay engages emotions such as 'melancholy'[49] and 'anxiety'[50] but is also curious.[51] According to Dillon, essays often consist of fragments[52] and incredible detail,[53] structured around divergence.[54] But at the same time I aim towards clarity, rigour and eloquence. The essay should be written with a clarity of thought and use literary means in a rigorous way: as when he describes Elizabeth Hardwick's essay writing as full of 'vexing repetitions and sly inversions'.[55]

Since Montaigne wrote his essays in the sixteenth century, the explorative and curious genre has gained foothold among writers, thinkers and filmmakers. Theodor Adorno's 'The Essay as Form' (1984) looks at the critical potential of the essay.[56] Adorno seeks a reader who 'interprets instead of accepting what is given'[57] – that is, a critical reader. One way that the essay operates critically is in its relation and references to already existing material: fragments, references, quotes, work and ideas by others. Adorno compares the essay with a densely woven carpet, where aspects of the argument are interwoven.[58] There is a precision in this construction, to which Adorno argues Walter Benjamin to be the unsurpassed master: 'the manner of expression is to salvage the precision sacrificed when definition is omitted, without betraying the subject matter to the arbitrariness of conceptual meaning.'[59] With this Adorno underscores the importance of the arbitrariness of meaning as a key element in the essay's elusiveness, urging the essayist to utilize this strategy. References, quotes and ideas could project or produce several divergent meanings, open for interpretation and critique.

While writers have explored various ways of experimenting with form in the written essay, film-makers have similarly adopted the defining traits of the written essay, outlined earlier, to make essay films, as theorized by film scholars such as Timothy Corrigan, Laura Rascaroli and Nora M. Alter who have outlined the genre's history, key traits and film-makers.[60] With 'Der Filmessay: eine neue Form des Dokumentarfilms' ['The Film Essay: A New Form of Documentary Film'], (1940), Hans Richter first coined the term 'film essay'.[61] Richter is critical of the falseness he sees in documentary film: 'castles bathing in moonlight, romantic perspectives, idealized shots, and completely artificial people on the screen'[62] as he makes an argument that 'a post-card is not an ideal model for a documentary film'.[63] Richter asks how film could answer more complex questions, and form arguments, thoughts and even ideas comprehensible to everyone.[64]

In this book, I draw upon the essay form both in my writing and in my film-making. I build upon Rascaroli's argument that the essay form above all *thinks* in the way that it offers both framing and reframing: of personal experience, existing footage, events, objects and place.[65] The frame as a concept encompasses several meanings, ranging from physical properties of the technology to the way that frame relates to ideology and to those who frame information, views and ideas.[66] Corrigan suggests the film essay's potential for bringing together the personal and the general, where movement stands as a central trait of the essay film, particularly films that are structured around a journey. He suggests that essay films about travel, taking place in different locations and the journeys between these locations, are a way to address the thinking self also as a mobile process.[67] Self-reflection also stands as a key trait of the essay film, apparent in the work of both Corrigan and Rascaroli, among others. According to Corrigan, the essay film explores the subjective experience in a public sphere.[68] Rascaroli argues that 'authorship in the essay film is interstitial and is played in the liminal spaces between the empirical author and his or her textual figures'.[69] As such Rascaroli sees the subjective and personal in essay film as a way to approach what occurs between the author and the figures surrounding her, highlighting fissures and gaps.

'Framing', 'mobility' and 'self-reflection' remain key terms throughout this book and in my approach to Norberg-Schulz's life and work. I wish to present alternative path towards Norberg-Schulz, where new aspects of his life and work are brought into the light. First, no scholars to date have looked at the role of the window in Norberg-Schulz's life and work, and the film *Livet finner sted* has to date been undiscussed. In this book, a focus on the window opens up a discussion about the role of travel, sound and poetry in the theorist's life and work, bringing forth new-found biographical information and architectural design, and links the theorist's thinking to other historical figures such as the poet Rainer Maria Rilke or the disabled author Helen Keller. Thus, the book offers a contribution to scholarship discussing Norberg-Schulz's oeuvre while additionally asking what it means to position oneself within the existing literature.

Slowly uncovering a variety of windows in Norberg-Schulz's life and work, this book takes its reader on a journey through landscapes, buildings, histories, films, creative practices and thoughts through the essay genre in film and writing. The book is structured around a return journey between Norway and Italy and explores a series of sites and windows which I see important in the life and work of Norberg-Schulz (see Map 1). Each window begins with a short presentation of each location, followed by a practice-led project and a written essay. The reader could choose to explore the book while travelling on the proposed itinerary outlined in Table 0.1. The essays can be read in sequence, but the essays are also written so they can stand alone. Because of this, the people mentioned in the essays will always be introduced by their full name the first time mentioned in each essay, and the books referenced will first be mentioned with title and subtitle, followed by title only. Although Norberg-Schulz's landmark treatise *Genius Loci: Towards a Phenomenology of Architecture* initially was published in Italian a year before as *Genius Loci: Paesaggio Ambiente Architettura* (1979),[70] I refer to the English version of the book from 1980 throughout this book, as this is the version I have read and consulted most closely.

When this book was in peer review, one of the reviewers described the overall book as follows: 'My initial impression is that this is a weird book (which is clearly the intention of the author). The ways in which the author presents the information are unusual.' This comment is poignant in its description of my objectives, but also offers a clue to the reader of what they can expect. The essay form invites for unusual twists and turns, and the reader is left with an experience rather than facts and dates that are to be noted down and memorized. That being said: enjoy the journey.

Itinerary

Window 1 | Trondheim

On a Saturday, take the 09:45 train from Trondheim to Oslo, ideally after having visited Gamle Kjemi (1910) at Gløshaugen. Change train twice and arrive in Oslo at 17:26. On this journey, explore Window 1 | Trondheim.

This window is focused on the death of Christian Norberg-Schulz's father, who died falling through a window in February 1926, and my visit to Gamle Kjemi, Norwegian University of Science and Technology (NTNU), designed by architect Bredo Greve. The essay film *The Death of the Chemist* (2016), which I made in response to this event, utilizes a technique where sound and image are separated. The camera frames the

TABLE 0.1 **Train schedule**

Day	Places	Transportation	Time
Friday	London–Trondheim	Flight D8 2832 Norwegian, LGW–TRD	17:40–21:10
		Airport train London	
		Airport bus Trondheim	
Saturday	Trondheim–Oslo	Train D 415, Trondheim–Røros	09:45–12:10
		Train D 2384, Røros–Hamar	12:17–15:45
		Train IC 324, Hamar–Oslo	16:07–17:26
Sunday	Oslo		
Monday	Oslo–Hamburg	IC 105/R 391, Oslo–Göteborg	07:01–10:40
		R 1063, Göteborg–København	10:55–14:28
		EC 32, København–Hamburg	15:37–20:21
Tuesday	Hamburg– Basel–Zürich	ICE 75, Hamburg HBF–Basel SBB	10:24–16:54
		IC, Basel SBB–Zürich HB.	18:37–19:49
Wednesday	Zürich–Roma	EC 15, Zürich HB–Milano Centrale	09:09–12:35
		ES 9639, Milano Centrale–Roma Termini	15:00–17:55
Thursday	Piazza Navona, Roma		
Friday	Calcata–Assisi	Rental car from Termini, Almo, Enterprise, Via Giovanni Giolitti 34, Rome, 00185	10:00
Saturday	Assisi–Roma–Sierre	Return car, Almo, Enterprise, Via Giovanni Giolitti 34, Rome, 00185	16:00
		ES 9642, Roma Termini–Milano Centrale	16:00–18:55
		EC 42, Milano Centrale–Brig	19:23–21:16
		IR 1838, Brig–Sierre/Siders	21:28–21:50
Sunday	Sierre–Hamburg	IR 1813, Sierre/Siders–Visp	11:08–11:24
		IC 1068, Visp–Basel SBB	11.28–13:29
		ICE 70, Basel SBB–Hamburg Hbf	15:06–21:38

TABLE 0.1 (Continued)

Day	Places	Transportation	Time
Monday	Hamburg–Oslo	EC 31, Hamburg Hbf–København H.	07:25–12:22
		R 19156 / R 1056, København H–Göteborg Central	13:08–17:05
		IC 398/IC 13, Göteborg Central–Oslo S.	17:55–21:49
Tuesday	Oslo–Trondheim	EX 41, Oslo S–Trondheim S.	08:02–14:31
Wednesday	Trondheim–London	Airport bus Trondheim	
		D8 2833, TRD–LGW	21:50–23:25
		Airport train London	

building, while the soundtrack explores movement through the building as the caretakers and I attempt to find the exact spot where the accident took place. My essay titled 'The sound of a window pane shattering' develops notes on how the accident had no eyewitnesses, opening up a discussion regarding the importance of sound in film and architecture, including Michel Chion's work on *acousmètre* and the film *E la nave va* (1983) by Federico Fellini.[71]

Window 2 | Oslo

On Sunday, in Oslo explore Window 2 | Oslo, and visit Ris and St Olavs plass.

This window is focused on windows in places where Christian Norberg-Schulz worked, particularly his office at Ris in Oslo, depicted in *Genius Loci: Towards a Phenomenology of Architecture*. The practice-led project *Windows: 'My Shack of Cinema'* (2015) is a spatio-textual response to the essay film in general: a box that responds to the way that windows in architecture, cinema and language move between the literal and figurative, opening up a discussion regarding the window's various uses and meanings. The essay titled 'By the window' places Norberg-Schulz's workplace by the window in his house, discussed in the context of other thinkers and writers who have also made working by the window part of their practice. I discuss the window's importance in articulating a relationship with place, as seen in the work of Rainer Maria Rilke and Martin Heidegger before questioning Norberg-Schulz's own working life in relation to the home, in reference to Agnès Varda's feminist film *Daguerréotypes* (1976).[72]

Window 3 | Journey

On Monday, leave Oslo by train at 07:01 to explore Window 3 | Journey. After changing trains in Gothenburg and Copenhagen, the train will arrive in Hamburg at 20:21.

This window starts with the opening scene in the TV documentary *Livet finner sted*, where Norberg-Schulz, positioned by a window in a train travelling through Østfold, describes how he had a theoretical epiphany by the window of another train, this time upon return from Italy. The essay film *Journey to Italy* (2016) springs from fieldwork I undertook between 2014 and 2016, where I followed Norberg-Schulz's many journeys between Norway and Italy through Europe. The footage consists of shots from the window of the train moving south, edited with moving images created with magnetic resonance imaging (MRI) technology. The essay 'At the window of a train' contextualizes Norberg-Schulz's journeys in a long history of travellers before him and my practices of following and film-making through the theoretical framework provided by Giuliana Bruno's *Atlas of Emotion* (2002) and the artwork of Justine Cooper.[73]

Window 4 | Hamburg to Basel

On Tuesday, leave Hamburg and travel to Basel on the 10:24 train, and explore Window 4 | Hamburg to Basel. Walk through Basel, before taking the train to Zürich for the night.

This window is based on the journey Christian Norberg-Schulz made through Europe in 1945, where he watched the damage resulting from war through three small windows of a military car. The essay film *Three Windows on Europe: September 1945* (2018) reworks archival footage used in *Livet finner sted* and repeats the specific archival excerpt three times. My own comments appear as subtitles that reframe the footage and journey from 1945. The essay 'Three windows on Europe: September 1945' explores historiographies related to war, and the importance of site-visits and how the historian might consult photographs. A focus on Norberg-Schulz's 1945 journey and my own following are seen in the context of artist Sharon Kivland's project *Freud on Holiday* (2006) as I address the difficulties architectural historians face when attempting to write history from a fragmented source material in reference to the work of Victor Burgin.[74]

Window 5 | Rome

On Wednesday, travel from Zürich to Rome on the 09:09 train, exploring Window 5 | Rome. You will change trains in Milan, arriving in Rome at 17:55.

This window focuses on Christian Norberg-Schulz's design for the Norwegian Institute in Rome, an unrealized design in Valle Giulia from 1958, and his renovations and design for an extension to a pre-existing building at Viale Trenta Aprile, 33, 1961–2. The essay film was developed out of material taken from an interview I conducted with Else L'Orange, the daughter of the co-founder of the institute, presented as a site-visit where we move through the building. The institute's roof terrace is framed next to plans of the building's various floors, and sound and image are separated until L'Orange and I eventually move into the frame. The essay 'Fill that window! Move into that frame!' discusses Norberg-Schulz's design and the problematic design process. I consider my own presence in the frame, as a film-maker and architectural historian, in light of the way Agnès Varda situates herself in her own films.[75] I reference Jacques Derrida's *Postcards* and his discussion of what it means for one thinker to come after someone else, before reflecting upon my own position in relation to Norberg-Schulz's life and work.[76]

Window 6 | Piazza Navona

On Thursday, visit the Norwegian Institute in Rome, followed by a Campari at Piazza Navona while reading Window 6 | Piazza Navona.

This window focuses on a moment discussed in one of Norberg-Schulz's autobiographical accounts from 1999. Here, he describes having an immediate, sudden epiphany of a theory of architecture and initial interest in *genius loci*, which happened while drinking Campari at Piazza Navona in Rome after a visit to rural Viterbo. The practice-led project consists of two unedited rushes that capture me re-enacting Norberg-Schulz's 'Campari-moment'. My essay 'A Campari-moment by the water fountain' springs from Norberg-Schulz's discussion of architecture and art at the Piazza, and examines the immediacy of his experience in the context of the autobiography of Helen Keller: a figure Norberg-Schulz uses to describe how knowledge can be formed immediately.[77] Here, prompted by my re-enactment of Norberg-Schulz's Campari-moment, I explore the more problematic aspects of my following of Christian Norberg-Schulz, in reference to the critical debate concerning artist Sophie Calle's *Suite Vénitienne* and writings by Peggy Phelan in which she considers troubling aspects of re-enactment.[78]

Window 7 | Calcata

On Friday, rent a car and travel to Calcata, inaccessible by public transport. Here I suggest exploring Window 7 | Calcata.

This window begins with an interview with the Italian architect and curator Paolo Portoghesi, discussing his friendship with Norberg-Schulz and their shared interest in the poetry of Rainer Maria Rilke. The essay 'Are we not *here* to say ... window' springs from these sources and the interview with Portoghesi, which reveals the two architect's shared interest in Rilke. I go on to consider Norberg-Schulz's use of Rilke in his writings, which I consider to be substantial. I uncover the theorist's emphasis on the connection between being and *saying*, and the role of architecture and poetry in articulating an I-world-relationship. I ask how this relates to his theory of *genius loci* and a Heideggerian understanding of language. A focus is on Norberg-Schulz's design for an installation for the 1980 Venice Architectural Biennale, to which Norberg-Schulz contributed with a panorama and poem expressing his theory of *genius loci* in spatial terms.

Window 8 | Sierre

On Saturday, return to Rome and catch the 16:00 train from Rome while exploring Window 8 | Sierre. Change trains in Milano and Brig, before arriving at Sierre at 21:50. Visit Foundation Rainer Maria Rilke early on Sunday before leaving.

This window focuses on the work of Rainer Maria Rilke, particularly his writings on windows from letters and his cycle of poems *Les Fenêtres* (Rilke, 1927). The latter is written in the period after moving to Sierre, where he began writing in French and departing from his native German. The practice-led project is a translation of Rilke's *Les Fenêtres IV* (1927) into the Norwegian. The essay 'Les Fenêtres – en norvégien' outlines Rilke's specific understanding of the window: not only as a separation between inside and outside, life and death, vision and hearing, but also as creating a unity – and a frame to measure our relationship with objects and distance, as discussed by Ji-Ming Tang.[79] Considering a highly mobile understanding of the window, I ask if Norberg-Schulz adopted Rilke's windows and how this relate to current critiques of the theorist's authorship. I propose a Norwegian translation of Rilke's poem as a gesture to Norberg-Schulz.

Window 9 | Oslo

On Monday, leave Hamburg with the train departing at 07:25, arriving in Oslo at 21:49 while exploring Window 9 | Oslo.

This window focuses on Norberg-Schulz's experiences of returning to Norway after his frequent travels abroad, particularly his house at *Planetveien 14* (1952–5), where he lived briefly in 1955, newly-wed to Italian-born Anna Maria Norberg-Schulz. The essay film *The Window and I* (2015) is a self-portrait focused on three sets of windows, asking how these windows filter air, light and view, consequently affecting my body. The essay 'Returned, X-rayed and exposed' looks at the difficulties Norberg-Schulz faced when continually returning to his native Norway. I look at the expansive modernist windows in *Planetveien 14*, seen in the context of

Beatrice Colomina's work on 'X-Ray Architecture' and women's experiences of modernism as discussed by Alice T. Friedman.[80]

Window 10 | Trondheim

On Tuesday, travel by train between Oslo and Trondheim (08:02–14:31), exploring Window 10 | Trondheim.

This window returns to Trondheim, where I install the film *The Death of the Chemist* into the staircase where I believe Norberg-Schulz's father fell through a window and died in 1926. The essay 'Reflections' functions as a coda and conclusion to the book. After ten windows into the life and work of Norberg-Schulz have been presented to the reader, the coda draws attention to the theorist as a figure whose life and work could be understood as resulting in a paradox. I position myself within a landscape of existing scholarship and aim to open up for a more nuanced discussion of Norberg-Schulz. The essay form in film and writing is highlighted as particularly helpful when tackling these themes of mobility, framing and self-reflection, before offering a concluding remark on the relevance of Norberg-Schulz for architecture today.

Window 1

Trondheim

Place

Trondheim, Norway
Latitude: 63.44.6827
Longitude: 10.421906
Language: Norwegian Bokmål (Vindu), Norwegian Nynorsk (Vindauge)

Practice

The Death of the Chemist
Anna Ulrikke Andersen
2016
HD video
13:50
QR1: Norwegian with English subtitles: https://vimeo.com/267983344

QR2: Norwegian: https://vimeo.com/530969056

Featuring: Stig Pallesen and Raymond Sterten.

FIGURE 1.1 *The Death of the Chemist*, 2016. Anna Ulrikke Andersen.

The Death of the Chemist (2016) is an essay film based around a visit to Gamle Kjemi and Hovedbygningen, NTNU (1910), by the caretakers Stig Pallesen and Raymond Sterten and me. Gamle Kjemi is shot using a Blackmagic Cinema Camera, played back in 50 per cent of normal speed. The sound, recorded with two wireless Philips radio microphones connected to a Zoom H4n recorder, captures the conversation between the caretakers and me, exploring the buildings and archival material. Sound and image are separated throughout the film. Language: Norwegian. Subtitles: English.

Essay

The sound of a windowpane shattering

Christian Norberg-Schulz never met his father, who died falling through a window at the age of twenty-eight. Christian Wilhelm Norberg-Schulz

(1896–1926) was a chemist, employed as a docent at the Norwegian Technical University in Trondheim. On 2 February 1926 the chemist was working at the chemistry building at the university when he went up to the rooftop to fetch snow needed for an experiment. He carried a small glass bowl usually used for this purpose, but he forgot his glasses. The nearsighted chemist must have tripped in the dark over a railing, falling through a glass construction and crashing in the floor below. No one witnessed the accident, but a group of students working nearby heard the sharp sound of glass shattering, and when they came running, they found the chemist in a horrible state. He was taken to St Olav's Hospital, but having fractured his skull, the young and promising chemist died the next morning, leaving his pregnant wife Lalla behind.[1]

As a consequence, Christian Norberg-Schulz never met his father. As an unborn child, he attended the funeral of his father in his mother's womb, from where he listened to the string quartet playing Oscar Merikanto's lullaby and the assembly singing the hymns 'Velt alle dine veier' and 'O tænk naar engang samles skal'.[2] As the coffin was lowered into the ground and covered with soil, the chemist disappeared.

'The greatest Acousmêtre is God – and even further back, for everyone of us, the Mother',[3] Michel Chion writes in his seminal work *Voix au cinema* [*The Voice of Cinema*] (1947), where he discusses the concept of *acousmêtre*. This term, according to Chion, is the definition of a sonic event in cinema, where the source of that very sound remains unknown, hidden and uncertain,[4] just like the sounds of a windowpane shattering, with no pane in sight.

Uncertainty marks the story about the death of Norberg-Schulz's father. There were no eyewitnesses to the event; students only heard the glass shattering, and those students are long dead. The existing sources reporting on the event are contradictory. Built in 1910 and designed by architect Bredo Greve, the building where Norberg-Schulz's father died was called *Chemistry* [*Kjemi*] until the department moved into a larger building designed by Pran and Torgersen architects between 1954 and 1967. The building from 1910 was renamed Gamle Kjemi, meaning 'old chemistry', and currently houses university administration. By doing some detective work when I visited the building with caretaker Stig Pallesen, I discovered that the glass construction mentioned earlier does not exist in the current building. Plans of the building kept in the Trondheim City Archive depict the changes undertaken in the intervening years: one of the plans shows a feature in the roof of the building from 1910 which could have certainly been a glass construction, more specifically a skylight (Figure 1.2). But these plans do not give any clear answer as to whether the discussed glass construction was located inside the building or was part of the roof.[5] Our closest guess for its location was a space above a staircase where we observed a new structure of plywood that might have replaced previous glass. However, an article from *Dagsposten* suggests that the chemist fell into a lab,[6] although there is no

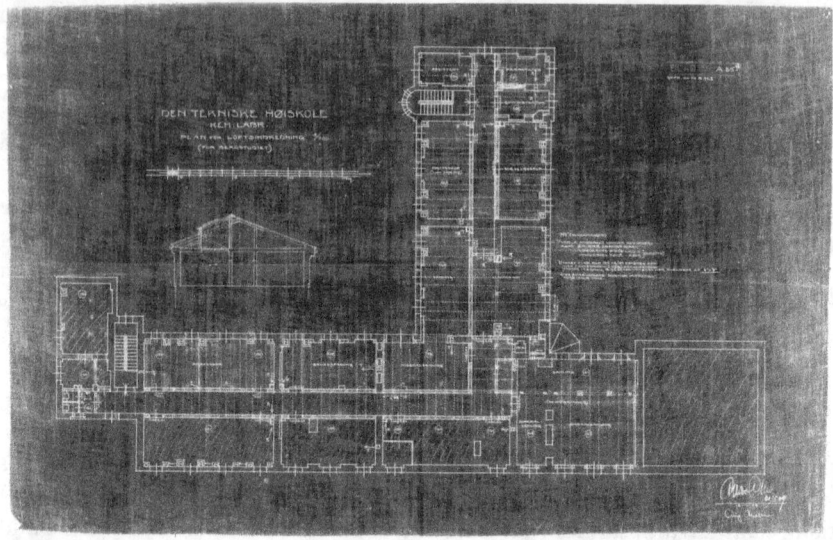

FIGURE 1.2 Plan for loftsetasjen [Plan for the attic], 12 November 1908, signed 20 May 1909. Box: PBE, Gløshaugen NTH, Tegninger fra 1905–20, 12. Trondheim Byarkiv.

lab beneath the plywood construction, only a staircase. And this staircase has always been a staircase. Attempting to situate the accident in the current building, we found ourselves making guesswork from fragmented pieces of information.

'The past carries a secret index with it, by which it is referred to its resurrection. Are we not touched by the breath of air which was among that which came before? Is there not an echo of those who have silenced in the voices to which we lend our ears today?',[7] Walter Benjamin asks in his seminal essay *Über den Begriff der Geschichte* [*Theses on the Philosophy of History*] (1940). Here, Benjamin addresses the problematics of history as a discipline aimed at addressing a past that is long gone. Only fragments remain, and it is up to the historian to interpret and frame these: to attempt what we might think of as a resurrection. On 2 February 2016, I moved through the building where the tragic accident had occurred. Ninety years too late, I listened for a windowpane shattering and a man falling to his death. It was perhaps as an attempt to capture the echo of resurrected voices silenced by history that I recorded the words and movements of myself and my companions. We walked, explored, discussed and investigated the past incident by looking at the architecture, the plans of the building and the newspaper articles together.

Although edited in post-production, our voices are played back at the same speed as they were recorded. The visual imagery of the building, *The*

Death of the Chemist, however, is not. The speed of this footage is slower than the sound: 50 per cent of normal speed. The camera located on a tripod captures a building that appears to stand still, almost a still image. But snow falls slowly from the trees; and people move past and into the building. The conversation reveals clues as to where exactly we are located. I ask Pallesen where we are; he answers that we are at the centre of the building, which draws the viewer's attention to that area of the façade. But the viewer cannot be certain of where exactly we are. Our movements through the building are not depicted visually with camera movements: instead, the clues from conversations locating us in the building or into the floorplans – like when we speak about being in room 164B – alongside the shifts occurring in acoustics covey that we are moving through the building's hallways, staircases and rooms. From one building to another, we move from the inside to the outside, to another inside.

The role of separating sound and image is one of the central features of the architectural window. When one is standing inside, one can look out, but the windowpane muffles the sounds of the outside, making the sound of the interior more noticeable. However, when the window is open, sounds from outside are let inside to fill the space. This position of the window as a threshold between inside and outside fascinated the poet Rainer Maria Rilke, who describes such a moment in his only novel *Die Aufzeichnungen des Malte Laurids Brigge* [*The Notebooks of Malte Laurids Brigge*] (1910).

In the opening sequence, the insomnia-ridden protagonist Malte is lying in the dark with his window open. As the darkness muffles his visual sense, all his attention is focused on the auditory. From his bed, he notices the noise from the streets: a screaming girl, a dog barking and a windowpane being shattered. At the same time, a sound also comes from within the house. Or was it coming from outside? Malte cannot tell for sure. As he lies there, tossing and turning in the dark, the sounds from the inside intermingle with those from the outside. No longer able to distinguish interior from exterior, he finally falls asleep by his window.[8]

A window can separate sound and image in the same way that cinematic techniques can. Iñigo Manglano-Ovalle plays with these ideas in his film *Le Baiser* [*The Kiss*] (2000), set at Ludwig Mies van der Rohe's iconic *Farnsworth House* (1945–51) (Figure 1.3) The artist plays the role of the window-washer, cleaning the large window panes of the exterior. Inside, a woman DJ plays music. As Lutz Koepnick comments:

> Whereas the window washer, as he eagerly restores the building's emphasis on breathtaking sight, appears caught up in a logic of pure and public visibility the dweller has chosen to dwell in an alternate and solipsistic universe of private sound.[9]

Jane Rendell argues that 'To focus on "listening" as an aesthetic act allows us to trace current interest in conversation and dialogue in art theory

FIGURE 1.3 Still from *Le Baiser/The Kiss*, by Iñigo Manglano-Ovalle, 2000. 12 min 30 sec. Courtesy of the artist and Galerie Thomas Schulte, Berlin. © Iñigo Manglano-Ovalle.

back in time to feminist criticism'.[10] Listening concerns the relationships between subjects. When one speaks and one listens, one is heard and the other listens. Hence, only one voice is heard. Rendell draws attention to Janet Cardiff's *The Missing Voice (Case study B)* (1999), an audio walk around Whitechapel in London. This sound recording guides the audience around in the area, telling stories about the site, the interior narrative sometimes synchronized with the exterior and sometimes not, 'highlighting our existence in a world that is simultaneously internal and external'.[11]

The viewer of *The Death of the Chemist* might have difficulties in distinguishing the different spaces of recording, as the bodies of the speakers are not visible during that thirteen-minute sequence. The missing presence of bodies connected with speech creates uncertainty for the viewer. As Mary Anne Doane argues in 'The Voice in the Cinema: The Articulation of Body and Space' (1985), a human voice is inevitably linked with a body.[12] The missing body is a fantasmatic body. This body acts as a point of identification for the viewers, even without the speaking body being visually present. The unity of sound and image produces, according to Doane, a sense of accordance and a point of identification.[13] So the intentional separation of sound and image could, on the contrary, be a form of critique. 'Sound carries with it the potential risk of exposing the material heterogeneity of the medium; attempts to contain that risk surface in the language of the ideology of organic unity',[14] she argues. The unity of sound and image suggests an organic unity which has ideological consequences. A physical and visual break between sound and image could simultaneously work towards breaking the organic unity presented to us by ideology.

Too much attention has been given to the verbal when discussing the essay film: *The Oxford Dictionary of Film* highlights voice-over and a strong authorial voice as defining features of the genre.[15] Laura Rascaroli is critical towards this emphasis in her book *How the Essay Film Thinks*

(2017), where she moves away from what she calls 'vococentricm' and focuses on the critical potential of other cinematic building blocks, such as montage, temporality and sound. She draws attention to scholars who, following Chion's writing on *acousmêtre*, have tended to think of a voice-over as coming from an extradiegetic space, a space that is outside that which is seen on screen. A voice coming from such a 'non-seen space' can more easily take on an authoritarian role and even inhabit threatening features, such as appearing didactic.[16] Instead, Rascaroli suggests that Gilles Deleuze's concept of 'sound images' is more relevant for understanding how the essay film thinks. This concept no longer places sound outside of the image but instead within it. According to Deleuze, a sound image 'is born, in its very break, from its break with the visual image',[17] which Rascaroli describes as a space in-between, rather than separated from each other. In this in-between space, something new can appear, she argues. Rascaroli also focuses on dissociation and dissonances occurring between sound and image and argues that these have the 'power to produce meaning that can contradict as well as complete verbal intelligence, contributing to the politics of the essay film a practice that unsettles the paradigm'.[18]

The making of essay films could be a way to unsettle the paradigm and offer critique. According to Rendell, engaging with sites through creative practice in a critical way can destabilize historical meanings.[19] When critical spatial practices bring new elements in a site – as during a site-visit or installation – the approach can 'draw attention to repressed aspects of the site and its history, bringing the what-has-been into direct relationship with the now, and inviting the viewer to take part in the making of a dialectical construction'.[20] Rendell's methodology of 'site-writing' offers a framework for artists and academics to engage with sites and history in a critical way.

This theoretical framework constitutes a main pillar in my approach to film-making and in the making of essay films. Through *being-there*, I situate myself within the fabric of the building and speak to the listening viewer. As an architectural historian and film-maker, I try to visually piece together a history, but my version is full of holes and gaps. Through the use of cinematic means – the slowed-down footage and the separated and edited soundtrack, I create a sense of movement through the building. Simultaneously, the film juxtaposes the visual imagery of the current building with my queries as an architectural historian when trying to find out where the accident once happened. Without attempting to arrive at a final conclusion, each reader could read the material differently.

> we have to understand that the past and history are not stitched into each other such that one and only one reading of any phenomenon is entailed, that the same object of enquiry is capable of being read differently by different discourses, whilst, integral to each, there are different readings over space and time.[21]

Keith Jenkins argues in *Re-Thinking History* (1991): Here, Jenkins sees what he considers to be past and history, as being separated. The past is gone, he argues, and history is the way we make sense of that past. As such, different people create different histories and that one might not be 'closer' to the past than the other. Instead of suggesting there is one history, there are multiple. In his postmodern historiography, the self is constructed from a series of fragments.

Jenkins's solutions for these problems arising when writing history is to approach the matter through a postmodern mindset, one that is marked by 'positive reflexive skepticism'.[22] What he understands as postmodern historiography is as follows:

> In any case, the aim here has been to help you to be reflexive; to develop a self-conscious reflexivity not only of the questions one asks and the answers one accepts, but why one asks and answers in the way one does and no other; further, of what such processes signify in terms of one's position.[23]

He urges historians to acknowledge that the past is gone and that any history that is to be written is biased, determined by the position of the historian. Historians should, therefore, approach the issue with scepticism and allow themselves to reflect on their position, considering which ideologies are at play when deciding what knowledge is and what methods to use.

Engaging with fragments could be a critical tool, and the way I play with fragments, as well as the separation of sound and image in *The Death of the Chemist*, is a way to critically engage with uncertainties and gaps, between the past and the history I write. Even the reporters writing in 1926 did not have all the details regarding the death of the chemist and had to negotiate uncertainties and gaps in the information. The account from *Dagsposten* shifts throughout the relatively short text. From reporting that the reasons for the chemist being in the attic were uncertain in one paragraph, the very next goes on to suggest that he had been there to collect snow due to the glass bowl found on the scene.[24] The reporter's lack of precision reads as an example of the precarious work of the reporter.

Orlando is the name of the reporter in Federico Fellini's *E la Nave va [... And the Ship Sails On]* (1983), a film that revolves around a cruise ship in 1914 set out to celebrate the death of a famous opera singer. The reporter Orlando is there to cover the voyage in the Adriatic Sea to scatter the opera singer's ashes on Erimo, the island where she was born. Depicting internal intrigues between the passengers and their lives on-board, their journey is interrupted as they pick a group of Serbian refugees, eventually leading to the sinking of the ship and coinciding with the breakout of the First World War.

Orlando in ... *And the Ship Sails On* is a reporter whose main task is to record what occurs, undaunted by his own puzzling question as to what exactly it is that he must report. Perhaps his portrayal reflects Fellini's own query concerning what must be filmed: events occur, and there is an observer who ought to record them, and that should suffice.[25]

As Joseph Perricone outlines earlier, Fellini's queries as a film-maker are reflected in the reporter's attitude, struggling to tackle the subjects and events at hand. Life makes its way into the film. Fellini addresses themes of death and loss through a final goodbye to a celebrated singer, but also marks the passing of his friend and year-long collaborator composer Giovanni 'Nino' Rota (1911–79). Rota had composed the music to many of Fellini's films, including *8 1/2* (1963), *Juliet of the Spirits* (1965) and *Amarcord* (1973). Theirs was a close friendship, Rota's music even being played in Fellini's funeral in 1993.[26]

Blanchard Gérard has argued that Fellini's film is a film about people who no longer exist, who have disappeared in time.[27]

> Fellini's entire film is a film about memory. It is a souvenir, retro-film *par excellence*: a homage to silent [mute] cinema. The first minutes of the film are silent. A port in Naples that had been reconstructed in Rome in a former pulp mill. The silence is the place of mystique, which was the first images that were to become cinema.[28]

On 6 October 1927 – the year after the chemist fell to his death in Trondheim – *The Jazz Singer* (1927) premiered in New York. According to Chion, this 'marked the moment when the entire previous cinema was retrospectively declared silent'.[29] New advances in technology allowed sound to be recorded and played synchronized with what was being seen on screen. *The Jazz Singer* was the very first feature-length film with a soundtrack, bringing with it a wide range of opportunities for film-makers. However, the prospects of sound film upset many of the film theorists of the era. Concerned with defining the unique qualities of the cinema, distinguished from literature, theatre or other art forms, many theorists suggested that the unique traits of cinema lay in the image and how these images were arranged and constructed.[30] Soviet film-maker and theorist Sergei Eisenstein was one of the theorists concerned about what would happen with the unique qualities of cinema when sound, speech and dialogue entered the art form. In August 1928 Eisenstein published the article 'Statement on Sound' in the *Leningrad Magazine* with his colleagues Vsevolod Pudovkin and Grigori Alexandrov. They were worried that sound could ruin the effect of visual montage and lead to commercial exploitation, only to 'satisfying simple curiosity'.[31] The theorists suggested that the use of contrapuntal sound, where the sound does not match the image, would be a way to avoid sound ruining the effect of montage and instead enrichen the expression. Written in capital letters the theorists claimed: 'THE FIRST EXPERIMENTAL WORK WITH SOUND MUST BE DIRECTED ALONG THE LINES OF ITS DISTINCT NONSYNCHRONIZATION WITH THE VISUAL IMAGES.'[32] With this strong encouragement, the theorists proposed an approach to sound in film in order to continue producing a similar effect to that of the juxtaposition of images in montage. A year later, Pudovkin wrote another article suggesting that asynchronous sound meant revealing complexity within the work.[33] In this way, sound was not a threat to the autonomy of cinema, but instead offered a new richness to the medium.

'Statement of Sound' was published on 2 September 1929, the same year that the first sound film *The Singing Fool* (1929) screened in Norway at Eldorado Kino.[34] And in Norway, the sound film brought with it a linguistic discussion. Whereas internationally produced silent films could easily be distributed in Norway, with a simple translation of the intertitles, the sound film was more challenging to translate. With a population of less than 3, 000, 000, making films specifically for the Norwegian language would be expensive, compared to the much larger English or German market. Alongside other smaller nations, such as the Netherlands and Greece, Norway and the other Nordic countries decided to translate films using subtitles rather than dubbing.[35]

The Death of the Chemist is recorded in the Norwegian language. The Norwegian-speaking audience can listen to what is being said, while their eyes rest on the slow footage of the building. The non-Norwegian speaker has a different experience. Whereas she can listen to the voices and change in acoustics and take note visually of how images shift, the precise content of the discussions and conversations is lost. I have therefore made two versions of the film: one, the original, in Norwegian and another, identical, except for the inclusion of English subtitles. In the Norwegian version, viewers can let their eyes wander across the screen while listening to the dialogue. In the English version, viewers would be preoccupied with the subtitles, allowing less attention to the visual image. With the subtitles, a new space on screen is created: a thin, transparent pane where text appears and disappears. English subtitles render the spoken word to writing, as if it was on a windowpane.

Subtitling and translating would not have been a concern – or offered the spatial potential of functioning as leaf-thin writing on windowpane – if the film had been filmed within the Italian studio tradition. Here sound was recorded separately and synchronized in post-production and so films were easily dubbed. Fellini worked within this system. Whereas the first scenes of *. . . And the Ship Sails On* were dedicated to the long-lost era of silent film, the rest of the film made a homage to sound as recorded and produced in Italian cinema. Fellini gathered 126 actors and singers from the English and Italian scene to partake in the film, constituting an elaborate example of sound and image synchronized in post-production, but not always perfectly executed.

> Speaking in a helter-skelter, post-synched Italian. There are nasty hiccups in the pacing, and the sea battle at the end with a passing warship is a jack-in-the-box fortissimo, accompanied by much 'Guerra!'-ing from Aida, that seems to have erupted from another film.[36]

As if erupting from another film, some of the actors and actresses on screen are not the sources of the voices heard in the film. The character Ines Ruffo Saltino, a jealous opera singer eager to uncover the secrets behind the fantastic voice of the deceased Edmea Tetua, is played by Linda Polan, but the singer's voice is that of Elizabeth Norberg-Schulz: Christian Norberg-Schulz's daughter.

Having grown up in Oslo, Elizabeth Norberg-Schulz moved to Rome in 1973, only fifteen years old. A year later she was accepted to the Santa-Cecilia conservatory, first as a pianist, graduating in 1978, and later as a soprano, graduating in 1982. Followed by studies in Zürich, her breakthrough as a soprano took place at the Spoleto Sperimentale in 1986. Between 1990 and 2000 she held a position at the Wien Staatsoper. Here, her 1992 performance as *Alida* in Gaetano Donizetti's opera *L'elixir d'amore*, staring alongside the Italian tenor Luciano Pavarotti, stands as the highlight of her career.[37]

The soprano shared her musical talent with her father. Before pursuing a career in architecture, Norberg-Schulz considered a career in music. In fact, music played great importance throughout his life. Norberg-Schulz's former home in *Planetveien 14* (1952–55), designed in collaboration with architect Arne Korsmo, where he moved as newly-wed in 1955, accommodated a grand piano. His wife Anna Maria Norberg-Schulz describes her husband as a talented pianist.[38] She recalls how they often invited musician-friends with whom her husband would play.[39]

Music made its way into his writing, most evidently in the article 'Frossen musikk'[40] ['Frozen Music'] (1996), dedicated to his daughter, the soprano. His exhibition design for the 1980 Venice Biennale in Architecture, consisting of a large panorama, displays the history of architecture as photographs located at different heights, resembling the notes on a five-line staff musical notation.[41] *Nightlands: Nordic Building* (1997) links the architecture of the Nordic region with music from those very countries. To Norberg-Schulz, the music of Jean Sibelius runs in tune with the landscape and building styles of Finland.[42] In *Genius Loci: Towards a Phenomenology of Architecture* (1980), a Norwegian spirit of the place is described through the sound deriving from walking on snow: 'Nordic man has to be friend with fog, ice and cold winds; he has to enjoy the creaking sound of snow under the feet when he walks around, he has to experience the poetic value of being immersed in fog.'[43] A similar statement occurs in the TV documentary *Livet finner sted* (1992): 'One cannot live in Norway without being friends with the snow, without enjoying skiing, or liking the sound of snow squeaking under one's feet.'[44]

Music – and sound – played an integral part in the life and work of Norberg-Schulz. His lecturing style was further affected by his musicality. Architectural historian Mari Hvattum, who heard him lecture many times, describes his style as unforgettable. She refers to how he would give with a nasal voice strong emphasis to certain words, stressing this emphasis with his whole body through the use of gestures. His extensive use of inverted commas and italics in his writing, Hvattum argues, recreates the way he spoke and lectured: rhythmic and accentuated.[45]

When Norberg-Schulz agreed to be involved in the TV documentary *Livet finner sted*, he could convey his lecturing style and interest in music to a larger audience. His correspondence and notes and sketches for the documentary are stored in his archive. I found there a note titled 'NRK Skisse til disposisjon' ['NRK Sketch for Disposition'] dated 28 September 1990 of particular interest. The note provides an overview of the film's structure with key themes, duration, order and soundtrack. In this note, Norberg-Schulz gives no attention to framing, camera work, montage or editing. However, he did seem to have an opinion when it came to music. Probably added to the note later, with a red pen, Norberg-Schulz suggested that music could be added as a soundtrack to the different sections and places covered in the film. In the section of the film which will be dedicated to Italy, he suggested *La serenata* and Bel Canto for music. For another sequence, which will discuss 'Nordic light, space, things and people',[46] he first suggested an organ piece by Bach or a Lied by Schumann. Later he crossed this out and instead suggested music played with the traditional Norwegian folk instrument hardingfiddle.[47] The shift is interesting. As Norberg-Schulz appears to suggest that certain music corresponds with certain places – and with this its spirit – it appears that he changed his mind when thinking about Bach and Schumann being in tune with Nordic *genius loci*. By pairing hardingfiddle music with footage from Norwegian rural areas he is making an evident link between traditional architecture and traditional music. When Norberg-Schulz applied his thinking to a TV documentary and added sound to it, he did so in a 'unified' way. He did not create a complex picture of place and sound, but rather suggested that it is all synchronized.

Norberg-Schulz's approach to film-making is, thus, radically different from my approach as a film-maker. In my work sound and image remain separated. Norberg-Schulz moved into the frame of the film with *Livet finner sted*: with his visual presence, his voice as voice-over, or speaking directly to the camera, and he made his mark on the soundtrack on the production: linking specific sounds, instruments and music with specific places. Sound played a vital role in Norberg-Schulz's life from his interest in music and attention to the sound of *genius loci*. Yet, Norberg-Schulz's cinematic soundtrack preaches the same attitude as the way that the *genius loci* does as a unified whole, as evident in his claims that Norwegians must love the sound of snow under their feet.[48] When I decide to separate sound and image in my essay film *The Death of the Chemist*, I do so as a critical tool. To underscore contradiction, uncertainty, fissure and *interstice* in my experience of place and my work as an architectural historian, and as such, I form a critique of phenomenology.

Window 2

Oslo

Place

Oslo, Norway
Latitude: 59.913869
Longitude: 10.752245
Language: Norwegian Bokmål (Vindu), Norwegian Nynorsk (Vindauge)

Practice

Windows: 'My Shack of Cinema'
Anna Ulrikke Andersen
2015
Box

This is a spatio-textual response to a set of literal and figurative windows created from plywood and Perspex. This light-box mimics my Blackmagic Cinema Camera, creating what I call a 'shack of cinema': a reference to Agnès Varda's *My Shack of Cinema* (1968–2013). The plywood was laser-cut with the help of Eva Sopeoglou, from drawings made by Quynh Vantu. The box is equipped with a battery-run light and contains pieces of writing and images and text printed on transparent sheets to be read and explored with the light-box. Language: English.

Essay

By the window

The very first photograph in Christian Norberg-Schulz's landmark treatise *Genius Loci: Towards a Phenomenology of Architecture* (1980) is that of a

FIGURE 2.1 *Windows: 'My Shack of Cinema'*, 2015. Anna Ulrikke Andersen.

window. Printed in black and white, the photograph depicts the window sills as clearly visible and the rugged panes of glass that frame a snow-covered landscape with a church. The photograph has been reprinted by multiple scholars and stands as a well-known motif of Norberg-Schulz's oeuvre.[1] Norberg-Schulz's close friend Raf de Sager stayed at the theorist's house in the 1970s.[2] It was a villa at Ris in Oslo, and the house in question was a wooden villa where Norberg-Schulz, his wife and three children moved in 1969.[3] Here, de Sager slept in the exact room where the photograph of the window was captured, and reflecting on his relationship with his late mentor, seeing that photograph brought de Sager back to conversations he had with the scholar. To him, the photograph stands as a bridge between thought and feeling.[4]

I travel to Oslo and visit the villa. With my camera I frame the window, seeking to capture Norberg-Schulz's view as depicted in his book (Figure 2.2). I have elsewhere discussed *where* Norberg-Schulz worked and wrote his book *Genius Loci*, concluding that the exact window depicted was

FIGURE 2.2 Christian Norberg-Schulz's former office at Ris in Oslo, 2014. Anna Ulrikke Andersen.

where he had his desk and office.[5] Standing in the villa with my camera in 2014, I imagine the theorist at his desk, writing, thinking and looking out the window.

When Norberg-Schulz picked up his camera and photographed the view from his workstation, he positioned himself within a long-standing tradition within the history of photography. Photography is reliant upon light, and many of the early advances in the medium took place by the window. In fact, the very first photograph by Nicéphone Niépce, *View from the Window at Le Gras* (1826 or 1827), was that of a window of his studio where the photographer worked. Karen Hellman sees the architectural window, thus, as the precondition for the photographic process. She argues that these spatial conditions of the photographer's studio further affect the way we think about the camera more symbolically. About the window she notes:

> it is the 'opening', of the 'viewfinder' through which images are seen and recorded in the camera, like the 'opening' in a wall of its ancestor, the camera obscura. As such, a photograph of a window is a representation of how a camera sees, a 'view of a view'.[6]

Alongside the reliance upon light that links the architectural window to the camera, so does the notion of framing. As the literal and architectural functions of the window have been described as providing air, light and view into the building,[7] the existing language already used to describe the architectural window influenced the way in which the camera was described from the outset. An inherent link between architecture and the medium is created with the window. The window itself becomes an intriguing and multifaceted concept, hovering between the literal and the figurative.

Anne Friedberg awards great attention to the many ways in which the architectural window links with cameras, film and screen culture. For her, the architectural window is not just a physical construct but also a widely used metaphor, which has greatly informed our screen culture of today.[8] This makes the window a quite intriguing concept to her: 'As a rhetorical trope, metaphor relies on the substitution of one thing for another, a transfer of properties from the plane of the literal to the plane of the figurative . . . we need to examine the slippage of meaning occasioned by the metaphor itself.'[9] The window as a metaphor relates then to both the literal and the figurative, and Friedberg's interest lies in the way that this creates slippages of meaning between the two.

Windows 'provide a surface or skin at which different symbolic or material worlds dynamically intermingle. They draw the viewer into what turns out to be an unpredictable and utterly unstable series of interactive exchanges and reciprocal transactions',[10] Lutz Koepnick argues in his writing on the window. The window, thus, becomes a flexible concept, something that lies in between: between language and architecture, between architecture and photography or between architecture and film.

Perhaps architectural historians have tended to treat interiors too literally, overlooking the metaphorical, as Diana Fuss argues in *The Sense of an Interior: Four Writers and the Rooms That Shaped Them* (2004).[11] Locating herself between architectural historians, on the one hand, and scholars of literature, on the other, which she understands to see interiors as subjective and figurative, she writes: 'It is by no means clear that literature is less embodied than architecture, or that architecture is less visionary than literature. Neither the materiality of writing nor the metaphysics of building can be quite so readily elided.'[12] As she moves between the literal and the figurative, she discusses the work of four selected writers and the architecture intimate to them.

One of these writers is the deaf and blind American author and lecturer Helen Keller. On a photograph, Keller is depicted writing on typewriter at a desk by a window (Figure 2.3). Behind her stands a radio. Unable to see or hear, the photograph reads as an emblem of Keller's remarkable life and how she learned to communicate with her surroundings, in spite of the challenges she faced because of her disability. Fuss describes how Keller felt 'particularly at home with these two modern machines'.[13] She could feel the vibrations of sound from her radio and had learnt how to type her thoughts and ideas on the typewriter. But I read the staging of the photograph, locating her desk by the window, as another sign of Keller overcoming the 'impossible'. Writing by the window would allow her a view of the outside world. The fact that Keller could not see appears unimportant. If she could learn how to type and enjoy the radio, why not write by the window? In

FIGURE 2.3 Helen Keller, typing at her desk by the window, 1929. Photograph by Alfred Tennyson Beals. Courtesy of the American Foundation for the Blind, Helen Keller Archive.

writing about Keller's room, Fuss asserts how 'architectural dwelling is not merely something we inhabit, but something that inhabits us'.[14]

The language used when discussing these literal and figurative windows is a spatialized language, which is the main concern for Jane Rendell in her discussion of the use of spatial metaphors of art criticism in *Site-Writing: The Architecture of Art Criticism* (2010) and in her work on architecture and psychoanalysis *The Architecture of Psychoanalysis: Spaces of Transition* (2017). Here, she refers to the work of Michael Schreyach, who in an essay 'argues that we have reached a position where self-reflective criticism is the norm and, making use of the spatial and visual term "frame" he suggests that critics are able to recognize and acknowledge the frame in which they write'.[15] Rendell builds upon Schreyach, as she turns to Sigmund Freud and his notion of framing as the setting for psychoanalysis. This setting includes the spaces, building and rooms, where therapy takes place, as well as aspects such as payment, which forms the relationship between analyst and analysed.[16] As such framing is spatial – in the way that the spatial conditions for the encounter help to construct the relationship – and social – in the way the relationships constructed are negotiated. The encounter of author and space is of great importance.

In my approach to Norberg-Schulz's windows, I adopt Rendell's interest in exploring the site where writing takes place – and her emphasis on the position of the reader and writer – and her attention to the window and the frame in this respect. In my approach to Norberg-Schulz, I consider the window as a specific site where thinking and writing take place. The window is a site for an encounter between writer and object.

In Norberg-Schulz's office the camera meets the window, photographed and let into his theoretical work.[17] Because Norberg-Schulz not only photographed his window and allowed it into his book, he also wrote about the window in *Genius Loci*, asking how this architectural feature relates to his phenomenological approach to architecture and notion of the spirit of the place. He writes:

> Among all *motifs,* the window is particularly important. It does not only express the spatial structure of the building, but also how it is related to light. And, through its proportions and detailing, it participates in the functions of standing and rising. In the window, thus, the *genius loci* is focused and 'explained'.[18]

In this passage, Norberg-Schulz draws attention to the important role the window plays in his theory of *genius loci*. Described as particularly important, the window stands as a pivotal architectural element where the spirit of the place is focused and explained. I read this claim in reference to Norberg-Schulz's argument on how certain elements in urban landscapes or architecture function as *foci* – focal points, 'which make manifest the meanings gathered by the place'.[19] By using the work 'gathering', Norberg-Schulz refers to Martin Heidegger's phenomenological understanding of being-in-the-world, where the concept of gathering is key. In his work, Heidegger aimed to understand being in relation to our surroundings, asking what the fundamental phenomena of our world are and how these are experienced. In his article 'Das Ding' ['The Thing'] (1950), he tackles the meaning of the thing, as of a simple object like a jug, and how it relates to our reality and being-in-the-world.[20] In his article 'Bauen Wohnen Denken' ['Building Dwelling Thinking'] (1954) he elaborates upon the same argument by understanding the building as a thing and describing the relationship we have with our built environment.[21] Central to both of these arguments is that the thing, whether it is a bridge, a jug or a window for that matter, relates to our world in a specific way: it *gathers*. What it gathers, Heidegger calls *the fourfold*. These are four fundamental aspects of our existence and of our world, namely the sky, the earth, divinities and the mortals. This reality must be gathered: by things or through building, dwelling and thinking. For instance, a bridge, built as a thing, relates to its surroundings by gathering the fourfold and making it tangible and understandable. The bridge gathers the two banks on each side of the river and relates to the flowing water below and the rain pouring from the sky. It allows for the godhead to be present and for mortals to cross in their everyday life. If this system of relations between the fourfold and what is built is broken or corrupted, humans would no longer find existence meaningful. They will not dwell. As such, Heidegger's phenomenology explores how the four elements of our world – the fourfold – are gathered, pulled together or focused, and become graspable and meaningful.

In Norberg-Schulz's development of Heidegger's phenomenology into the field of architecture, architecture can gather a place and allow for dwelling in a meaningful way. Norberg-Schulz suggests that the architect should be 'analyzing the functions of standing, rising and opening, it follows that the critical parts are base, roof, corner, and opening (window, door); that is the "elements" which relate the building to its environment and defines how it "is" on the earth'.[22] By experiencing and exploring openings in buildings, architects, thus, can gain a greater understanding of how we, as human beings, *are* in this world: the window gathers.

Heidegger often wrote in his hut in Todtnauberg in the Black Forest, where his desk faced two windows and overlooked a water well (Figures 2.4 and 2.5). The hut was Heidegger's escape from his life in Freiburg, and in search of a more basic lifestyle, his hut had neither water nor electricity. Water had to be acquired by the water well.

FIGURE 2.4 Heidegger writing by the window in his hut in Todnautberg, 1968. By Digne Meller-Marcovisz. Courtesy of BPK Bildagentur. © bpk / Digne Meller-Marcovisz.

FIGURE 2.5 The water well at Todnautberg, the windows from Heidegger's workstation in the back, 1968. By Digne Meller-Marcovisz. Courtesy of BPK Bildagentur.

'A split-hollowed log is fed with water from a spout in another, upright log connected to a natural spring',[23] Adam Sharr writes in reference to Digne Meller-Marcovisz's photographs taken of the philosopher in his mountain recluse. In *Heidegger's Hut* (2006) Sharr sees Heidegger's phenomenological understanding of being-in-the-world and dwelling to have been shaped by the philosopher's lifestyle in the mountains and refers to Heidegger's article 'Bauen Wohnen Denken'. The daily routine, of writing, going for walks or helping local farmers in their work, shaped a specific attention to traditional lifestyles. According to Sharr, Heidegger saw philosophy as 'no arcane bookish pursuit, but a life lived through inquiry. In this spirit, many of Heidegger's students and interpreters framed Todnautberg as the ascetic retreat of a mountain recluse'.[24] In Todnautberg, Heidegger experienced building, dwelling and thinking at first-hand by being outside fetching water or helping local farmer, or by thinking and writing by his window overlooking the water well.

The water well makes an important feature in Sharr's argument, where he links that specific water well to Heidegger's reading of Friedrich Hölderlin's poem *Der Ister*, which the philosopher discussed in detail in his article *Hölderlin's Hymne 'Der Ister'* [*Hölderlin's Hymn 'The Ister'*] (1984) first given as a lecture in 1942.[25] The poem looks at the *Ister* – the classical name for the Danube – as a source which leads to Greece, which is considered both literally and figuratively: geographically through the waters and culturally in terms of the philosophers of antiquity. Some of the waters from Todnautberg flow into Danube, and Sharr explores how the water seen from Heidegger's hut, thus, could be considered as a potential source of ancient Greece's rich philosophical tradition. He argues how 'this landscape, for Hölderlin and Heidegger, was somewhere that great things could and should take place'.[26] As Heidegger's hut overlooks the water well, the philosopher at work would literally be located at the source of knowledge and at a site where thinking takes place. This architecture 'framed its inhabitants and surroundings acutely tracing flickers of insight'.[27] Looking out of his window, and observing the water well, Heidegger's experiences are flickers of insight that the water well itself made into his philosophy.

Hendrik Andries Auret argues how 'works of architecture, as acts of precession, are not only "spatial places", but become guardians of the care of their inhabitants'.[28] Here, Auret creates a close link between the places where writing takes place and how these places are connected with that very thinking in the authorship of Norberg-Schulz. I build upon this assertion in my approach to Norberg-Schulz's window and had Auret's words in mind as I visited Norberg-Schulz's former home in Ris in September 2014. Autumn was about to set in, and as I looked out the window I imagined the view in the winter, when Ris church yet again would be covered in snow. The window before me was double glazed, appropriate to the cold Norwegian climate. When writing in the winter, Norberg-Schulz would be protected from the cold draft by two panes of glass. Comfortably warm and indoors he could watch and appreciate the snow before him.

Snow made it into his theoretical oeuvre. When describing the Norwegian weather in *Genius Loci*, he argued that the sound of snow under one's feet was vital to the Norwegian spirit of the place.[29] Snow gave Norberg-Schulz a foothold in Norway. Weather and temperature, here, are filtered and controlled by architecture and its double-glazed windows. At the window he could experience the snow and simultaneously write.

> We have to use the word 'dwelling' to indicate the total man-place relationship. To understand more fully what this distinction between 'space' and 'character'. When man dwells, he is simultaneously located in space and exposed to a certain environmental character. The two psychological functions involved may be called 'orientation' and 'identification'. To gain existential foothold man has to be able to *orientate* himself; he has to know *where* he is. But he also has to *identify* himself with the environment, that is, he had to know *how* he is a certain place.[30]

As such, Norberg-Schulz proposes that dwelling allows for identification and orientation: a correspondence between being and place. I read these windows at Ris as an example of Norberg-Schulz's claim that 'In the window, thus, the *genius loci* is "focused and explained"'.[31] If the window was where the *genius loci* was at its strongest and could be most readily articulated, the windows in Norberg-Schulz's office offered two panes of protection from the Norwegian climate, as well as offering existential foothold and dwelling. To Heidegger, the view from his window brought him closer to a traditional way of life: the origin of ancient Greece springing from a water well. To Norberg-Schulz, working at the window moulded a theory of place, focusing on the important place and architecture have in shaping our understanding of dwelling and existential foothold, focused and explained by the window.

On my visit to Ris in 2014, I had brought with me my camera and framed the view that I knew so well from that photograph on the seventh page of *Genius Loci*. But I did not get the framing exactly right. My lens, different to Norberg-Schulz's, did not replicate the same sense of distance. So, I discarded the footage and I forgot about it until I decided to make another visit, this time with headphones. I noticed something interesting. Whereas the visual imagery depicted houses, trees and Ris church, the soundtrack reminded me of what lay just outside of the frame. The sound alerted me to the fact that Norberg-Schulz's house was located right next to the train tracks of Holmenkollenbanen: a tram line connecting the city of Oslo with its surrounding woodlands. As Norberg-Schulz worked from home, he must have been repeatedly reminded by the train as it passed at regular intervals, of the city centre of Oslo and through the broader international rail network. As a chord leading from his home and his windows, this network connected him with the entire world.

The poet Rainer Maria Rilke considered working by the window as a way of tackling a struggle with an external world of ideas (Figure 2.6). A frequent traveller, the poet often mentioned windows in letters written to his friends, patrons and lovers, as quoted in Tang:

> My windows are big; I can see the park stretching, the grand sky, and therefore also great darkness. In front of one of them stands a desk. And the high desk, which I use the most, stands in the middle of the room, so that it can enjoy both windows.[32]

This letter, written on 21 January 1904, was sent to Lou Andreas-Salomé. In it, Rilke describes his workstation in great detail: how two desks are placed before two windows. By these desks and in front of these windows was where the poet worked that January day. Discussed in detail by Ji-Ming Tang, she argues that for Rilke working by the window had a particular effect on his thinking and writing.

> When I wake up in the morning, the mountains lie well rested before my open window, the room crisp, [. . .] and now I am sitting there, watching and watching until my eyes start hurting. And I show myself and tell myself, if I should learn it by heart. And yet I cannot grasp it, and then I am none to whom it does not come.[33]

FIGURE 2.6 Rilke by his desk at Villa Strohl-Fern, Rome, 1903–4. Courtesy of AKG images/NTB.

Facing trouble with his creative process, Rilke turned to the window. The quote outlines how he looked and looked until his eyes started hurting, hoping to learn from the outside. Whereas the passage earlier describes a moment when he neither learned nor prospered, looking out the window sometimes did spark his creativity. Tang calls this Rilke's *Fensterblick* – a view from the window – where looking out the window became a way for him to negotiate and struggle with the external world, still safely indoors with pen and paper at hand. According to Tang, Rilke's *Fensterblick* becomes a method to wrestle with the outside.[34] Thinking by the window, as such, suggested a sense of mobility between the thinking self that is located inside and the world of ideas and thinkers that are outside, ready to grasp by the window. Tang sees Rilke's struggle with the external world as also a main theme for his poetic authorship.[35] Rilke even wrote a cycle of ten poems dedicated to the window: *Les Fenêtres* (1927).[36]

Rilke's workstation by the window and his *Fensterblick* formed a specific space where the poet could wrestle with his difficult relationship to the world around him and result in poetry. Rilke's *Fensterblick* became a specific way to negotiate struggles with the external world, a struggle that was intellectual rather than physical. Physically, Rilke was standing still by his desk, but his thinking was constantly moving through the world.

Norberg-Schulz's windows offered foothold but at the same time linked the theorist to a larger international network. Norberg-Schulz's *Fensterblick*, shaped by the sound of the train, appears rather unrestricted.[37] Connected by the rail network, his view was full of professional potential. The Italian architect Paolo Portoghesi writes about his friend: 'As a typical exponent of international culture, this "flying Norwegian" . . . has spent a great part of his time moving between the universities of the world (showing a mobility which may be compared to that of the famous Gothic architect Villard de Honnecourt).' I see his extensive authorship is evidence of how he could travel, research, publish and lecture, and the window as an emblem of the world that was open to him.

On the contrary, Agnès Varda's film *Daguerréotypes* (1976) 'bear[s] witness to the world that is open to women, to a woman who goes shopping'.[38] The film is based around Varda's home, as she investigates a series of windows in the street where she lives, Rue Daguerre. Having just given birth to her son Mathieu, Varda could not venture far from home when she was commissioned to make a film for German TV. Fatigued from lack of sleep and her child requiring her attention, she also wanted to stay at home to enjoy her new baby. 'So I told myself that I was a good example of women's creativity – always a bit stuck and suffocated by home and motherhood. So, I wondered what could come of these constraints. Could I manage to restart my creativity from within these limitations?'[39]

Varda's limitation tool was the physical form of a long electric cord for her camera connected to a power source in her home. The chord provided electricity, making her film-making possible, but its length determined how far she could venture, so defining her limits to her neighbourhood.[40] Varda framed the shop windows of the many shops on the street, providing various services and products. She went beyond these windows and into the buildings behind, creating portraits of the people inside. The title itself plays upon the early photographic process of Niépce's partner Louis-Jaques-Mandé Daguerre (1787–1851), who was known for developing a photographic technique: the daguerreotype. The earliest reliable daguerreotype *Still life with plaster casts* (1837) depicts objects placed by the window.

Creating a series of daguerreotypes from Rue Daguerre, the early history of photography taking place by the window, lurks as an undercurrent, bringing together the figurative with the literal. Similarly, this film remained determined by her very physical eclectic cord, which she described as an umbilical cord symbolically connecting the film-maker to her child at home[41] (Figure 2.7)

Norberg-Schulz's domestic reality was rather different. As I have previously discovered, Norberg-Schulz worked from home and this made his writing more proximate to his children.[42] Yet, Norberg-Schulz could travel and nurture his international career. If he had not been a man, Norberg-

FIGURE 2.7 *Daguerréotypes*, 1976. Courtesy of Agnès Varda and Cine Tamaris. All rights reserved.

Schulz's mobility would probably have been compromised, restricted by an expectation to build a traditional home. 'If I had not met my husband and I had followed that route which I had started, I would have been a professor of American literature in Rome',[43] Anna Maria Norberg-Schulz said. But instead, she got married and followed her husband's career, as many women did.

Also Varda followed her husband Jaques Demy to California where she made a series of films, the focus of the exhibition *Agnès Varda in Californialand* at Los Angeles County Museum of Art, 2013–14. This exhibition was dedicated to her work in California, including *Documenteur* (1981) *Mur Murs* (1981) and *Lions Love . . . (and Lies)* (1967). The latter informed the centrepiece of the exhibition: an architectural structure constructed from Varda's film stock from this very film. The audience could walk into her work titled *My Shack of Cinema* (1968–2013) and move among her celluloid strips. 'If you recognize the house of a symbol of the self, then you'll get the subtle joke of Varda's film house installations', Emily Kramer writes in her review of the installation, seeing the work as both a homage to Varda's work and her 'limited desire to build a traditional home'[44] (Figure 2.8).

Varda's entire oeuvre inhabits a different structure – the box – in the DVD box set *Toute Varda – L'intégrale Agnès Varda* (2012).[45] This DVD box set consists of thirty-six films, on twenty-two DVDs, as well

FIGURE 2.8 *My Shack of Cinema*, 1968–2013. Photograph of installation by Agnès Varda. © 2021. Digital Image Museum Associates/LACMA/Art Resource NY/Scala, Florence.

as postcards, booklets, objects and a strip of film from one of her films and is a collector's item. But the box also reveals her attention to film as something moving beyond the space of the cinema, including the materiality of film itself: the celluloid stock and the postcards taking the presence of a film to be distributed, sent and received, handed over in person or sent through the post service. Just as *Daguerréotypes* exposes the constraints of a (female) film-maker where the physical frame of her film-making forms a limitation that sparks creativity and defines the film *My Shack of Cinema*, *Toute Varda* treats film as much more than a screening in the darkness of the cinema space, as she moves between literal and figurative meanings (Figure 2.9).

Varda is not an architect per se and does not explicitly refer to herself as someone who is creating space. She does, however, use a spatialized language when she talks about her work. 'I'm not behind the camera. I'm in it.'[46] There is certainly no way Varda could be inside her camera in a literal way, unless her camera was very large. Being in her camera is more figurative, reflecting the way she thinks about her work and involvement. *Tout(e) Varda* (2012) contains a series of postcards, objects and a celluloid strip of film, alongside a small booklet and the DVDs. 'All of Varda' is not just films screened but the literal and material aspects of film-making – the stock of film that one can attach to an architectural structure and move into and through (Figure 2.10).

FIGURE 2.9 Twenty-two DVDs, postcards and film stock, Toute Varda – L'integrale Agnès Varda. ARTE, 2012. Photography by Anna Ulrikke Andersen, 2018. Courtesy of Agnès Varda and Cine Tamaris.

FIGURE 2.10 Agnès Varda peeping through her shack of cinema, 2013. By Gary Freidman. Courtesy of Getty Images, Agnès Varda and Cine Tamaris, Los Angeles Times.

My own camera is heavy, but I find it suitable for the filming of windows. I decided to purchase a Blackmagic Cinema Camera due to its affordable price and great potential for reworking the digital footage in post-production. The camera can shoot in different modes, including RAW: the original bitrate, quality and size of the digital film. Using this mode, twenty-five high-resolution RAW stills are created per minute, which gives high flexibility in adjusting exposure, grading colours and manipulating the image later on. Setting out to film windows is not an easy task because the light conditions of the exterior and the interior always differ. But with this camera, as with many other much more expensive digital cameras, I can potentially capture the same scene with two different settings before combining the two in *Adobe After Effects* in post-production.

Drawing upon Rendell's interest in the position of the author, I started reflecting upon my own position as a follower of Norberg-Schulz and the

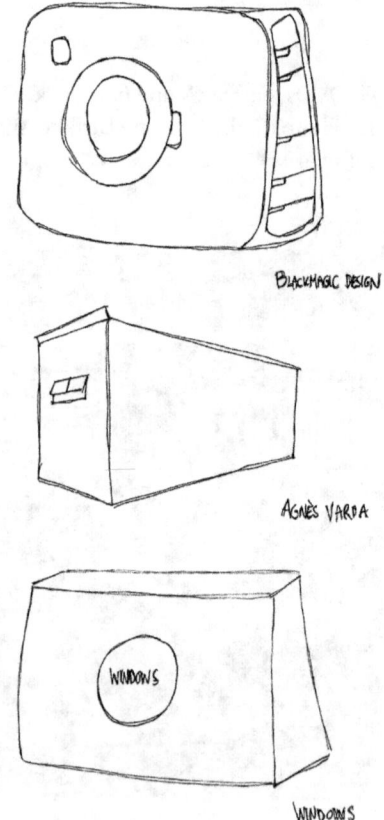

FIGURE 2.11 Blackmagic Design Cinema Camera, Agnès Varda's shack of cinema and my box, 2021. Anna Ulrikke Andersen.

FIGURE 2.12 *'My Shack of Cinema'*, 2015. Anna Ulrikke Andersen.

spatial preconditions of my engagement with his work and windows. I became attracted to the shape of my camera, which I thought resembled the form of a shack. Not too dissimilar to Varda's shack, the camera has a 'slanting roof', where one of its sides does not follow the otherwise 90-degree angles of the other sides (Figure 2.11). Where Varda's shack had windows and a door for people to walk inside, my shack has a lens and a digital screen resembling windows, and a 'door' where the SSD could be taken out to do back up and edit.

Windows: 'My Shack of Cinema' (2015) responds to these spatial qualities of my cameras and the meaning of the window as both literal and figurative as proposed by Friedberg. The box is constructed from Finish plywood, each side resembling the sides of my camera. Laser-cut and glued together, the windows of my camera are replaced with other windows. Instead of a lens I have written the word 'windows', and the digital screen is replaced with translucent Perspex. The 'shack' can be opened, large enough to contain my films and writing, in the form of a book, transparent sheets with images or text, DVDs or a USB stick. A light is attached to the lid, and when turned on the box becomes a light-box, a tool for watching the transparent sheets placed within, including Norberg-Schulz's photograph from his window at Ris, where he wrote and developed his theory of place (Figure 2.12).

Window 3

Journey

Place

Norway, Sweden, Denmark, Germany, Switzerland, Italy
Longitude: 63.446827 (Trondheim) Latitude: - 41.905777 (Rome)
Language: Norwegian (Vindu/Vindauge), Swedish (Fönster), Danish (Vindue), German (Fenster), French (Fenêtre), Italian (Finestra).

Practice

Journey to Italy
2016
Anna Ulrikke Andersen
HD video
13:42
https://vimeo.com/267985536

Springing from fieldwork where I travel by train between Norway and Italy, the film *Journey to Italy* (2016) is shot with a Blackmagic Pocket Camera equipped with a Røde Pro-Microphone. The footage shows the views from the train window shot every full hour of the journey. Sound is recorded in sync. The film includes several sequences made by using magnetic resonance imaging (MRI) technology. Language: Danish, Italian, German, Norwegian.

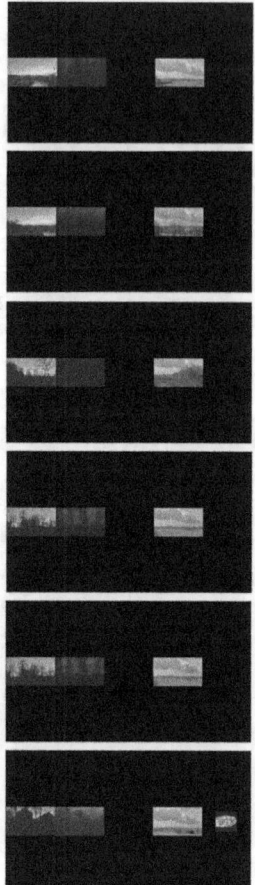

FIGURE 3.1 *Journey to Italy*, 2016. Anna Ulrikke Andersen.

Essay

At the window of a train

Giuliana Bruno returns to Naples after her father's death. Having lived and worked in New York for years, she travels back to settle his affairs.[1] In her writing, she describes how her journey reminds her of another journey to Italy similarly prompted by a death in the family. In Roberto Rosselini's *Viaggio in Italia* [*Journey to Italy*] (1954), a married, British couple named Katherine and Alex travel to Naples to settle their inheritance. Their journey to Italy – a voyage through a foreign land, landscapes and architectures – brings up questions regarding their marriage and their relationship.

There are places where one allows geography to speak history; places where one's trajectory is somehow shaped by the feelings left by the arrivals and departures of others, even imaginary – or filmic. Italy is one of them. Like Katherine, many have travelled Italy with a map that others as well have used, and have transformed themselves en route.[2]

Bruno's journey to her late father's house, moving through land, city and house, engages not only the history of lives once lived but sparks emotions related to place: 'the voyage through landscape pictures the paths of emotion.'[3] In Bruno's work, emotion and motion are inevitably linked. Her book *Atlas of Emotion: Journeys through Art, Architecture and Film* (2002) navigates the reader through a series of emotional journeys across borders and between disciplines.

* * *

If this should make good TV, and serve CNS justice, the film must depict a journey in time and space, a circle from Hjartdal to Rome, and back again to rural Norway, with its 'communal' architecture. Thus, this will be an expensive film to make.[4]

Director Sven-Erik Helgesen wrote this to the NRK in June 1990, when negotiating the budget for the film about the life and work of Christian Norberg-Schulz. The film, potentially expensive to make, was to be directed by Helgesen and co-written by Ulf Grønnvold. Norberg-Schulz was himself involved in its making and contributed to the process with text and ideas.

Helgesen had experience as a director, especially working with TV programmes about architects and architecture.[5] But the project was Norberg-Schulz's first and only attempt to use moving images to disseminate his thinking and biography to an audience. A folder titled 'NRK Livet finner sted' containing documents related to the making of the film, currently kept in the Norberg-Schulz archive in Oslo, shows the film-maker's initial ideas for the film as extensive and ambitious. The film was to be shot internationally: in a loop from Hjartdal to Rome and back again. And furthering the film-maker's ambitions, it was to cover the life and work of the architect, historian and theorist, and outline current issues concerning architecture in Norway and abroad. Norberg-Schulz's problem with contemporary cities was their lack of meaning caused by architects and planners that did not take the spirit, structure and character of place into account.[6] The film would further propose Norberg-Schulz's theory of place, as proposed in *Genius Loci: Towards a Phenomenology of Architecture* (1980) as a solution to these problems, offering a way to design that would consider the spirit of the place: *genius loci*.[7]

The archival material I consulted from the folder includes a six-page essay where Norberg-Schulz discusses the theoretical issues connected to place, carefully constructed and argued, appropriate for a written essay or a lecture.

But if this essay were to have been read out loud on film, then the content of that essay would cover over half of the duration of the film.[8] The essay appears to be written in a similar manner to how one would write for print. But film is different, as I have experienced. A film would have difficulties conveying a densely written text. As a film-maker, I would instead use both sound and image to convey a message. I could not possibly find a way to include a full essay in a way that would make sense to a general audience in forty-one minutes. Norberg-Schulz appears to be planning a lecture or a book, rather than a film. From this I infer that Norberg-Schulz was less involved in the production and planning of the film, and that Helgesen, who had experience as a film-maker, would work through Norberg-Schulz's material to appropriate it to the screen.

Developing the project would take time: no wonder Helgesen asked for a larger budget in his letter of 1990: 6000 NOK for developing the project further. Eventually, the film was shot during a three-week period in 1991.[9] *Livet finner sted* (1992) – a title which translates as 'life takes place' – was broadcast on 7 October 1992.

In the film that was broadcasted, only a few sentences from Norberg-Schulz's six-page essay have been included as a voice-over.[10] One section forms the opening scene of the film:

> When I think back, the meaning of place occurred to me many years ago. It was an early morning in the corridor of a train, heading towards Oslo, after a year spent in Italy. The forest of Østfold flew by, with its spruce trees, heather and moss. Suddenly, a strong feeling came over me: This I know. This is part of me![11]

These are the words spoken as a voice-over during the opening scene, depicting Norberg-Schulz looking out the window of a train moving quickly through a forested landscape. He recalls a moment many years prior when the meaning of place came to him as a sudden inspiration: 'This is part of me!' He exclaimed when passing through the forest of Østfold. This thinking took place at the window of a train returning from a journey to Italy (Figure 3.2).

> As a typical exponent of international culture, this 'flying Norwegian' . . . has spent a great part of his time moving between the universities of the world (showing a mobility which may be compared to that of the famous Gothic architect Villard de Honnecourt).[12]

Making a play on words from the ghost story of the *Flying Dutchman*, a ship that is doomed to sail not able to make port,[13] the Italian architect Paolo Portoghesi describes close friend Norberg-Schulz as 'flying Norwegian'. A visit to Norberg-Schulz's archive in Oslo makes the nature of his international career and extensive travelling strikingly clear. Norberg-Schulz's CV, included as an appendix, outlines his major journeys: studies in Zürich, a Fulbright scholarship for Harvard, guest-lectures at the world's leading universities and research stays in Italy, Sudan and Germany.[14] Two

FIGURE 3.2 *Livet finner sted*, 1992. Sven-Erik Helgesen and NRK. All rights reserved.

longer research-related stays in Italy are mentioned: 1956–8 and 1973–4.[15] He visited Japan with his wife Anna Maria Norberg-Schulz,[16] whom he met during his Fulbright stay in the United States, and Jordan with Portoghesi and their common friend Vittorio Gigliotti.[17] Anna Maria Norberg-Schulz was Italian, and although Norberg-Schulz had travelled to Italy already as a student in Switzerland, his first trip to Rome was in 1947,[18] and their marriage inevitably led to many more trips to Italy.

Anna Maria Norberg-Schulz recalls how they spent every summer holiday in Italy and travelled between Norway and Italy by car.[19] And when Norberg-Schulz travelled, he travelled with a purpose. The itinerary was separated into different stages, carefully planned to expose his family and himself to new architecture, towns and landscapes. I ask Anna Maria Norberg-Schulz if her husband took notes or made sketches. She responds: 'He knew everything, he knew the place. He had prepared himself.'[20] Norberg-Schulz had already read what he needed to know about the place and did not bring his notebook onsite. 'But he wanted to see. He wanted the experience of seeing. That was important. It was very important for him to go there.'[21] On the journey, he had his camera with him, capturing photographs for his books to come.[22]

Through his travels, Norberg-Schulz developed his experience of seeing and experiencing place, a road to knowledge that has a long history in European culture and the tradition of the grand tour.[23] Architectural historian Anne

Hultzsch has argued that the grand tour radically changed the way thinkers and philosophers of the time understood perception. Tracing the history of travelling thinkers, she sees travelling as forming a sense of I through the process of 'eye-witnessing', a tradition springing out of the fifteenth-century thinking of Francis Bacon, who emphasized observation and experience, and external stimuli as method for inquiry. Hultzsch describes how Bacon's suggestion of encountering the unfamiliar at first-hand and categorizing this experience became the cornerstone of empiricism, which differed from the earlier scholastic tradition, where the text itself was a road to knowledge. Through studies of text, the thinkers would arrive at a greater knowledge of a subject, opposed to travelling somewhere to explore the object or subject of study at first-hand. As Hultzsch argues, travelling in the age of the grand tour became a way to investigate the world, described and reflected upon en route or once returned.[24] The idea of the grand tour as *Bildungsreise* – an educational tour – builds upon this principle: travel, seeing, experiencing and reflecting are ways to gain knowledge of a subject. Travelling becomes a tool for thinking, and the result is a new way of seeing the world.

'Through the act of walking new connections are made and remade physically and conceptually, over time and through space',[25] Jane Rendell argues in a chapter dedicated to walking in her book *Art and Architecture: A Place Between* (2006). Here she sees walking as a way to reconfigure our relationship with the urban fabric of the city, but also to understand ourselves in space and time, which could be a critical tool.[26] As such 'walking temporarily positions the subject in motion between a series of scenes that at times might resemble dialectical images'.[27] Rendell shares her interest in walking as a critical tool and a tool for getting to grasp with our position in the world with feminist author Rebecca Solnit. In *Wanderlust: A History of Walking* (2011) she traces the history of walking, focusing on how walks can render the walking subject.[28] In *A Field Guide to Getting Lost* (2006) she gives emphasis to the importance of getting lost: when travelling in space, thinking or writing.[29] 'Leave the door open for the unknown, the door into the dark. That's where you yourself came from, and where you will go. . . . It's the job of the artist to open doors and invite in prophesies, the unknown, the unfamiliar.'[30] Travelling, walking, venturing, getting lost and moving, the unknown could be encountered and from it art can derive.

When the poet Rainer Maria Rilke was asked about what influenced him in his work, his answer included landscapes and places.[31] To encounter these landscapes and places, Rilke travelled, and Italy was a recurrent destination. *Rilke: Les jours d'Italie/Die italienishen Tage* (2009) – available only in its original dual language in German and French – shows travelling to have had a profound impact on his work.[32] Rüdiger Görner suggests that Rilke travelled to 'find the ideal conditions for writing and cultivating his oeuvre'.[33] With a similar focus on travel, Curdin Ebneter draws attention to Rilke's first Italian journey took place as a young child, accompanying his mother to a spa in Arco.³⁴ Ebneter draws attention to Rilke's stay in Duino with Fürstin Marie von Thurn und Taxis in 1911–2, where they discovered Italy by car.³⁵ Being based in Duino, this was where he started his seminal work *Duino Elegien [Duino Elegies]* (1922), only to be completed ten years later. The Italian island Capri affected, according to Jo Catling, Rilke's understanding of landscape as expression of an inner world. Evident in his letters and work from the period, his stay on the Italian island particularly moulded his attention to the sea and the sky.³⁶ He was also a great admirer of Renaissance art, prompted by a stay in Florence, discussed in Rilke's *Florenzer Tagebuch* (1942).³⁷

'I knew and loved Italy since my eight year, – distinctly multifaceted and full of form, Italy, so to say, became a textbook for my mobile being [*beweglichen Daseins*]',³⁸ Rilke wrote in a letter in 1926. Rilke's journeys formed a specific understanding of being in relation to place. First, it was through experiencing the ambiguity within Italy itself that his attention was formed towards what has been described by Ebneter as antagonistic forces relating to cultural, literary or climatic references.³⁹ Ebneter's account suggests that Rilke could only understand and grasp this idea of active resistance and opposition between two places – for example Rome versus Paris – after experiencing how such forces also come into play within one nation, and this was Italy. Ebneter sees this attention to antagonistic forces in one place, or between two, as central in Rilke's understanding of a relationship between places, but also as a way to understand the relationships between being and world. Ebneter describes Rilke's way of life – constantly travelling – as *beweglichen Daseins*: mobile dwelling. And he uses the same term to describe how Rilke understood experiences of a singular place itself as a mobile experience. Visiting Rome implied earlier journeys to Paris and an inner, mental movement between the two. Experiences of the antagonistic forces within the nation of Italy itself suggested again that dwelling was not fixed, as Ebneter argues from looking at Rilke's biography, journeys in Italy and his letters. Dwelling, according to Rilke, always had strong mobile aspects to it: *beweglichen Daseins*.⁴⁰ 'It is evident to me that Rilke's "mobile being" also involved a relationship to countries, landscapes and place as something floating and changeable',⁴¹ Ebneter argues in reference to Rilke's life on the move.

The specific way Norberg-Schulz travelled, saw, experienced and reflected is evident in his travel journal from 1973 to 1974, when he spent a year in Italy to research his next project, a stay he himself referred to as researching *genius loci*.⁴² Beginning in September 1973, this research involved journeys in the area surrounding Rome where he visited villages, such as Bracchiano, Subiaco and Assisi. Alone, or accompanied by his son Emanuel, wife or friends, he visited places, before carefully writing down ideas, experiences and impressions in his travel journal.⁴³ His destinations in and around Rome that year were many, making these excursions a central element in his approach to the research stay.⁴⁴

Norberg-Schulz's observations and experiences of the villages he visited are detailed, describing the architecture and the surrounding landscape of places he visits; he notes that each one has its unique *genius loci*. On 20 May 1974 he writes about how he understands Piazza Navona as a Tuscan valley that the *genius loci* is the same in the valley and the piazza,[45] a central idea in his chapter on Rome.[46]

On his way he photographed, later to publish these photographs in his books. When comparing the destinations of his travel journal with the illustrations of *Genius Loci* there is striking correspondence.[47] Illustration no. 39 of Subiaco corresponds with his journey on 2 October 1973, and he visited no. 238, Nordica, on 20 June 1974. Along with photographs from Khartoum, where he worked in 1975, photographs from Jordan illustrate the *genius loci* of the desert and Norberg-Schulz visited Jordan with Portoghesi on 27 July and 4 August 1974. His photographs from the United States are exclusively from Boston and Cambridge, Massachusetts, which runs on accord with his stay at MIT in 1974. Illustration no. 55, Lüneburger Heide, is described in his journal (18 August 1974) along with Einbeck, no. 317. Norberg-Schulz's specific approach to researching *genius loci* involved travel, journal writing and photography.

But with *Genius Loci*, Norberg-Schulz represented Italy with a specific objective in mind: to develop a phenomenology of architecture. Evident in his travel journal, Norberg-Schulz's experiences are often related to specific philosophical ideas: in describing his experience of Rome (9 October 1973), he quotes Edmund Husserl 'Back to the things themselves'.[48] Husserl's infamous quote is central for the field of phenomenology and phenomenologists whose aim is to focus on things and its relationships to our being, in order to understand our world.[49] The first traces of Heidegger's phenomenology occur after his stay in Boston in spring 1974, when he makes attempts to explain places he visited, such as Subiaco or Palestrina, through the Heideggerian concept of the 'fourfold', here referred to as the German *Geviert*. In Heidegger, the 'fourfold' is described as fundamental elements: earth, sky, divinities and mortals, and these elements in interplay can create meaningful dwelling and being-in-the-world.[50] Norberg-Schulz's journal entry has been later annotated with a red and blue pen. Dated 23 May 1974 this appears to be an early attempt to find concrete, architectural and geographical counterparts to Heidegger's fourfold. Norberg-Schulz lists the four elements introduced by Heidegger: earth, mortals, sky and divinities, referred to in Norwegian, and he matches these to four specific characteristics of nature and geographical locations: for example, mortals (*menneske*) refers to personification of the character of place, as in Colli Albani, and sky (*himmel*) is nature as cosmic order, the eternal and distant Palestrina.[51] He does not go into greater detail regarding these Italian examples, and although the specific link between the fourfold and specific landscapes reoccurs in *Genius Loci* the geographical location has shifted. In the book Norberg-Schulz claims the sky to be the dominant feature of the natural place of Jordan and Sudan, which is a landscape he sees as distinctly different from what he had seen and experienced in Italy.[52]

The correspondence Norberg-Schulz finds between the Italian regions that he visited and Heidegger's concept of the fourfold appears to be an early attempt to develop a phenomenology of architecture, which later evolved into considering a larger scale and larger geographical area. Italy is his point of departure, but as he travelled to other places in the world – including the United States, Jordan, Sudan and Norway – his horizon broadened, and he was able to include more suitable examples for his theory of place.

Phenomenology is defined by the *Stanford Encyclopaedia of Philosophy* as 'the study of structures of consciousness as experienced from the first-person point of view'.[53] To a phenomenologist, knowledge can only come through direct and personal experience. By visiting place, seeing and experiencing, Norberg-Schulz's thinking evolved. And to be able to think about the spirit of one place, he had to have experienced more than one. The Piazza could not be described without being in reference to the valley: they were the same, not similar. Or at a larger scale: Norberg-Schulz could not articulate the *genius loci* of his native Norway, until he had experienced Italy. Leaving Italy, and returning to Norway, the meaning of place occurred to him, as described in the aforementioned opening scene of *Livet finner sted*. The longer stay in Italy, described in this film, was quite likely to have been in 1973–4, as he did return to Norway in August 1974 and wrote about a similar experience in his journal.[54] I argue that the processes of travelling, observing, reflecting and writing architecture and place appear central in Norberg-Schulz's life affecting his understanding that different places have different *genius loci* and that architects should concretize this in their design. To do so, the architect needs to understand the structure, character and spirit of the place, and Norberg-Schulz makes his argument by contrasting his native Norway with Italy in the south. As such, the depiction of Norberg-Schulz at the train window in *Livet finner sted* forms a poignant picture of the 'flying Norwegian': his thinking taking place between Norway and Italy, occurring at great speed, en route. At the window, Norberg-Schulz experienced the spirit of the place at first-hand.

Whereas Norberg-Schulz recurrently travelled from his home in Oslo to the south, he seldom travelled in the opposite direction: north from Oslo. Anna Maria Norberg-Schulz once did travel to the northern parts of Norway but recalls that her husband did not join her.[55] In general, the northern parts of Norway appear to have no interest to the theorist, underscoring an Oslo-centric understanding of Norway. One of Norberg-Schulz's earliest books written with Gunnar Bugge is about traditional Norwegian architecture. The book begins with a map.[56] Entitled 'Map of Norway', it is striking that the map only covers the southern parts of the country, leaving out two-thirds of the country's length. The map stops right above Trondheim. Instead of going north, Norberg-Schulz focused his attention to the south and west. His books do include some examples from outside Europe, such as Northern America, Jordan and Sudan.[57] Norberg-Schulz's interest in Northern America is easy to understand, as the American architectural scene has long been established within the canon. It was Norberg-Schulz's friendship with the Italian architect Paolo Portoghesi which allowed him to work and travel to Sudan and Jordan. The two worked together on a plan in Sudan in 1975, which led to the two being invited to Jordan. But the project in Jordan remained a study only.[58] In Norberg-Schulz's authorship a great emphasis is given to the western world, particularly structured around his many journeys between Norway and Italy.

The opening scene of *Livet finner sted*, as well as the many sources documenting Norberg-Schulz's extensive travelling to Italy, informed my approach and research methods, shaping the nature of my fieldwork and my film-making. Seeking the windows that he left, travelled behind, arrived at and returned to, I completed two journeys where I followed in his footsteps: Oslo to Rome via Venice in September 2014 and Trondheim to Rome in February 2016. My journeys were not tracing one specific journey by Norberg-Schulz, but instead they were constructed out of fragments from a series of journeys he undertook, fragments I found in published texts, archival material or became aware of in interviews with his family members. With my camera at hand, I travelled, and I reflected on how my journeys related to those of Norberg-Schulz. I allowed myself to venture into the unknown, to research and explore. Equipped with fragments only, I hoped that following in Norberg-Schulz footsteps would open up for something new and reconfigure what I already know.

> Through film as process of being elsewhere, that self becomes another and different self, and the travel essay in particular has been a notable literary and cinematic practice that has discovered complex ideological and psychological significance through the journey, the walk or the exploration.[59]

Cinematic travel and essayistic excursions, Timothy Corrigan argues, are central features of the genre of the essay film. In this genre, which investigates and tackles a destabilized self's engagement with a fragmentary world, the journey stands as a suitable theme, motive and metaphor. Through travel, that very self is developed and changed, and becomes something different.[60] Thinking takes place, and the essay film-maker is ready to capture it all on camera, edit and disseminate.

Floating and changeable are the views, landscapes and buildings passing by the train window as I travel north to south, first in 2014 and later in 2016. Alongside the panoramic views provided by the railroad, a culture of panoramic and dioramic shows developed, offering the audience visiting these shows a view of distant places.[61] Bruno links the early years of the motion picture to the development of the railway and rail network, where the era's new 'network of architectural forms produced a new spatiovisuality'.⁶² These new architectural forms include the railway, but also other spaces of transit, which moulded a culture that depended upon mobility and an appreciation of all things mobile: moving images, rail-travel or strolling through an arcade. Although distinctly different, Bruno, in her essayistic writing, links these spaces through the keyword mobility.⁶³

Travelling by train, the itinerary is predetermined by the train tracks, many of the routes having been established in the early years of railway history. As Wolfgang Schivelbusch argues of the nineteenth century:

> Route and vehicle became technically conjoined on the railroad: there was no leeway between the rails and the vehicle running on them, nor was it possible for one train to pull to one side when confronted by another.⁶⁴

I set out on my journey to Italy travelling by train, a journey mapped out from the possible routes determined by the railway network. My compartment cannot leave the predetermined route and I watch a landscape in passing that many travellers before me have experienced. Such panoramic scenes passing by the window, Schivelbusch suggests, form a panoramic vision, specific to the railway. This entails an experience of space that no longer is three-dimensional but instead a set of images, passing by the train window.⁶⁵

As I move, my mind wanders off to Frederico Fellini's 1984 advert *Ragazza in Treno [Girl on the Train]* for the Italian drink Campari.⁶⁶ The advert, described in *Sight and Sound* in 2016, stars Victor Poletti and Silvia Dionisio, the latter playing a young, blonde woman on a train. Looking out onto a landscape that does not excite her,⁶⁷ Dionisio picks up a remote control, pointing towards the window and then she 'changes channel'. Landscapes and architecture from around the world pass by them: pyramids, cathedrals, temples. Yet, Dionisio appears bored and dissatisfied, and finally throws the remote control away. Poletti picks it up, smilingly, and changes the channel again, this time to Italy. Once the Cathedral of Pisa appears, easily recognizable by its leaning tower (1173–1372), Dionisio's attitude changes and she leans excitedly towards the window. As a large bottle of Campari appears before the Pisa Baptistery of St. John (1152–1363), the door to their compartment opens, and a waitress serves them each a glass of Campari. Travelling by train, looking out the window, becomes a way to travel the world. As the woman's attitude changes when she can see Italy from her seat, the advertisement depicts Italy as a favoured destination for travellers, best to be enjoyed with a glass of Campari. The window of the train is like a TV screen: a frame for moving images.

When Norberg-Schulz located himself at the window of a train in *Livet finner sted*, he is saying something rather different. Here, the views that pass by his window are not merely flat, two-dimensional images resembling a TV where the channel could be shifted at any time. Norberg-Schulz's filmic train window represents a deep connection with the landscape beyond the pane of glass. Through his film, Norberg-Schulz aims at conveying a sense of dwelling that is in deep, inevitable and intimate connection with place. To Norberg-Schulz this connection is revealed through travel, experienced as he is standing at the window of a train.

'"Viewed" through the lens of travel, the relationship between film and the architectural ensemble unfolds as a practice of mobilizing viewing space that invites inhabitation',[68] Bruno argues, and she describes journeys in film, art or architecture as haptic. She writes:

> the haptic [is] an agent in the formation of space – both geographic and cultural – and, by extension, in the articulation of the spatial arts themselves, which include motion pictures. Emphasizing the cultural role of the haptic, it develops a theory that connects sense to place. Here, the haptic realm is shown to play a tangible, *tact*ical role, in our communicative 'sense' of spatiality and motility, thus shaping the texture of habitable space and, ultimately, mapping our ways of being in touch with the environment.[69]

Sensuous, embodied and mobile: this is how Bruno maps out a cultural history of the spatio-visual arts in her book *Atlas of Emotion*. For her, motion and emotion are interconnected, and the haptic links these (e)motions to a place. From this standpoint, she writes her cultural history.

Atlas of Emotion 'came together through a diverse set of intellectual journeys, even passing through the fabric of my body',[70] Bruno writes, to reflect upon her own process of thinking and working as scholar. She sees her thinking as a form of intellectual journey, which is haptic: that is, connected to place. Bruno travels in the external and inner worlds, as the motion and emotion traverse through her body.

In my film *Journey to Italy* (2016) I capture the shifting views and landscapes, as I travel south from Trondheim. The train compartments only give me the option of looking to the left or right: west or east. I aim my camera towards the west reinforcing and critiquing Norberg-Schulz's western focus. Norberg-Schulz travelled, experienced, reflected and wrote. As I travel, I film and think about all those places Norberg-Schulz did not include in his *oeuvre*. And in my later editing, I add footage created by MRI: an alternative imaging technology creating alternative views of the body, moving through it.

Travelling affects the body. In her project *Freud on Holiday* (2006), artist and writer Sharon Kivland travels in the footsteps of Sigmund Freud, tracing his holidays in Europe. When reflecting on her fieldwork and journeying, Sharon Kivland involves a discussion of her own migraines and mild depression as an integral part of her travelling.[71]

Helgesen, Grønvold and Norberg-Schulz had initially planned that a return journey between Norway and Italy would be the structural backbone of the film. The NRK agreed to the proposed budget in 1990 and funding was secured. But around that very same time, Norberg-Schulz was diagnosed with cancer. Due to his health issues, the journey to Italy had to be redesigned to accommodate Norberg-Schulz's health and availability, Helgesen recalls.[72] The film was shot during a three-week period in 1991.[73] The proposed physical journey was replaced by shots of Norberg-Schulz lecturing with his slides from previous journeys[74] or by using footage from other productions.[75] For instance, the exact same footage used to illustrate Norberg-Schulz's lecture on the spirit of the place in *Livet finner Sted* derives from an earlier NRK production about the Norwegian architect Sverre Fehn, *Rommet og Lyset* (1988), depicting Fehn's journeys to Morocco.[76] The only remains of the journey from Norway to Italy and back again are in the scenes with Norberg-Schulz on the train. I recognize the location of filming as the county of Østfold, located south-east of Oslo, towards the Swedish border. I know the region intimately. It is where I grew up.

Norberg-Schulz never recovered from his illness and died of cancer in March 2000. The ambitious film project including international travel was altered. The journey between Norway and Italy was replaced on screen with what I recognize as the two-hour train journey from the Swedish border towards Oslo through Østfold. The film-maker's choice of locating Norberg-Schulz at the window of a train in Østfold, rather than on a *Piazza* in an Italian village, I read as a manifestation of the immobility caused by his illness: an illness that eventually led to his death.

The film team did not travel to Italy, instead they went on a two-hour journey to Halden (my hometown) and the Swedish border at Kornsjø, then back again to Oslo. For years, my father also travelled by train through Østfold towards Oslo. Working as a radiologist at Ullevål Hospital in Oslo, while living in Halden, the four-hour daily commute took him through that very same forest of Østfold depicted in *Livet finner sted*. Around the time that Ullevål Hospital got their very first MRI machine in 1993, my father started a new job at a hospital closer to home.

MRI technology is different from the X-ray, the latter using radiation to create images of the body's interior. MRI, in contrast, uses both magnetic fields, radio waves and field gradients to move into the body and create images. The subject must go into a narrow tube and lie completely still. Large magnets are turned on, affecting the way protons move in the hydrogen atoms in the body. A radio signal with the same frequency as the protons is sent in affecting the way the protons in the hydrogen atoms move, before they soon return to their normal state. This movement can be captured and read by the MRI machine. Within the body, the MRI, thus, can localize water. From this information it is possible to create a visual image. The ways that the hydrogen atoms return to a state of equilibrium are communicated by the radio frequencies. The images constructed differ depending on the properties of the water molecules.

At the same time, the MRI signal tells us where in the body the water is located and constructs a three-dimensional representation of the body thereof. The medical professionals can create still images to investigate in greater detail or look at an animated movement through the three-dimensional body. In this way, fluid in an inflamed joint can be depicted accurately. In contrast to the bone, which does not contain any fluid, tissue, fat and water do and will react to the magnetism. As such, an image of the water and fat in the body can be constructed, showing the soft tissues, leaving out the bones so famously depicted with X-ray. In contrast to the X-ray, MRI does not contain ionizing radiation, which is bad for the body.[77]

I had my first MRI scan right before I turned six, on 11 April 1994. To do so, I travelled with my father to Oslo. It was incredibly exciting, as we walked through the large hospital, using the routes and entrances for staff. In the scanner, I had to lie completely still, while contrast liquid was injected intravenously into my left arm.

My father was a radiologist. With his machines, he could see through the body, slice it up without a knife, explore what is there and create an image or animation of that very body. He knew what is underneath our skin, behind our face and what organ lies next to the other. All-knowing, he saw through you. As a child, I found his work fascinating and loved to visit him at the hospital where he worked. The people dressed in white were his friends and colleagues. Always friendly, the hospital was a grown-up world, where X-ray, ultrasound, CT and MRI results were dictated into machines, to be transcribed, journaled and archived.

Four years after my first MRI, artist Justine Cooper was the first to use MRI in an artistic context.[78] The video work *RAPT I* (1998) (Figure 3.3) and the installation *RAPT II* (1998) shown at the exhibition *Probe: Explorations into Australian Computational Space*, at the Australian Embassy, Beijing, China 1998 (Figure 3.4), question what new visions of self can be explored through this new technology. The project does not break up the body; it seamlessly joins it, Robyn Donohue argues.[79] The film *RAPT I* takes the viewer through Cooper's body, slowly, and beautifully, its different parts and sections evolve, spring forth and grow, while our point of view constantly moves. *RAPT II* presents the sliced-up body drawn out, extended in space. In Donohue's critique of Cooper's artwork, she argues how the use of MRI creates new-found image of the self, herself, by taking the viewer through the inside of her body (Figure 3.5).[80]

But the importance of movement in Cooper's piece appears to be rather overlooked. Turning the gaze inward, MRI makes slices through the body but leaves it intact, mapping it by coordinates that can be converted into images or animations. It is not static. Just as each slice is cut and framed and frozen joined together and reanimated, it once again comes alive. Related to movement, MRI also locates the body in a space. I see MRI, as a process, experience and concept as highly haptic.

Cooper's artwork is from 1998: the same year that Bruno wrote her prologue to *Atlas of Emotion*, an introduction which she claims 'can be drafted only after one has already finished the work'.[81] Having completed her work at this time, it is quite understandable that the book does not give any attention to the MRI or artworks utilizing this technology. When Bruno discusses medical imagery and their view of the internal body – central in her thesis – Bruno refers to X-ray, rather than MRI. To her, film is

> an analytical 'cyborg': a relative of the X Ray, it can dissect somatic traces. It can even freeze the body, as only death can, transforming it into a *nature morte*. In so far as it is fundamentally 'still' photography, film is inhabited by death. Like waxwork or a mummy, its illusionary movement can return us to a state of stillness.[82]

Although suitable for a discussion on the relation between the X-ray and cinema that focuses on stillness, the X-ray does not involve many traces of

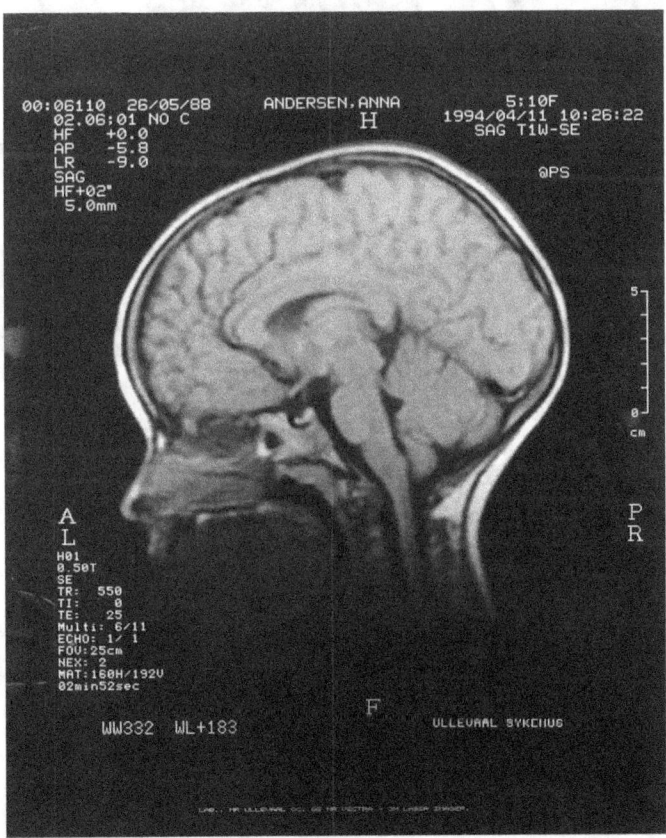

FIGURE 3.3 MRI scan of head, 11 April 1994. Anna Ulrikke Andersen.

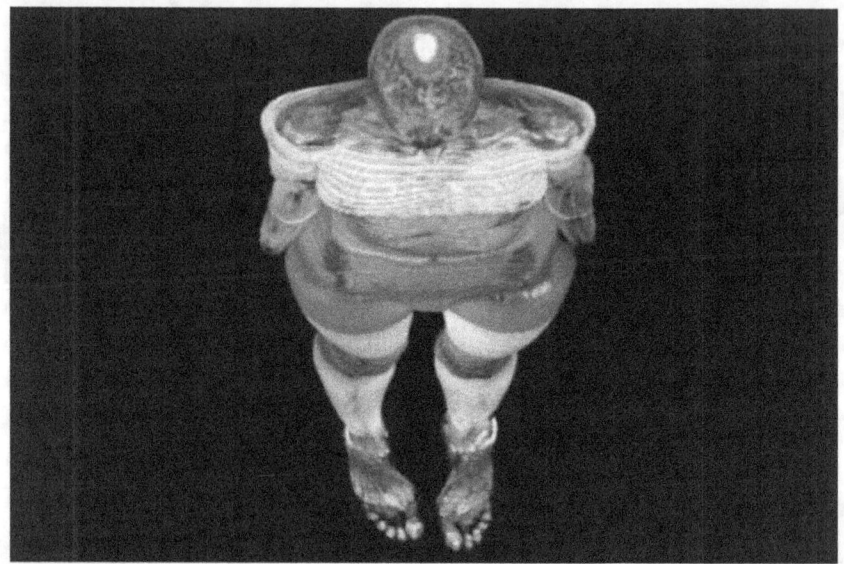

FIGURE 3.4 *RAPT I*, 1998. Courtesy of Justine Cooper.

FIGURE 3.5 *RAPT II*, in *Probe: Explorations into Australian Computational Space*, at the Australian Embassy, Beijing, China, 1998. Courtesy of Justine Cooper.

motion that stands as essential to both motion pictures and travel culture that Bruno discusses.

MRI, on the other hand, does. Lying completely still in an MRI machine, apparently immobile, the body is in fact in constant motion. The water- and fat-molecules inside the body are reacting to the strong magnetic field created by the machine. Forming new, alternative views of the body and the body in space by translating sound into image, a view through the body becomes possible. The view of the body is three-dimensional, and water and fat are located in space. Compiling animations out of these images, we can journey through the body itself.

Bruno argues the camera itself is a means of transportation: the moving camera makes moving images.[83] My practice as a film-maker utilizes the train window as a camera making moving images, as I press the lens of my camera towards the pane of glass, hold it still and record. My shots are determined by the railway engineers and planners who determined the route long before I was born. I travel through forests, fields and tunnels. Norberg-Schulz's process of thinking involved travel, direct experience, reflection and a process of writing. His phenomenological approach to place involved these stages of thinking. Similarly, I travel, experience, reflect and write, but also film, as I adopt Bruno's attention to journeys in film, architecture and art as a history that is haptic and Rendell's emphasis on mobility as a critical tool. As such, I bring the haptic into Norberg-Schulz's phenomenology of architecture.

I do not encounter one place but several. Five small frames correspond with five days of travel, showing the different light, climate and architecture from Norway to Italy. To Rilke seeing multiple places, or experiencing antagonistic forces, was pivotal in his understanding of being-in-the-world not as static but as mobile.[84] As such I consider my dwelling as mobile, as I travel through Europe, looking out the window of a train, I negotiate that exterior world with my '*Fensterblick*'.[85] My moving camera certainly makes moving images, engaging with emotion and with the haptic, as Bruno argues. But as I am engaging with Cooper's *RAPT I*, I allow my moving image practice to move into and through my body. An animation using MRI of my foot is included in the editing and stands as a reminder of the travelling, walking and mobile subject. In Cooper's piece, the moving point of view ventures through space and the body and captures a series of MRI images put into motion. Bruno, perhaps, wrote her book too early to see that the MRI technology as a moving image camera makes moving images by creating movement within the body, a body that evidently rests completely still as if dead – immobile – captured from within that narrow tube that is the MRI machine.

Window 4

Hamburg to Basel

Place

Hamburg, Germany
Latitude: 53.551085
Longitude: 9.993682
Language: German (Fenster)
Basel, Switzerland
Latitude: 47.559599
Longitude: 7.588576
Language: German (Fenster)

Practice

Three Windows on Europe: September 1945
2018
Anna Ulrikke Andersen
SD video
02:33
Re-edited: *Livet finner sted*, directed by Sven-Erik Helgesen, co-written with Ulf Grønvold, NRK, TV documentary, 1992. 41:00. 03:27–04:13.
Voice by Anne Lie Nymoen. Subtitles/Commentary: English
https://vimeo.com/266009551

Password: anna

FIGURE 4.1 *Three Windows on Europe, September 1945*, 2018, by Anna Ulrikke Andersen. Archival source and date unknown. Broadcast by NRK, 1992.

Three Windows on Europe: September 1945 (2018) is an essay film created from footage used in *Livet finner sted* (1992). The footage used in this documentary is archival footage from the end of the Second World War, narrated by Anne Lie Nymoen. This footage loops three times, where comments are added as subtitles in English. The original 3:4 format archival footage used in the TV documentary is recorded from an online source using QuickTime. Language: Norwegian. Subtitles: English (Figure 4.1).

Essay

Three windows on Europe, 1945

On the first day of my fieldwork in September 2014, I visited Anna Maria Norberg-Schulz in Oslo. I had told her about my project and my interest in Christian Norberg-Schulz's extensive travelling when she suggested that I have a look at her late husband's photographs. She pointed me in the direction of a bookshelf stacked with photo albums, and I pulled out one of them. That was his first photo album, she explained, containing the photographs from summers in Norway in the early 1940s, his studies in Zürich and his travels and excursions in Europe.

Norberg-Schulz was nineteen years old when he made the decision to study architecture. It was 1945, and the Second World War had just ended, and with this, the five-year-long occupation of Norway by Nazi Germany. But the war had left the country in a poor state. As the Russian troops had advanced from the north, German forces withdrew south, burning towns, cities and villages. The northernmost part of Norway was left in ruins, and the country had to be rebuilt.[1] Architects were needed.

Having contemplated studying music, Norberg-Schulz instead decided on architecture and was admitted to a national initiative educating Norwegian architects abroad. With 124 other Norwegian students, he travelled to Zürich and the renowned Eidgenössische Technische Hochschule Zürich (ETHZ).[2] Travelling through Europe in 1945 was the first international journey for the nineteen-year-old Norwegian.[3]

Norberg-Schulz boarded a train in Oslo and with the group, he travelled south through the county of Østfold and crossed the border into Sweden at Kornsjø. In Helsingborg, in Sweden, the group took the ferry over to Helsingør in Denmark and continued the journey by train to Copenhagen and eventually arrived in Hamburg. But from Hamburg, the rail network could take them no further. Instead, the students continued south to Basel in military cars. Jan Carlsen notes how these military cars had been used to transport former prisoners from the concentration camps.[4] Venturing through a destroyed country, Norberg-Schulz observed the destruction of war from three small windows of that military car.[5]

This experience had a profound impact on the young student. The destruction of war stood in stark contrast to what he experienced when arriving in Basel, Switzerland. Neutral throughout the war, Switzerland had not been bombed and damaged. Structures were still standing; infrastructure remained intact. The students were handed beers, and Norberg-Schulz went for a short walk up to Basel cathedral. Here, he could hear Friedrich Händel's *Samson* oratorio from within the building, reminding him of all that was stable and good.[6] From the darkness of war, he had arrived at the structural stability and brightness of peace.

> Total eclipse! No sun, no moon!
> All dark amidst the blaze of noon!
> Oh, glorious light! No cheering ray
> To glad my eyes with welcome day!
> Why thus depriv'd Thy prime decree?
> Sun, moon, and stars are dark to me![7]

* * *

When I visited Anna Maria Norberg-Schulz in September 2014 and opened up Norberg-Schulz's photo album, I realized that he had photographed his journey through Europe in 1945. The photographs captured the entire journey from Oslo through Sweden, Denmark, Germany and eventually Switzerland. Anna Maria Norberg-Schulz allowed me to make copies for research purposes, but the family later decided that the photographs were considered too private to publish and should remain out of sight for the general public. When I left Oslo by train on the very next day, I had the theorist's photographs with me, printed and pinned into my notebook. Embarking on my journey from Norway to Italy, I was following in the footsteps of a man who was long dead.

Death, Roland Barthes argues, rests in the nature of the photograph. A photograph refers to that which is depicted, an umbilical cord tying the present to the past. A photograph captures a moment in time, but in the very next second, that moment is already gone. Photography, thus, is always 'that which has been',[8] as the aperture of the camera has fixed time and movement in a single, motionless picture.

'When we define the photograph as motionless image, this does not mean only that the figures it represents do not move; it means that they do not *emerge,* do not *leave* the photograph: They are anesthetized and fastened down, like butterflies.'[9] With this, Barthes's sees the photograph as a motionless image that is still, without direction. His take on the photograph can be linked with a specific understanding of history, which highlights a separation between me and them, now and then. The past is available to those who come after, like pinned butterflies, Barthes argues.[10]

The photographs offered me clues to the exact places Norberg-Schulz had travelled before me, what he had seen and what he had decided to frame and capture with his camera. There are several photographs from Hamburg showing the destructions of war. These are scenes we are used to seeing: black-and-white images of buildings that have been bombed and structural arches about to collapse, the roof having been blown off.

I was excited when I approached Hamburg, studying Norberg-Schulz's photographs of the bombed-out city, its structural arches reaching up from the rubble. Archival material and oral history mapped my itinerary, but the photographs offered me a chance to re-enact his views and link his experiences to precise locations. On that journey towards Hamburg, looking at his photographs, I felt that I was travelling to get closer, closer to Norberg-Schulz, and the places that he had known and visited.

Photographs were integral to Victor Burgin's experience of visiting Ludwig Mies van der Rohe's infamous German Pavilion in Barcelona, Spain (Figure 4.2).[11] Designed for the 1929 World Exposition the pavilion stands as a prime example of modernist architecture and well-established within the canon. According to Alan Colquhoun, the pavilion earned this standing because of its radical open plan design, which prompted visitors to flow through the building as if the walls were filters.[12] The pavilion was

FIGURE 4.2 Ludwig Mies van der Rohe, The German Pavilion. Barcelona, International Exhibition, 1928–9, digital image, ©1928–9 The Museum of Modern Art/Scala, Florence. © 2021. Digital image, The Museum of Modern Art, New York/Scala, Florence.

demolished in 1930, war eventually erupted and the architect fled Europe and emigrated to the United States. For years, the pavilion only survived in photographs until it was reconstructed in 1986.[13] Open to the public, visitors today can flow through Mies's modernist masterpiece in Barcelona.

Burgin's experience of visiting the reconstructed pavilion accounted for in his book, *The Remembered Film* (2004), included consulting photographs. He had seen photographs of the original building from 1929, the reconstructed pavilion from 1986, as well as the site of land in between before his visit. Upon visiting, more photographs were presented to him. Looking at these photographs was, to Burgin, a way to travel in time.[14]

As he walks through the building, Burgin feels as if he would emerge on the other side in the year 1929: 'with history poised motionless before it plummets towards the fascist occupation of the city a decade later'.[15] The building, and the photographs, brought Burgin back to a time before war, horror and destruction. To him, time travel occurs when the photographs and the experiences of being at a certain place intersect.

In 2014, I had left Copenhagen by train in the morning and taken the ferry over to Germany, from Rørby to Puttgarten. But in Puttgarten we were told to leave the train. The trains continuing south to Hamburg were cancelled, and I had to wait and continue my journey by bus. As I slowly approached the city centre of Hamburg, the Hamburg that I had imagined from the photographs and located on maps as a predetermined route along the rail network became more and more unclear. I could see no rubble, no ruins in black and white. The railway was replaced by highways, streets, rush hour and traffic lights. That Hamburg of 1945 which existed on the photographs was no more.

To me, the vibrant city concealed the city of the past. The horrors of war were long gone. With my camera, I filmed the station, yet the footage was nothing but bland and uneventful. I zoomed in on a structural detail, parts of a window, without really knowing why. Attempting to recreate Norberg-Schulz's views – to resurrect a pinned butterfly – appeared to be impossible (Figures 4.3 and 4.4).

In the light of the present day – September 2014 – that darkness of the Second World War that Norberg-Schulz had encountered was not there for me to see. The past was concealed, difficult to grasp and impossible to claim. For once, David Loewenthal writes in *The Past Is a Foreign Country* (1985) how the past is always 'viewed and celebrated . . . through present-day lenses'.[16] Through my present-day lens, I could not see Norberg-Schulz's Hamburg. In following Norberg-Schulz this was what I wanted to.

In her artistic practice Sharon Kivland follows Sigmund Freud. She re-enacts and recreates a series of his journeys, as in her project *Freud on Holiday* (2006) where he sets out to recover the 'missing Freud',[17] where archival work forms an attempt to bring back the dead.[18] In doing so, Kivland's experiences are comparable to mine. Freud travelled before her

FIGURE 4.3 Hamburg, 2014. Anna Ulrikke Andersen.

FIGURE 4.4 Hamburg, 2014. Anna Ulrikke Andersen.

but is not present anymore. The information she has at hand is often too fragmented for her to find precisely where it was that Freud had been before her. For example, when Kivland wanted to find the exact place where Freud conducted his research on eels, she could not find the place, and had to venture off route, and do something else.[19] Such detours form a common part of the historian's work but are seldom addressed as part of the argument. As I engaged with Norberg-Schulz's photographs and followed him to Hamburg, my experience was marked by disappointment, of detours and fragmented remains of the past.

I see this practice of following as closely related to practices of re-enactment, which involve re-staging – re-enacting – an event or experience of the past, which brings up questions relating to what separates the then and now. Re-enactment can transfer these issues that the historian often encounters into an embodied and powerful experience. Sven Lütticken argues how the tradition from German historicist Leopold von Ranke, who so infamously aimed at writing history '*Wie es eigentlich gewesen*'[20] (how it really was), still remains prevalent among some historical re-enactors, where others engage with the way re-enactment never really can be a time machine.[21] Attention to minute details to make the experience more historically 'accurate' is rooted in nineteenth-century historicism, 'fuelled', as Lütticken argues, by romanticism and German idealism.[22]

Yet to Rebecca Schneider the temporalities at play in the practice of re-enactment, both in historical amateur practices of war re-enactors and in the work of performance artists, are not simply that linear. She writes:

> To some who ridicule the activities of reenactors as naïve, the faith that linear time is the one true time couples with an investment in the

contingency offered by the linear temporal model to reassure that any *true* temporal return or overlap would be impossible because *different*.[23]

The picture Schneider paints of re-enactment is far more complex than naïve attempts to resurrect something that happened before and, instead, re-enactment offers a different understanding of time. Although re-enactment can never be precisely like the event of the past, the past and present coexist in what she describes as 'cross- or intra-temporal negotiation, even (perhaps) interaction of inter(in)animation of one time with another time'.[24] To Schneider, re-enactment brings up something new, something different and valuable.

Perhaps I needed to return to Norberg-Schulz's photographs, and instead of expecting that they could link then and now to specific locations, I need to see them differently and allow the complexity and detour to come forth. To Burgin, associations between images, albeit place or photographs, can 'form like involuntary memories, at times in the form of involuntary memories, a solicit interpretation'.[25] They can evoke specific memories

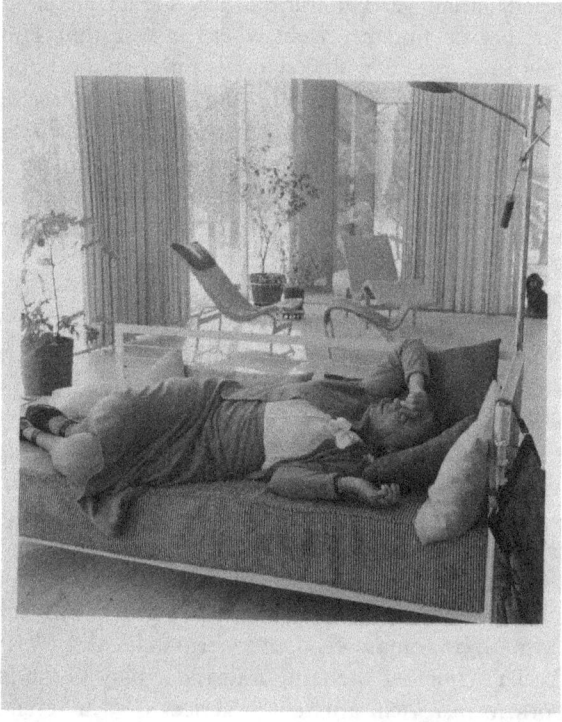

FIGURE 4.5 Unidentified woman, perhaps Edith Farnsworth, at Farnsworth House, undated photograph. Unknown photographer. Courtesy of Newberry Library, Chicago, Illinois.

through associations and wander off on detours. A sculpture of a woman surrounded by water in the reconstructed German Pavilion in Barcelona reminds Burgin of Mies's *Farnsworth House* (1945–51) outside of Chicago, where the villa's owner Edith Farnsworth spent her time surrounded by transparent glass walls (Figure 4.5).[26] His associations do not stop there. To Burgin, the female sculpture also evokes another memory of a female figure, whom he read about in an exhibition about the Second World War during a previous visit to Barcelona. This woman was arrested for having anti-fascist leaflets and tortured to death. In the photograph Burgin had seen exhibited, the woman used her arm to cover her face, a gesture Burgin recognizes in the sculpture located in the pavilion. One associates the other.

I suddenly recalled another memory of Hamburg Hauptbahnhof from a journey that I had undertaken in 1994. This was my first international journey. Travelling by train from Norway through Hamburg to Düsseldorf, I accompanied my grandfather to his mother's funeral, the last remaining member of that erstwhile large German branch of the family. My grandfather grew up in Düsseldorf, and being born in 1930, his childhood was marked by the Second World War. When he died in 2016, and we emptied his house in Norway, we found several items from this period, including an elaborate and extensive book with photographs of Hitler, glued in between handwritten text.

The war was a traumatic event for my grandfather. Since Düsseldorf was frequently bombed and considered unsafe for children, he was sent to a boarding school in southern Germany. As the war progressed, the school was eventually shut down, and the children were sent in groups through Germany by train, my grandfather heading to Düsseldorf. But after a while, the trains could take them no longer, because the tracks had been bombed. Alone and without anyone to help them, the children had to make their way across the country on their own, my grandfather told me in a letter. He reached Düsseldorf and reunited with his mother. His father was working in transportation in the army. At a later point, the family travelled to see in Poland in 1944. During this journey they allegedly crossed through Auschwitz the very same week that Anne Frank arrived there by train. My grandfather might have met Anne Frank. They were the same age. I am not sure what to do with that information, nor what to think about what my grandfather as a fourteen-year-old would have felt when he passed through Auschwitz in 1944. Or are these events simply stories that we tell each other in a family?

The Second World War is difficult to approach. The war is marked by violence, horror and death, and Timothy Corrigan awards this specific war great importance for what he calls an essayistic experience of modern space. As bombs exploded cities and buildings, social and cultural spaces were also destroyed. The social and the architectural became fragmentary. Moulded from these conditions the post-war self, he argues, 'must often travel directionless paths in search of homes that no longer exist and through landscapes strewn with colonial and other historical wreckage'.[27] The essay as a form, in either film or writing, could be a way to negotiate such fragmentary experiences, Corrigan suggests.

How I could approach the thematic brought up in this essay through essay film-making? I look at the way Norberg-Schulz's journey through Europe in 1945 was depicted in the documentary *Livet finner sted*. Whereas Norberg-Schulz's own photographs are terribly silent, the film is not. Music and female voice-over accompany footage of a bus travelling through a landscape destroyed by war. The footage is not Norberg-Schulz's journey – who travelled by car – but the film-makers probably used archival material.[28] I re-watch the sequence over and over, focusing on different aspects of the film: the voice-over, the music or the moving images. I create a new file in Premiere Pro and place the sequence after each other three times, before I make subtitles. In the first sequence the subtitle translates the voice-over. The second time, I write [Norwegian voice-over]. The third round, I allow my own comments and thoughts to be expressed through the subtitles. The result is the essay film *Three Windows on Europe: September 1945*. Although being arguably rather precise in depicting my experience of following Norberg-Schulz through land, archives, photographs and film, the result, however, is not necessarily representative of Norberg-Schulz's own experience.

Norberg-Schulz travelled through the historical wreckage of war between Hamburg and Basel. The experience was confusing and horrific to the young student. With his camera, he captured the suffering before him. He caught glimpses of architecture fragmented, torn apart, through three small windows of a military car, until finally arriving in Switzerland, where structures were still intact. As he reflected later in life, this experience reminded Norberg-Schulz of the importance of the built environment in creating meaningful existence, a central theme throughout his authorship.[29]

'Christian Norberg-Schulz was first and foremost an architect and a theorist, rather than a historian: by understanding the past one could understand what needed to be done today and tomorrow',[30] Mari Hvattum argues in *Genius Historiae* (2009). She argues that Norberg-Schulz himself understood history in an organic way: 'a living being that germinates, grows and dies'.[31] Historical epochs, thus, are driven by such development, striving towards fulfilment before withering away, but could be reinvented and reused by the architect-historian, such as Norberg-Schulz himself. His own present was governed by an urge for a new architecture and new place, a reality where the horrors of war were left in the dark and other historical epochs and building styles grew and were brought into the light.

My approach to history is rather different. Drawing upon scholars such as Barthes, Burgin, Lütticken and Schneider, I see a complex interplay between then, now, place, photography and architecture. These discussions around historiography, the inaccuracy of re-enactment and its engagement with Ranke's take on history could be seen in the context of the postmodern historiographical approach as outlined by Keith Jenkins. In his book *Re-Thinking History* (1991) Jenkins addresses a series of fragile aspects of historiography related to the epistemology and methods of history. He separates the past from the practice of history, suggesting that what we write about the past is different from what the past was really like. Even with a wide range of sources, Jenkins argues that 'no account can re-cover the past as it was because the past was not an account but events, situations, etc. As the past has gone, no account can ever be checked against it but also against other accounts'.[32] Because of this gap between past and history, it is up to the historian to make her own account, to write her own version of history. Norberg-Schulz's Hamburg was gone, and what remained was a series of temporalities brought into play through my visit, my writing, my research and my following in 2014.

Following Norberg-Schulz's through Europe had opened up these historiographical concerns, where it had become clear to me that my view on history differed from his. Where I was struck by an insight into the complexities involved in bridging then and now, Norberg-Schulz's experience of seeing a Germany that was changed, fragmented and ruined was different. To him, watching Europe through three small windows of a military car fostered specific attention to place, where habitation eventually would grow out of and replace the destructions of war.[33]

In his landmark treatise *Genius Loci: Towards a Phenomenology of Architecture*, Norberg-Schulz suggests that the architect needed to understand the structure, character and spirit of place to create meaningful relationships between being and world.[34] Norberg-Schulz found a framework to support his theory of place in the philosophy of Martin Heidegger, a philosopher who was similarly concerned with the destructions of war. Heidegger was invited to give a lecture about the issue on post-war reconstruction, published later as 'Bauen Wohnen Denken' ['Building Dwelling Thinking'] (1954). Here, his emphasis on the importance of building to create meaningful dwelling is outlined, infamously adopted by Norberg-Schulz.

However, those photographs of the ruins of Hamburg from September 1945 never made it into *Genius Loci* or any of his other books or publications. This is noteworthy since his own photography plays such a vital role in his published work. Jorge Otero-Pailos, who has explored Norberg-Schulz's use of photography, claims that architects are visual thinkers.[35] As such architecture can be strongly communicated through images as well as word, and Norberg-Schulz's work stands as an excellent example of such non-verbal communication. Otero-Pailos awards great attention to Norberg-Schulz's use of photographs in the theorist's books *Intentions in Architecture* (1963) and *Genius Loci*. Norberg-Schulz's approach to historiography is a 'photo[historio]graphy', Otero-Pailos argues. Seeing the history of architecture as a series of recurrent visual patterns from where all architecture originates, Norberg-Schulz sets out to uncover, describe and learn these patterns to form a theory for architects. To communicate an approach to architecture that awards great emphasis on visual structures, and how these structures form our relationship to place, photography becomes central, as Otero-Pailos points out. Visual structures in landscapes and buildings can be captured on camera.[36]

Meaning as well as architecture was important to Norberg-Schulz, and I would suggest that when Norberg-Schulz took pictures, he mainly did so to capture that which was meaningful. Perhaps that is why his photographs from September 1945 never made it to any of his publications. The photographs depict ruins, destruction, wreckage, war and death. With his camera, Norberg-Schulz had captured the opposite of meaning: chaos of fragments, a world in the aftermath of war. He had seen the wreckage of war through three small windows of a military car, and he had framed his experience with his camera. Both framing practices – the window of a car and the photographer framing their motif – offer fragments of place. What we see on the photographs would not fit a theory suggesting 'Architecture means to visualize the *genius loci,* and the task for the architect is to create meaningful places, whereby he helps man to dwell'.[37]

Paradoxically enough, ideas related to our belonging to a place were pivotal to the Nazi ideology that fuelled the Second World War, a line of thought that Heidegger himself contributed to. As Hitler rose to power, Heidegger was appointed rector of Freiburg University and joined the Nazi Party in 1933. In his book *Heidegger and Nazism* (1987) Victor Farias opened up the discussion regarding Heidegger's contact with the Nazi Party and the connections between his philosophy and the *blut und boden* rhetoric that the party promoted. Heidegger's writing explores how our being is structured in relationship with the world, developed in his book *Sein und Zeit [Being and Time]* (1927).[38] In his writing, this often led to an emphasis on a close connection between being and specific places, with a preference for rural farm life. This emphasis on specific humans belonging to specific places runs on accord with a *blut und boden* ideology based on the idea that the German people and the German blood were connected to German soil.

To Hilde Heynen, Heidegger's philosophy, and its influence on fields such as architecture, is worthy of question.[39] In her account, Heynen also questions Norberg-Schulz's use of the philosopher's work. She is critical towards certain aspects of Norberg-Schulz's theory, particularly how *genius loci* presuppose an emphasis on rootedness over mobility:

> Norberg-Schulz interprets Heidegger in a fairly simplistic and instrumental way, by which the Spirit of the place and the organic relationship between man and house takes on a mythical character. Rootedness and authenticity are presented as being superior to mobility and the experience of rootlessness. What is more, he seems to be completely unaware of the violence that is implicit in concepts like this. It is no coincidence these words are part of the basic vocabulary of Nazi-ideology.[40]

The Second World War stands as a horrific example of a violent result of Nazi ideology. I share Heynen's concerns as she hints towards a parallel between the rhetoric Norberg-Schulz uses and the basic vocabulary of Nazi ideology. For instance, Norberg-Schulz explicitly stated how the wandering of 'modern man' – which I read as travelling mobility and movement – was a divergence from how we lived prehistorically. 'Today we start to realise that true freedom presupposes belonging, and that "dwelling" means belonging to a concrete place.'[41] There are similarities between Norberg-Schulz's dismissal of mobility and his emphasis on belonging to a concrete place, and the *blut und boden* rhetoric discussed earlier. I will return to these issues throughout this book, especially in Window 8 | Sierre. I agree with Heynen that Heidegger's influence on architectural culture is both worthy of question and must be approached with caution.[42] But whereas Heidegger had clear links to the Nazi Party in Germany, no evidence exists to suggest that Norberg-Schulz had any connections with the Norwegian Nazi party. Instead, Norberg-Schulz viewed the Third Reich at a distance post-capitulation, through three small windows of a military car between Hamburg and Basel in September 1945.

Window 5

Rome

Place

Rome, Italy
Latitude: 41.902782
Longitude: 12.496365
Language: Italian (Finestra)

Practice

The Norwegian Institute in Rome
Anna Ulrikke Andersen
2016
HD video
19:44
Featuring: Else L'Orange
Norwegian with English subtitles: http://vimeo.com/164027129

Norwegian without subtitles: https://vimeo.com/503937447

The Norwegian Institute in Rome (2016) was made during a visit I made to the Norwegian Institute in Rome with Else L'Orange, whose father co-founded the institute. A long shot of the roof terrace of the institute is shot

FIGURE 5.1 *The Norwegian Institute in Rome*, 2016. Anna Ulrikke Andersen.

with a Blackmagic Cinema Camera, and archival material of plans of the building is added in the editing. The sound is recorded with two Philips radio microphones, capturing the conversation between L'Orange and myself. Sound and image are separated, until we move into the frame of the roof terrace and sound and image are united. Language: Norwegian. Subtitles: English.

Essay

Fill in that window! Move into that frame!

When Christian Norberg-Schulz visited the construction site of the Norwegian Institute in Rome at Janiculum west of the city in early 1962, he made the following decision: to fill a large window located in the library with plaster. On the exterior, he suggested keeping the blinds permanently shut, covering the solid wall to maintain the façade's symmetry. This solution would allow for a slide projector to be installed in the library, he outlines in a letter to the building committee dated 31 January 1962, also informing the committee that he has started the design for the interiors.[1] There is nothing to suggest to the reader that the architect had probably already decided to leave his architectural profession for good and turn to teaching and researching theory and history in a university environment.

Norberg-Schulz's prospects as an architect were nevertheless quite bright at the outset of 1961; he had just completed a design proposal for the Norwegian Institute in Rome that was to be built among other nations' cultural and educational institutions in Valle Giulia (Figure 5.2). A note dated 1958

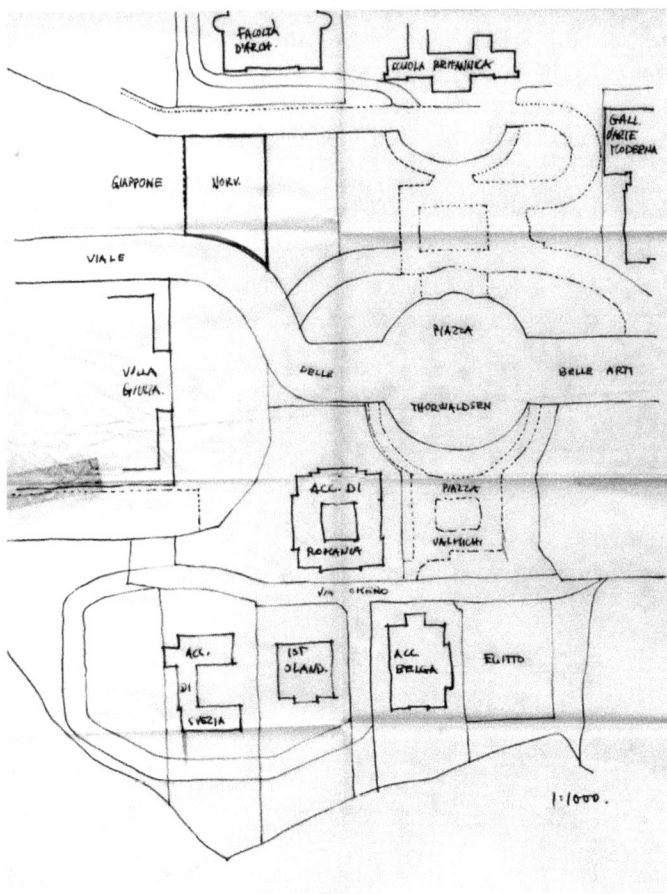

FIGURE 5.2 Map of Valle Giulia, with the proposed Norwegian plot, undated, hand-drawn map. Box: 1959–2002, 003.4. Diverse, Avisklipp, Opprettelse. Istituto di Norvegia in Roma. Courtesy of the Norwegian Institute in Rome, University of Oslo.

outlines the agreement between Italy and Norway, securing a 'Norwegian' plot located on a prime location: next to the Japanese Institute, close by the British School and overlooking the Swedish Institute across the valley.[2]

Hans Petter L'Orange and Hjalmar Torp had been working on founding the institute since 1955, arguing that 'Modern research categorically demands scholarship not be isolated, but integrated within an international scene: a whole universe of knowledge operating on a global scale'.[3] A plot at Valle Giulia would literally locate the institute right at the centre of such global research exchange. And for the design, young and promising Norberg-Schulz was involved as an architect. Dated 1958, his plans, facades and sections show the two-storey institute (Figure 5.3).[4]

But on 5 March 1961, Norberg-Schulz wrote an urgent letter to L'Orange, in which he expresses concern. In the Italian newspaper *Il Messaggero* he has read that the Japanese Cultural Institute is planning a garden exactly where the Norwegian Institute is to be built, and the issue requires immediate attention, Norberg-Schulz writes.[5] And if that plot goes to Japan, perhaps the land next to the Belgians (promised to Egypt) still might be free? Or he suggests how about attempting to negotiate with the Municipality of Rome for a new plot next to the planned Japanese garden?

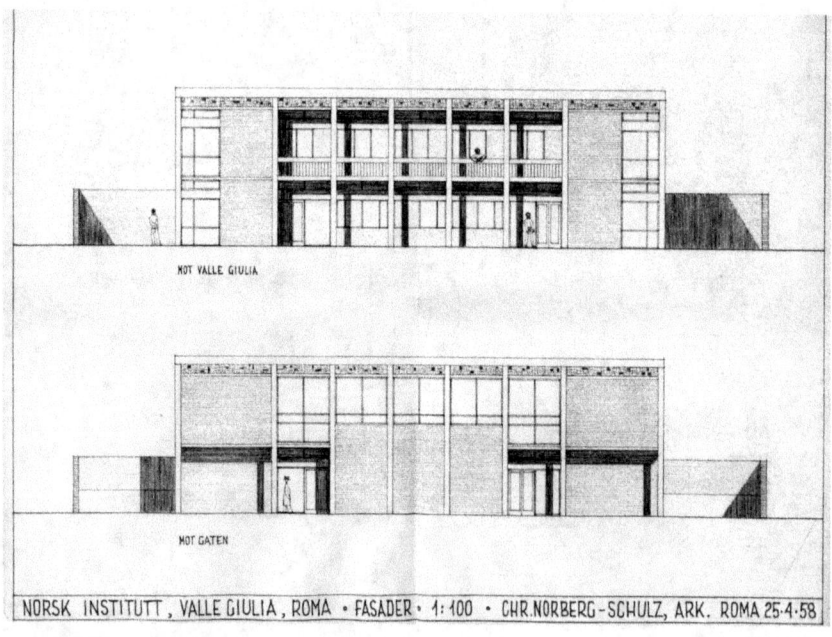

FIGURE 5.3 The Norwegian Institute in Rome, facade, 1958, architectural drawing. By Christian Norberg-Schulz. Box: 1959–2002, 003.4. Diverse, Avisklipp, Opprettelse. Istituto di Norvegia in Roma. Courtesy of the Norwegian Institute in Rome, University of Oslo.

A telegram of 9 March 1961 confirms Norberg-Schulz's suspicion: the Municipality of Rome would rather give the plot promised to Norway to the Japanese garden project in order to prevent any new construction in the area.[6] And so the Norwegians were in effect pushed out of the valley, and Norberg-Schulz's design was consequently discarded.

However, later in the year, the institute founders L'Orange and Hjalmar Torp found a suitable villa at Janiculum, close to the American Academy of Rome, which would suit the institute's needs if extended and renovated, and Norberg-Schulz was once again involved as the architect.

Knowing the project's difficult funding situation, Norberg-Schulz agreed to 50 per cent of a normal fee to design a two-storey extension, a roof terrace and the overall renovations. The work had to be completed by 31 December 1961, which gave Norberg-Schulz less than five months to finish the building and renovations. Throughout the process Norberg-Schulz worked closely with L'Orange and Torp, as well as Verga, the Italian construction company involved. But the project was marked by delays, conflict and miscommunication. L'Orange went away for an arthritis rehabilitation in Vicarello on 3 September, and on his return ten days later, he found that important building materials had not been ordered. Work had been delayed, but Verga claimed the order was the responsibility of the architect. Yet Norberg-Schulz appeared to have left for Naples.[7]

'My contract does not include ordering materials',[8] Norberg-Schulz wrote on 19 October. But the damage was done. Verga left the project, due to 'conflict with Norberg-Schulz'.[9] The situation was tense, and Norberg-Schulz wrote to L'Orange: 'I solemnly hope that this [letter] can end our discussion, as it is of importance for the build that the collaboration remains friendly.'[10] L'Orange and Norberg-Schulz remained lifelong friends, but as New Year's Eve 1961 approached, the building was far from finished, and the work would continue long into 1962.

Architectural historian Jorge Otero-Pailos, for one, identifies post-war bureaucracy as the main reason for Norberg-Schulz leaving architecture and becoming an 'architect-historian: a person who authors architecture by redefining how others see it'.[11] Leaving out the disappointing events of 1961, Norberg-Schulz himself in 1993 addressed his own professional shift in the following way: 'My interest in architectural history was sparked by studies in Italy. I thought I would be able to combine design and writing, but eventually had to make a decision.'[12] Faced with the impossibility of doing both, Norberg-Schulz chose writing history and theory, research and teaching.

Ordering materials might not have been for Norberg-Schulz, but he did propose that the window be filled with plaster. The window is a frame filled with glass, separated by window sills. This was the physical reality of the window – the literal window – that Norberg-Schulz ordered to be removed and discarded, before the empty frame was filled with cold, solid plaster.

Polished, painted and then covered up by a permanently shut blind, this window was to no longer hold the promise of view and air. Light or light projector? The architect made his decision, and the darkness of the library triumphed those fragile panes of glass. The window was removed, filled in with plaster.

If the window is not only a physical construct but also widely used as a metaphor for framing, exposing or for discussing that strange boundary or threshold that both separates and connects, and which can create unexpected relations, then filling a window frame with plaster is a strong statement: both in architecture and in language.

Norberg-Schulz knew how to master languages and was fluent in many that were foreign to his mother tongue. His successful authorship of books, articles and lectures listed on his CV stands as solid evidence on this.[13] And whereas Italy surely sparked his interest in architectural history, his choice of words when describing his decision is peculiar. In Norwegian, he said: 'Jeg hadde tenkt til å kombinere tegning og skriving, men jeg måtte ta et valg',[14] which translates into 'I had planned on combining drawing and writing, but I had to make a decision'. In describing his decision, he uses the word 'had'. Deriving from his initial plan, he did not *make* the decision, which would suggest some kind of agency, but he *had* to make the decision. This I read as if it was external pressure that led to him having to make up his mind. If this was the case, he fails to tell his listener the reason behind what I read as a somewhat forced verdict.

But to me, the frustrating events of 1961 stand as crystal-clear reasons why he left the architecture profession and never looked back. Instead of stating his frustration and resignation in words that January day in 1962, I believe that he wrote his statement in architecture, and he did so with assertion. *The Norwegian Institute in Rome* (1961–2) remains Norberg-Schulz's final, and southernmost, design project. As he filled in that window, he permanently pulled down the blind on the architectural profession.

* * *

When I visited the Norwegian Institute in Rome at Janiculum west of the city in early 2016, I made the following decision: to leave my camera on the rooftop terrace. I left it there before meeting with and interviewing Else L'Orange. As the daughter of the institute's co-founder, Hans Petter L'Orange, she partly grew up in the building and knew its history well. With two radio microphones connected into a Zoom H4n, I recorded our conversation. Starting in the institute's garden, we slowly made our way through the building, floor by floor.

Later, as I sat down with the footage to edit *The Norwegian Institute in Rome*, I made another decision. Within the frame of the editing software, I created two separate sections: to the right, I used the continuous footage from the roof terrace, while the left is dedicated to Norberg-Schulz's original

FIGURE 5.4 *The Norwegian Institute in Rome*, 2016. Anna Ulrikke Andersen.

plans from 1961 to 1962. These still images from the archive are juxtaposed with the slowness of time passing in the one-take shot from the roof terrace. A third element of the film is the audio capturing our movement through the building, without seeing a visual image of the people who speak. That is until 13:21 of the film when Else and I walk into the frame. And we do so with surprising effect (Figure 5.4).

Up to this point, the viewer has become accustomed to the disembodied voices and the subtle shifting of architectural plans and the footage of the roof terrace shown in one take. But then at 13:21, the viewer suddenly and unexpectedly sees us – as figures carrying those two voices – walk through a door, hidden in Norberg-Schulz's large panoramic window. I hold the door open and let Else out before we both walk over to the edge of the terrace. We face away from both the window and the camera. We stand on the terrace, overlooking the city and its surrounding hills towards the south-east. Else tells me how her father used to go hiking in those very hills, before rheumatoid arthritis affected his ability to walk. A typical Norwegian activity, as she describes it, her father's hiking was a little piece of Norway that he brought with him as he settled in Italy. Through the duration of almost four minutes, Else and I claim the frame with our visible presence, in the film and on the terrace.

I face away from Norberg-Schulz's large window, leaving my back exposed. It is exposed to the camera that is recording, but also framing my body is that large window designed by Norberg-Schulz. As a viewing device, his architecture overlooks and frames the city, echoing Pauline Gjøsteen's account of previous designs of his, in both Norway and Italy.[15] Fortress-like structures are what she describes: overlooking and dominating the landscape, there his buildings lie as lenses in the landscape.[16] As such, these carefully constructed windows frame a view they watch and control. As I face away from Norberg-Schulz's *bastille*, my exposed back is an easy target only waiting to be watched – branded and marked from behind, perhaps without my even knowing so.

To be branded and controlled from behind, this is what Jacques Derrida refers to in his notion of a *pancarte*: 'a billboard that we have on our backs and to which we can never really turn round'.[17] In his writing, such cards are written and sent by those who came before us. Derrida calls them *envois*, French for 'shipment', 'posts' or 'sending'. This is the same word with which he titles the series of short texts that form his book *La carte postale: De Socrate à Freud et au-delà* (1980),[18] known to most English readers as *The Postcards: From Socrates to Freud and Beyond* (1987).[19] Addressed to an unknown receiver, written and sent between 3 June 1977 and 30 August 1979, a series of *envois*, texts or postcards form an enigmatic piece of writing and thinking: fragmented and at times difficult to read. This style of writing runs in accord with one of the book's central themes – the interesting relationship which occurs between thinkers, as they refer to each other's work or when their own work is referenced by others. Thought is sent like postcards addressed to unknown receivers. What happens in this process can be unpredictable and what eventually gets delivered might be as fragmented and difficult to encode as Derrida's cards in the book.

The sender in his book comes across a postcard while conducting research in Oxford. It is a print of Plato and Socrates, from *Prognostica Socratis basilei*. The Bodleian Library holds the original thirteenth-century work by Matthew Paris, showing Socrates sitting on a chair, dipping his pen in ink to write on a piece of paper. Behind him stands Plato, pointing one finger into Socrates' back, the other pointing up, past his writing arm. The author underscores how the card depicts the spatial positioning. '[Socrates] is in front of Plato, no, Plato is *behind* him, smaller (why smaller?), but standing up' (Figure 5.5).[20]

From this remark we understand the spatial organization of the two thinkers, depicted on the postcard in question: one before, the other behind. Is the younger thinker before or behind the older? Who is dictating to whom? And this is not just a question that is relevant when looking at Socrates and Plato but includes the history of intellectual thought: from Socrates and Plato to Freud and beyond. Derrida does not give a clear idea of how these thinkers relate, who is behind whom, but through his text, instead, complicates the relationships.

The *pancarte*, then, is part of this generational configuration, one that cannot be avoided. Freud, Plato and Socrates are related to each other over time and through writers, thinkers, archivists and librarians, 'sent' from one to the other, as one thinker picks up and engages with the thinking of someone else. As Derrida writes: 'Plato sticks him with a *pancarte* and Freud who has it on his back can no longer get rid of it.'[21]

My back facing his large window, I become an easy target for Norberg-Schulz's *pancarte*. I feel his weight following me, as I follow him, and seek to frame his views with my camera, walk onto his roof terrace with my body or read his letters, plans and sections in the archive, taking notes

FIGURE 5.5 Socrates and Plato, thirteenth-century manuscript, by Matthew Paris (1217–59). The Bodleian Library in Oxford, MS Ashmole 304, 31v. Courtesy of the Bodleian Libraries, University of Oxford, Courtesy of Digital Bodleian, University of Oxford via Creative Commons. CC-BY-NC 4.0 89.

with my pen. I wander through the archival boxes in the library of the Norwegian Institute, a space dimly lit as my desk is facing a window that no longer exists as he ordered it to be filled in with plaster years ago (Figure 5.6).

As I work, examining this material, the building and its architect hover around, over, below, behind and in front of me. Derrida blames our 'bibliopedic' culture and how we have organized our books and boxes on cards and maps. Doing so dictates how we see and think. Placing one before or after the other, in front or behind it, ideas in words are placed next to each other: 'This is how to orient one's thought, this is the left and this the right, march.'[22] I think of Norberg-Schulz as I stand on the roof terrace. Speaking with Else, I might not see Norberg-Schulz's ghost, but as a *pancarte*, he is there with me.

If Freud was stuck with a *pancarte* on his back, possibly pondering on his position with regard to his forebears (or may I say forefathers?), his query was not gendered. Nor did Derrida consider what it might mean to a

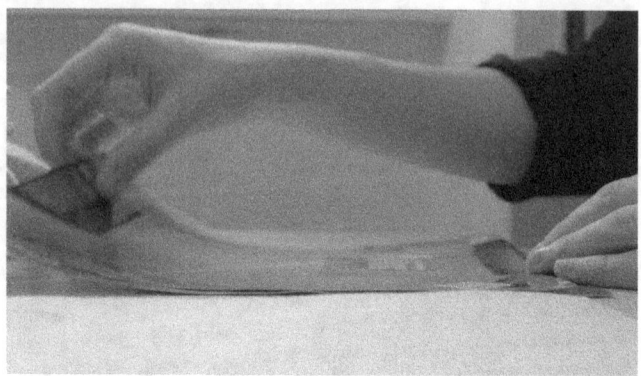

FIGURE 5.6 In the archive, 2016. Anna Ulrikke Andersen.

woman, how she might relate to a *pancarte* created, sent and stuck on you by a man.

Perhaps I must look elsewhere to find someone who did work and establish herself as a woman in a man's world, someone like Agnès Varda, as she claimed her space within the French new wave and became *the* female, feminist film-maker.[23] And she did so by allowing herself into the frame.

'I'm not behind the camera. I'm in it',[24] Varda claimed, as she, again and again, would allow herself into the films she was making: either as an actor[25] or by choosing locations close to her home or history,[26] or even by defining her films as self-portraits.[27] Her seminal work *The Gleaners and I* (2000) is no exception. A film about the somewhat forgotten activity of gleaning, Varda traces its history and searches for gleaners in contemporary culture. Through her film, she looks for people who pick things up from the ground, and by doing so, the film opens up a wide range of questions about gender, class and the environmental concerns of consumer culture. And Varda herself becomes a gleaner in the film, portrayed carrying grains or with a close-up where she picks up potatoes with one hand, while the other hand holds the recording camcorder. In the film, she is simultaneously the object and subject at hand (Figure 5.7).

Varda's tendency to enter her films as subject-maker and subject matter, and to be both the object of the film and the subject who makes the film, Kate Ince describes as an act of feminism. As Varda gleans by picking up her camera, potatoes or references to artists, thinkers and film-makers before her, she is doing so on, behind and in the camera, taking different positions. The consequence, according to Ince, is that Varda's films resist femininity as a cultural construct.[28] '*The Gleaners and I*, then, offers plentiful evidence that for Varda, female subjectivity is always "lived", that is, embodied and actively animated, even when it remains a viewed object.'[29] To Ince, Varda's location behind the camera and in it addresses this in a poignant way. In *The Gleaners and I*, the lightweight camcorder allows her to pick it up and film her own

FIGURE 5.7 *The Gleaners and I*, 2000. Agnès Varda and Cine Tamaris. All rights reserved.

hand: one hand on the camera, the other framed by that very same camera. I see Varda's body as engulfing the camera, literally, but also figuratively as she allows her own experiences to affect the subject matter of the film.

In Varda's use of her own body, the first-person pronoun *I*, Varda draws attention to women and their experiences at large.[30] By discussing Varda's feminist and filmic *I*, also I as a subject wish to draw attention to my own presence as a film-maker within the frame of my film. I position myself next to, rather than in front or behind the woman I am speaking with. I not only speak to Else and walk through the building with her. Eventually, the bodies of those speaking subjects move into the frame. I set up the camera to capture this moment. I conducted the historical research preceding this film-making moment, prepared for me by the (female) librarian Manuela, my stay organized in collaboration with the (female) administrative staff Anne and Mona. Whereas I have presence in the frame, the presence of female helpers and their labour is not visible. They are invisible around its edges, and this strikes me as quite poignant.

I becomes visible in my film and inspired by Varda's use of herself in her films, I consider my entrance as an act of feminism. I am following Norberg-Schulz, who was a man. Just as Norberg-Schulz took his stand, made his point and filled in that window, I move confidently into the frame. As I moved into the frame and claimed attention, what *exactly* was my position following a man: Norberg-Schulz?

* * *

When, towards the end of his life, Norberg-Schulz was asked what in his *oeuvre* he was most proud of, his answer was the following: a short piece of writing about a pond in the woodlands surrounding Oslo. 'Båntjern' (1986) was published in *Et sted å være: Essays og artikler* (1986) and is relatively short: four pages with a full page covered by a photograph of the pond. Here, he brings together his phenomenological project, a call for an architectural design that shows care for its surroundings and a story told through accounts of his personal experience of walking to this pond in the woods.

> When we arrive at the pond, we sit down and feel calm. We remember the woodland we have just walked through, the path we have followed, and we experience the pond as a destination. Now, we have arrived; we do not have to walk any further, at least not right away. We first want to experience the place, know what the pond is telling us, and understand why exactly this pond invites us to stay. 'We have arrived', we say.[31]

Norberg-Schulz uses his own experience in this article, as he so often did in his writing.[32] He certainly builds his experience of walking into his writing. But instead of *I*, he uses the pronoun *we*. And the sentence 'when I arrive at the pond, I sit down and feel calm' would read quite differently from the one he wrote: 'When *we* arrive at the pond, *we* sit down and feel calm.'[33] The first example is an account of one person's experience, whereas the latter suggests that one person's experience already speaks for a larger group. With this text, he suggests that we all walk the same way in woods, ignoring the fact that *we* as a group consists of different individuals, who experience the world differently. When Norberg-Schulz speaks on my behalf, I do not feel that it resonates – first, my position as a woman. Second, my position as a Norwegian.

The way Norberg-Schulz describes the experience of large groups of people as unified and coherent is recurrent in his writing, and it has also been the basis of much criticism of his authorship. The criticism aimed at his work is persistent, even harsh, as touched upon in previous essays. In the critique Norberg-Schulz has received, he is described as a traditionalist[34] and worthy of question.[35] Rowan Wilken claims that Norberg-Schulz's focus on locality and place is traditionalist and nostalgic.[36] Similarly, Alberto Pérez-Gómez outlines the generalization of experience in Norberg-Schulz's thinking. 'To expect that one can isolate regional or cultural characteristics and reflect them in architecture through a conscious, externalized operation is naïve',[37] he writes. Pérez-Gómez advocates instead a more nuanced conception of place, as he argues: 'Making architecture with a desire to acknowledge local identity we must recognize the priority of embodiment and our connections to the natural world, and yet neither the world nor the body is simply given unmediated, as permanent and unchanging essence.'[38] The persistent critique that Norberg-Schulz is often aimed towards the universalist aspects of phenomenology. The way Norberg-Schulz convert *I* into *we* is an example of this way of thinking. Following Pérez-Gómes emphasis on embodiment, my focus is on *I* instead of the more general, universal *we*.

I am inspired by Gro Lauvland's use of Hannah Arendt's reading of Heidegger's phenomenology. Lauvland reads Arendt's *The Human Condition* (1958) as a way of seeing place as political.[39] Within this argument, Lauvland draws attention to how Arendt's work opens up for a greater sense of diversity and a politics of place that is free and inclusive.[40]

'Norwegians love nature',[41] Norberg-Schulz claims at the outset of 'Båntjern'. And by doing so, he makes a generalized claim that accounts for Norwegians as a whole. And as I make my way into the frame at the roof terrace and claim my position, I realize the following: *I* do not like the way Norberg-Schulz talks about *me*. As a Norwegian, I am part of this group of people that he claims to love nature. But what if I don't? What if I prefer staying in the Italian sun, in a big city, surrounded by noise, dust and concrete?

Standing on the roof terrace, looking south-east, I am tempted never again to turn north. Yet, I walk back through that framed panorama, into and through the building, I return to wherever I 'came from'. But having followed and framed Norberg-Schulz's movements from Norway to Italy, I experienced and reflected: upon what it means to follow and what my position is as a follower. The claim that all Norwegians love nature does not allow for different kinds of experience. Different bodies experience place differently. When I read Norberg-Schulz, I sometimes get the feeling that he regards his own personal experiences to speak objectively. To me, this objectivity is epitomized in his use of *we*, rather than *I*. As a Norwegian, feminist film-maker, I object to what Norberg-Schulz claims in 'Båntjern', the article he understood as his most important and accomplished piece of writing.

At the same time, being in his building and looking through its archive create a sense of empathy. I feel frustrated when I think about Norberg-Schulz's final years as an architect. I feel his ambition, enthusiasm and vision for what the building in Valle Giulia could have been, and his passion and genuine interest in the project once it moved to Janiculum, as he agreed to half his pay for the job on the renovations and extension. The correspondence between the involved actors is both agonizing and touching. The duration of the project, the lack of funding and the idealism that went into the build are all very impressive. As he filled in the window, and I move into the frame, my position is filled with ambiguity.

Window 6

Piazza Navona

Place

Piazza Navona, Rome, Italy
Latitude: 41.899163
Longitude: 12.473074
Language: Italian (Finestra)

Practice

I: Campari-Moment
2014
Anna Ulrikke Andersen
HD video
03:08
https://vimeo.com/268140434

Password: CNS

II: Campari-Moment
Anna Ulrikke Andersen
HD video
13:50
https://vimeo.com/268140713

Password: CNS

FIGURE 6.1 *II: Campari-Moment*, 2016. Anna Ulrikke Andersen.

I: Campari-Moment (2014) and *II: Campari-Moment* (2016) are unedited rushes of films showing me ordering and drinking a Campari at Piazza Navona. The films were shot with a Blackmagic Design Camera and a Philips radio microphone recording into the Zoom H4n, with the help of Mikkel Due (16 September 2014) and John Øyvind Hovde (15 February 2016). Language: English.

Essay

A Campari-moment by the water fountain

Christian Norberg-Schulz was sitting at Piazza Navona in Rome after having spent the morning in the valleys north of the city. He was enjoying a Campari and watching life at the *piazza*, when he was struck by a sudden feeling: that the *piazza* and the valleys that he had visited earlier in the day were the *same*. Not similar: the valley was rural with steep tufa-rock formations in the landscape, coloured yellow and brown. The *piazza* was surrounded by buildings, filled with fountains, sculptures, restaurants and people. Yet, the architectural theorist marked a sameness between the two places as he later wrote:

> Suddenly, I had a feeling of still being in a 'tufa-valley': this is the same, (despite not being similar)! So started my study of the *genius loci*. Because of sudden inspiration, and not at all a logical line of thought.[1]

Published in 1999, this was Norberg-Schulz's own account of how his study of the *genius loci* began. The realization of the fact that the valley and the *piazza* shared a sameness, and that the Roman term *genius loci* could be a way to describe sameness, came to him immediately and suddenly when drinking a Campari at Piazza Navona. He had what I am describing as 'a Campari-moment'.

The history of Piazza Navona far exceeds that of Campari: an aperitif invented in 1860 by Gaspare Campari. Piazza Navona's history goes back to antiquity, built on the site of the Stadium of Domitian from the first century AD, when the *piazza* was a circus: a place for horse races, gladiator fights and entertainment. The elongated shape of the *piazza* still owes much to the antique horse race, a shape that remained even as the *piazza* was radically changed in the Baroque period under the papacy of Pope Innocent X. A *palazzo* for the Pamphili family was designed by Girolamo Rainaldi in 1644, Francesco Borromini designed the church Sant'Agnese in Piazza Navona (1652) and Gian Lorenzo Bernini designed the fountain Fontana dei Quattro Fiumi [Fountain of the Four Rivers] (1651). A favoured tourist destination, the Piazza Navona of today is known for these Baroque masterpieces – among them, the fountain (Figure 6.2).

This very fountain figures in Norberg-Schulz's writing. Before his authorship turned towards theory and phenomenology, Norberg-Schulz had focused his historical authorship on Baroque architecture. In fact, his first book was dedicated to the architecture of Michelangelo,[2] and his passionate interest in the Baroque remained with him throughout his career. In his many books, articles and essays, Piazza Navona makes its way into his argument: historically and later theoretically. In the close to identical texts from *Baroque Architecture* (1979) and 'Piazza Navona' (1986), he saw Piazza Navona, with its buildings and artworks, as employing certain characteristics of the era. Ideas of enclosure,[3] openness and movement are brought up as distinctly Baroque,[4] a period formed by the achievements of exploratory travel, colonization and scientific research.[5]

'In general, Piazza Navona represents the typical space of Roman Baroque architecture, a space that is eminently dynamic, vital and various',[6]

FIGURE 6.2 Piazza Navona, 2016. Anna Ulrikke Andersen.

he writes in *Baroque Architecture*. A specific kind of centralization that was fluid and dynamic rather than static stands as a significant trait of the era, and Norberg-Schulz describes the Baroque city as centred around specific *foci*, focal points, that could be buildings, such as Sant'Agnese, or fountains, such as Four Rivers.[7] Although separate works, they relate to each other, Norberg-Schulz argues. As such, Norberg-Schulz sees Baroque architecture and planning always to create a whole: the totality of a city.[8] The focal points are not standing alone; they are part of a greater correlation and a whole.

The Baroque also seeps into Norberg-Schulz's theoretical oeuvre. *Genius Loci* (1980) has a chapter dedicated to the city of Rome, where Piazza Navona makes its appearance. He articulates Rome's character, structure and spirit of the place, similarly forming a whole and a totality. Norberg-Schulz's position on Baroque architecture appears suitable for a theory of place, considering different places – such as a rural valley and Piazza Navona – as being the *same*. He saw Rome as a whole, rather than a collection of single buildings, which Norberg-Schulz adopts as part of his phenomenological project.[9]

In Norberg-Schulz's *Genius Loci* the totality is made up from a series of places, following a similar line of thought as presented in his discussions on the Baroque. He suggests that the Baroque city was constructed out of elements in the context of a greater whole. On the larger scale: the city. The *piazza* at a smaller scale.

But in *Genius Loci* this totality goes beyond even the urban structure of the city, to include the structure of the surrounding landscape. Norberg-Schulz describes the landscape using two terms: *forre* and *campagna*.[10] *Forre* is a term used to describe the steep rock formations in the landscape surrounding Rome. The volcanic rock here has been dug from rivers, creating the steep, surprising formations in the landscape. At the top, there is a sharp edge, where the *campagna* begins and stretches out. The *campagna* is defined by Norberg-Schulz as open and wide and provides an overview of the large spaces.[11] From the structure of the *campagna*, Norberg-Schulz argues that axis seen in the planning in the city of Rome forms a similar structure. The axis structure stands as a central urban theme of Rome that Norberg-Schulz relates to the structures seen in the *campagna* surrounding the city.[12] Norberg-Schulz, thus, sees the city of Rome as being compiled out of *forre* in terms of small narrow streets and the axis in terms of the axis in the city planning. These structures are directly linked to the landscape.[13] The ides of the *forre* and the axis remain a central thought in this theory of *genius loci*.[14]

Norberg-Schulz concludes his chapter on Rome at Piazza Navona in this way:

> At Piazza Navona we are really 'inside', close to the earth, close to the palpable things of everyday existence, at the same time as we feel ward of a comprehensive cultural totality. No wonder that it has become the popular place of Rome *par excellence*. The synthesis of nature and culture is condensed and visualized in Bernini's great fountain, where natural elements such as water and rocks are combined with human figures and religious symbols, as well as the *axis mundi* of the obelisk.[15]

Here, he argues, Rome's archetypical form can be found in both the idyllic form of the *forre* and the grand axis of the *campagna*. The large-scale structures of place affect individual examples of architectural design, Norberg-Schulz argues.

It was this idea that came to him – suddenly – with a drink at hand, sitting on the *piazza* overlooking the fountain – four river Gods springing out from a rock-formation and with them, water: flowing from inside the fountain. The dynamic, forceful, Baroque sculpture is crowned by a tall obelisk decorated with hieroglyphs. The fountain stood as a *foci* to Norberg-Schulz, sharing similar structures to its surrounding landscape and city planning. The *piazza* and the *forre* are the same. Not similar, but the *same*. At the water fountain, with a drink at hand, Norberg-Schulz suddenly realized how the *foci* of the *piazza* related to a whole.

* * *

I went to Piazza Navona first in 2014 and then returned in 2016. I had been intrigued by, and drawn towards, Norberg-Schulz's anecdote of how he suddenly understood that places can share a similar *genius loci* while drinking Campari in Piazza Navona.[16] I sought out both the place and the drink that had triggered his thinking. Thirsty for knowledge, I needed a glass of Campari to gain a greater phenomenological understanding of my subject at hand. As part of my following of Norberg-Schulz, I re-enacted the Campari-moment on those two occasions. The two re-enactments share some similar traits: both are recorded from the other side of the *piazza*, with my Blackmagic Cinema Camera, the sound from a radio-microphone attached to my clothes. Twice, I walked into the frame from the left, sat down at one of the restaurants and ordered a Campari.

On both occasions, the experience was quite uneventful. That is not to say that I didn't experience the two re-enactments as different. On my first attempt in 2014, I was tired after too many appointments and too much travelling. My following of Norberg-Schulz's journey from Hamburg and Basel had been marked by disappointment, as the present day conflicted with the photographs from the past. Sitting in Piazza Navona in Rome, I no longer expected proximity to my subject of study. My attention was mainly on the practicalities of film-making: being there, with the camera, setting it up, recording, performing, packing it all down again before leaving for the next shot. It was hot, early in the morning, and I felt dizzy from the strong alcoholic drink. From the corner of my eye, I paid attention to the camera across the *piazza*. It was more about me than it was about Norberg-Schulz.

My second re-enactment took place in 2016 after almost two years of thinking and planning my next journey. In that time period, I had developed my ideas and had time to reflect. I had travelled, followed, experienced, filmed, reflected, written and edited, before again travelling to experience and to film. My thinking was not sudden and immediately, I understood my argument to develop in time, being questioned by various departures and returns. On the second visit in 2016, I was facing the exact same direction as in 2014, but two years earlier, I had not paid much attention to Bernini's fountain. Perhaps the rain on that February day not only reminded me that the two visits had taken place during different seasons and that time had passed but also made me more aware of the water pouring from the water fountain. Drinking Campari at Piazza Navona twice shaped two different experiences of place that felt more different than Norberg-Schulz's suggestion of *sameness*. Norberg-Schulz's Campari-moment is described as a singular, immediate moment where insight and understanding took place. When such a moment occurred, there were no need to visit again, to rethink, or rephrase. According to Norberg-Schulz's own accounts of this Campari-moment, a flicker of insight was all he needed. There was no need to visit twice.

'Some research projects are pure with fulfilment, intellectual enterprises that gratify both mind and fancy. This book was just such a guilty pleasure, the culmination of a persistent desire to occupy, if only for a moment, the private lives of celebrated authors',[17] Diana Fuss wrote this phrase in regards to her project *The Sense of an Interior* (2004). Here she explores the life of the four authors, Emily Dickinson, Sigmund Freud, Marcel Proust and Helen Keller, with a focus on the rooms where they lived and wrote. As I followed Norberg-Schulz and had arrived at Piazza Navona to drink my

Campari, I no longer expected to occupy or get close to Norberg-Schulz's private life. What, then, was the purpose of my visit and my 'following' of his journeys, and as part of this, my attempts to re-enact his experiences? Watching Bernini's fountain, I took another sip of my drink and started thinking about guilt and the notion of being guilty.

In 1981, John W. Hinckley, Jr., attempted to assassinate President Ronald Reagan, and during his trial, Hinckley claimed that he was re-enacting a scene from Martin Scorcese's *Taxi-Driver* (1976). In this film, Vietnam War veteran Travis Bickle, played by Robert De Niro, plans the assassination of presidential candidate and Senator Charles Palantine. As his attempt fails, he instead goes to Iris, a prostitute he has befriended, played by Jody Foster. Taking out his aggression towards the senator, Bickle instead kills Iris's pimp. But instead of being seen as a murderer and villain, the public treats Bickle as a hero who saved the young woman. Perhaps Hinckley also dreamed about becoming a hero, as he dressed like Bickle and drank the same alcohol that the character drank.

Discussing the aspect of re-enactment in Hinckley's crime, Peggy Phelan describes a potentially questionable behaviour that is often seen in re-enactments:

> Imitative behaviour, such as buying a jacket that looks like Travis Bickle's, or drinking the same liquor as the character, expresses identificatory logic that is the bedrock of both capitalism and advertising's *raison d'être*. Imitative behaviour becomes dangerous, when the imitation is so complete it erodes a sense of self, and a sense of a world independent of one's own relationship to it.[18]

In Hinckley's case, such behaviour could have had fatal consequences for the president. I was also following someone I had never met and drinking what *he* had been drinking. I had been following Norberg-Schulz through Europe twice. Yet, it was at those moments at Piazza Navona while drinking Campari I started feeling uncomfortable (Figure 6.3).

When discussing Sophie Calle's work *Suite Venitienne* (1980), Jean Baudrillard suggests that the kind of shadowing, or following, that she had performed takes the responsibility away from one's life as he writes: 'she who folles is herself relieved of responsibility for her own life as she follows blindly in the footsteps of the other'.[19]

In *Suite Venitienne* Calle followed a stranger, a man called Henri B., from Paris to Venice. Equipped with a blond wig and a camera, she purchases her ticket in Paris and arrives by train in Venice on Tuesday 12 February 1980. Not knowing where Henri B. is staying, she calls hotels, wanders around the city and looks for him through windows of restaurants.

Calle hides behind windows. When she discovers where Henri B. lives, she makes an agreement with a doctor who owns the flat across the street to sit at a window overlooking the hotel's entrance. Calle finds herself by

FIGURE 6.3 Campari moment, 2014–16. Anna Ulrikke Andersen.

the window on 20 February 1980 and writes: 'At 7:30 PM: I leave. I will be back tomorrow at 9:00 to station myself at this window. *Why this obstinacy, this window now?*'[20]

Why this window now? A transparent, but also potentially reflective (and self-reflective) barrier, the window makes the following safer. It removes an aspect of the confrontational, as well as provides protection, and I wonder if it also assigns some of the responsibility for the act of following to the window itself, the architecture that frames her experience.

I had no such boundary between my camera and the objects and subjects I choose to frame. Twice, I record my Campari-moment with a radio-microphone attached to me, while the camera captures the scene from across the *piazza*. This is a technique similar to the one that I have used in my other films: *The Death of the Chemist* (2016). As I have described in Window 1 | Trondheim, this film uses sound recordings separated from the visual imagery of a building's exterior. *The Norwegian Institute in Rome* (2016) discussed in Window 5 | Rome, similarly, separates sound and image, until Else L'Orange and I eventually walk into the frame and the voices become attached to bodies. In my films, my separation and then the connection of sound and image enhance the uncertainty involved in my work as an architectural historian or is a powerful means to make myself as a writing, speaking and making subject visible in the discussion.

But in my footage from Piazza Navona, the radio microphones and footage bring up other questions and issues. The way the camera is located so far away from the restaurant, and the fact that this is a public space, has resemblance to the practice of filming using a hidden camera, where the people being filmed are unaware that they are being filmed and recorded. Attaining permission to film at Piazza Navona proved to be incredibly expensive and difficult, and my budget simply did not allow for it. Hence, I did not ask the restaurant for permission to film, nor did I ask the waiter if I could record his voice. The waiter could not be recognized from the footage, so I did not see any legal issues around consent. But does this make my covert practice acceptable?

Perhaps I should include only the unedited rushes, footage I even wasn't that happy with from a technical perspective. I put the two sequences into Premiere Pro, which adds titles and exports: *I: Campari-Moment* (2014) and the other *II: Campari-Moment* (2016). As I had no permission to make films, the result of my visit to Piazza Navona are two mov. files that I decided would not become films to be viewed publicly. Instead, the footage remains raw, as if their fate has not been decided yet. I start considering the footage itself as floating and even fickle, as if I cannot really get a good grasp of their potential meaning, as if I cannot really get a good grasp of what it might mean. In his poem *Les Fenêtres IV* (1927), Rainer Maria Rilke describes windows 'as fickle as the sea'[21] – windows, just as water is moving, changing and difficult to grasp. I think about the different meanings and uses of the window that Lutz Koepnick describes intermingle on its surface.[22] The fickleness of windows could be read both figuratively as a concept and literally, linking the window pane to water flowing through the fingers.

> I stood still, my whole attention fixed upon the motions of her fingers. Suddenly I felt a misty consciousness as of something forgotten – a thrill of returning though: and somehow the mystery of language was revealed to me. I knew then that 'w-a-t-e-r' meant the wonderful cool something that was flowing over my hand. That living word awakened my soul, gave it light, hope joy, set it free.[23]

These were the words of Helen Keller (1880–1968) describing the experience of learning language described in her autobiography *The Story of My Life* (1903). The American author, political activist and lecturer had caught an unknown illness when she was nineteen months old. She survived, but the illness left her blind and deaf. So, Keller as a child had problems communicating with her surroundings.

That was until the family hired the teacher Anne Sullivan. After Sullivan had attempted to teach the child language by presenting her with objects she could touch and repeatedly giving her a sign language in her hand without success, a breakthrough occurred one day by the water fountain. Up until this moment, Keller had learned hand-movements but had not made the connection between object and word. But at the water fountain in the wellhouse, Sullivan placed the child's hand under the spout and the other hand on Sullivan's mouth. Sullivan said the word 'water', and Keller felt the vibrations with her hand. This moment is described in Keller's autobiography *The Story of My Life* quoted earlier and later depicted in the two films *The Miracle Worker* (1962) and *Deliverance* (1919). This was a moment when Keller suddenly felt a misty consciousness and could understand the connection between water as a phenomenon and the word 'water' (Figures 6.4 and 6.5).

To Keller, language opened up new possibilities of communicating with others, either through sign language and touch or eventually through reading, writing and speaking – literature she saw as 'enchanted windows'[24] that gave her sight.

> I left the well-house eager to learn. Everything had a name, and each name gave birth to a new thought. As we returned to the house, every object which I touched seemed to quiver with life. That was because I saw everything with the strange, new sight that had come to me.[25]

FIGURE 6.4 *The Miracle Worker*, 1962. Arthur Penn and Playfilm Productions. All rights reserved.

FIGURE 6.5 *The Miracle Worker*, 1962. Arthur Penn and Playfilm Productions. All rights reserved.

'Remember Helen Keller <u>"Water"</u>',[26] Norberg-Schulz wrote this in his travel journal after a trip to Spoleto, Assisi, and Todi 29–30 September 1973. Written as a reminder to himself, the note suggests that he returned to his travel journal later on. Initially having made this note with a blue pen, he later added red marks next to the initial blue, the red marks reminding him to revisit his notes later on.

Keller's experience of object and language intrigued thinkers in many fields. The philosopher William James even reached out to Keller, and the two discussed her sense perception, without the nature of this exchange being clear to me from Keller's autobiographical accounts.[27] Phenomenologist Maurice Merleau-Ponty draws attention to Keller in his discussion on sensible signification. He writes: 'The table that I touch and the one that I see are the same table. But must it be added, as we have said, that I hear the same sonata that Helen Keller touches, and that it is the same man whom I see and whom the blind painter paints.'[28] According to Merleau-Ponty, Keller's touching rather than hearing a sonata related to the same signified object. Diana Fuss relates Merleau-Ponty's reference to Keller to his attention to touch: the importance of the hand and touch in creating contact with the world.[29] (Figure 6.6).

And for Norberg-Schulz, the story of Keller by the water fountain sparked a different discussion:

> In *The Story of my Life,* the deaf-blind, American author Helen Keller recalls how the world opens itself up to her. It happened when she was seven years old, and she says herself that was the understanding of the fact that all things have a *name* that liberated her.[30]

The sequence is taken from an article titled 'Water', in which Norberg-Schulz sees water as a mobile element that is the origin of all things.[31]

FIGURE 6.6 Helen Keller, typing at her desk by the window, 1929. Photograph by Alfred Tennyson Beals. Courtesy of the American Foundation for the Blind, Helen Keller Archive.

This article on water is rather short, published in an edited collection of essays, opening with Norberg-Schulz's reference to Helen Keller and her experience of water with her teacher, followed by a discussion on how she made a connection between the thing and its *name*. To Norberg-Schulz the connection between the phenomena of water and the word associated with it – spoken by Keller's teacher and experienced by Keller's hand touching the teacher's mouth – seems most interesting.

'Water' is a word with an image and a sound, and in chemistry, it is referred to as H_2O, but both the word 'water' and the formal denomination H_2O are, according to Norberg-Schulz, far from our experience of the wetness of water.

> By explaining all things being in the world, phenomenology is the starting point for all science. As Heidegger says 'Science does not open the world, it explores that which is already opened.' We must, in other words, understand water phenomenologically before we can define it as H_2O.[32]

In this quote, Norberg-Schulz underscores how water is not only H_2O, since this clinical name for water does not account for the experience of water as a phenomenon. If science does not open the world, experience does. According to Norberg-Schulz, the articulation of water – or windows for that matter – happens immediately. It is not a line of thought that develops over time. Norberg-Schulz's Campari-moment is, thus, comparable with his moment on the train, as depicted in the opening scene of *Livet finner sted* (1992).[33] They link to Keller's experience by the water fountain. All these moments are sudden, where gaining knowledge is like being struck by lightning, as it is informed by a physical experience. To Norberg-Schulz knowledge is formed through experience, taking place either by the train window or while drinking a Campari.

Norberg-Schulz writes in *Genius Loci* that the window focuses and explains the *genius loci*.[34] If the previous discussion is taken into account, the focus and explanation that he refers to happens immediately, forcefully and with an exclamation point. Whereas the Campari-moment does not directly involve any actual windows, what this moment represents is closely related to the way Norberg-Schulz uses the window in his writing or the film: both suggest that certain ideas come suddenly and immediate, to be focused and explained by the experiencing subject. Norberg-Schulz's experience by Bernini's fountain with a drink at hand or at the window of a train and Keller's experience by the water fountain all suggest the same immediacy in the way these experiences are being re-told. Keller becomes the poster-child for Norberg-Schulz's phenomenological way of thinking.

Window 7

Calcata

Place

Calcata, Italy
Latitude: 42.204533
Longitude: 12.423730
Language: Italian (Finestra)

Practice

Calcata
2017
Anna Ulrikke Andersen
HD video
12:37
Featuring: Paolo Portoghesi
https://vimeo.com/208204366

Password: anna

Calcata (2017) is based on an interview with Paolo Portoghesi in his home in Calcata, Italy. Here, he speaks about his friendship with Christian Norberg-Schulz and their shared interest in the poetry of Rainer Maria Rilke. The interview was shot with a Blackmagic Design Camera, and sound was recorded with a Zoom H4n. The B-roll is shot with a Blackmagic Pocket

FIGURE 7.1 *Calcata*, 2017. Anna Ulrikke Andersen.

Camera, and sound was recorded with either Røde Video-Mic Pro or Zoom H4n. Languages: English, French, German, Italian. Subtitles: English.

Essay

Are we not here to say . . . window

I drove to Calcata on a bright February day to interview the Italian architect Paolo Portoghesi, as I wanted to learn more about his friendship with Christian Norberg-Schulz. When I arrived, I set up my Blackmagic Design Cinema Camera in his office, took out my H4n Zoom recorder and started recording. Portoghesi politely answered my questions about how and when the two architects met, their shared interest in Baroque architecture and his choice of inviting Norberg-Schulz to contribute with an installation for the first Venice Architecture Biennale in 1980. After an hour, the interview came to an end, and Portoghesi invited me to his nearby home to show some drawings and photographs. The architectural historian in me was intrigued, as I was interested in having a closer look at the material and continue our conversation. The film-maker in me was, however, not all that excited. The camera would be too heavy and complicated for me to bring, especially with a sound being recorded externally on a Zoom H4n. I quickly decided to leave my camera behind and only carry my sound recorder as I followed Portoghesi into the dark February night (Figure 7.2).

The first section of the film *Calcata* (2017) is edited out of my interview with Portoghesi, but as he suggests leaving, the screen becomes black. The viewer is left in the dark and can only follow our movements through the soundtrack.

As expected, the conversation did become more interesting in Portoghesi's house. I met his dog, his wife, and he showed me an original drawing by Borromini. As I had noticed many books by or about the poet Rainer Maria Rilke in Norberg-Schulz's private library, I eventually asked Portoghesi if he could tell me more. 'Rilke, my passion!',[1] Portoghesi exclaimed, before showing me his original copy of *Duino Elegies* (1922) published by Insel Verlag. Portoghesi then explains how he and Norberg-Schulz found a common friend in Rilke.[2] He sees his own *oeuvre* as influenced by six people. The first group defines his early work and consists of the architect Francesco Borromini and the poets Giacomo Leopardi and Arthur Rimbaud. Portoghesi outlined how he, in the second phase, studied Rilke, Martin Heidegger and Friedrich Hölderlin 'The second three are strongly influenced by Christian

FIGURE 7.2 Paolo Portoghesi suggests to leave his office, *Calcata*, 2017. Anna Ulrikke Andersen.

[Norberg-Schulz].'³ Beyond the two architects' interest in architecture, and collaboration for the 1980 Venice Biennale, it is clear that the two shared a passion for poetry.

Portoghesi and Norberg-Schulz were friends long before the 1980 Biennale. The two had met, as Portoghesi recalls, in Rome at some point between 1959 and 1961.⁴ Norberg-Schulz had seen the construction of Portoghesi's *Casa Baldi* (1959–62) and was intrigued. Their friendship developed as they explored a shared interest in the history and theory of architecture. In the 1960s their friendship was 'so strong like in my life I had never had',⁵ Portoghesi explains before showing me a photograph of the two friends immersed in conversation in Calcata while eating polenta (Figure 7.3). 'I invited him to the Biennale for the exhibition for *The Presence of the Past*',⁶ Portoghesi adds.

Although described as a relatively small event in 1980, *The Presence of the Past* –the first Venice Biennale of Architecture – has later been pinpointed as the moment when postmodern architecture was defined, discussed and exhibited for the very first time.⁷ The main feature of the exhibition consisted of a series of facades designed by invited architects, which formed a street in the Arsenale, in Venice. At the end of this Strada Novissima was the aforementioned *mostra dei critici*, or 'critic's section'.

In this section, Norberg-Schulz's immense panorama engulfed the installations of the two other invited critics and their work: Charles Jenck's design of a grand, blue, slanting pencil placed in the middle of the room and Vincent Scully's video work. Described as an 'immersive environment',⁸ the audience could walk along the panorama exploring a series of photographs placed on five horizontally separated fields, depicting Norberg-Schulz's take on the history of architecture (Figure 7.4).

FIGURE 7.3 Portoghesi and Norberg-Schulz eating the polenta, undated. Courtesy of Paolo Portoghesi.

FIGURE 7.4 The critic's section, 1980 Venice Architecture Biennale. Courtesy of Archivio Storico della Biennale di Venezia, the Historical Archives of Contemporary Arts (ASAC), Venice.

Léa-Catherine Szacka, who has written extensively on the history of this first architectural Biennale, briefly discusses the often-overlooked critic's section and its role in theorizing postmodern architecture. The critics were initially invited to interpret, discuss and correspond with Strada Novissima, yet the outcome did not receive as much attention as the rest of the exhibition. Szacka describes the critic's section as 'less memorable'[9] and draws attention to how the section was seldom mentioned in reviews of the 1980 Venice Architecture Biennale.[10] The critic's section has received far less attention by historians than the Biennale overall, except for Szacka's work and an article titled 'Christian Norberg-Schulz at the Venice Biennale.'[11]

In a folder titled 'Venice 1980', kept in the Norberg-Schulz archive in Oslo, I find Norberg-Schulz's notes, correspondences and sketches for an exhibition design for the critic's section.[12] He titled his exhibition design *Life Place Architecture*, and his contribution took the form of an installation consisting of a 52 metre-long panorama, a poem he had written himself and an article for the Biennale catalogue.[13]

Szacka successfully links Norberg-Schulz's panorama to his phenomenological work and interest in Heidegger's seminal essay 'Building Dwelling Thinking' (1954). She sees clear connections between Norberg-

Schulz's *Genius Loci: Towards a Phenomenology of Architecture* (1980) and *Mellom himmel og jord: en bok om steder og hus* (1978), and the panorama in the way that it expresses the importance of dwelling in architecture, locating architecture on a grid of horizontal and vertical features.[14]

> Norberg-Schulz argued that man's identity is defined by 'the identity of the place' and that places have a spatial structure that must first be understood as a relationship between the horizontal and the vertical lines present on site. Whilst the horizontal lines represent the rhythms of the life-world, the vertical ones represent a tension that transcends the spherical world: 'Earth and Sky constitute a "landscape", which is the basic form of concrete space'.[15]

The panorama presents a history of architecture, expressed through photographs depicting a series of visual structures. Norberg-Schulz locates these between earth and sky that is represented with the colours brown and blue. His drawings make this explicit. A human figure is drawn next to the panorama. In Norwegian he has written 'menneske, horisont, jord og himmel',[16] which translates into human, horizon, earth and sky. In other words, between earth and sky, life takes place. Probably built by technicians from the Italian film studio Cinecittà as the rest of the exhibition had been,[17] Norberg-Schulz was able to express his theoretical ideas in space and not in his usual books, articles or lectures. And whereas he also wrote a more traditional article to go in the Biennale catalogue, his main contribution was this panorama and a poem that expressed his phenomenological approach to architecture in a new way.

The poem has not received any scholarly attention, but is currently available in the Norberg-Schulz archive at the National Museum in Norway. Written in two languages, the poem expresses Norberg-Schulz's emphasis on dwelling as instrumental in creating meaningful places.[18] The words and themes in the poem correspond with key themes from *Genius Loci*, for example identification, orientation, meaning, place, character and space.[19] But instead of expressing these ideas in the form of a book or article, Norberg-Schulz wrote a poem.

In fact, Norberg-Schulz often turned to poetry in his approach to architectural theory. His book *Minnesjord* (1991) consists of a series of poems dedicated to a second home he acquired in the rural Telemark in Norway.[20] His article 'Den poetiske forståelsesform' (1996), which translates into 'Poetic Understanding', outlines how poetry could offer an alternative to the knowledge formed by scientific means. For poetry to describe what science cannot, Norberg-Schulz argues that 'a substantial contact with things is required'.[21] Phenomenology can offer this substantial contact, and poetry could readily articulate this very contact. 'A poem is neither theory of practice, it neither describes nor acts. A poem rather *depicts* things in a way which interprets its essence or nature.'[22] The architect should adopt this poetic understanding to grasp and express that which cannot be measured and counted.[23]

In his theoretical and historical work, he often turned to poets when making his argument. For instance, the Norwegian author and poet Tarjei Vesaas is quoted by Norberg-Schulz in *Mellom jorg og himmel* (1978).[24] At the outset of the book, Norberg-Schulz quotes Vesaas's short story 'Siste-mann heim' (1952) where the protagonist Knut is working in the woods:

> *Here, you are at home Knut.*
> What? –
> No one had said it. But today it had happened. Here, you are at home. At the place where he was born a beautiful and true and simple world opened itself up to him.[25]

In this passage, the protagonist Knut experiences a feeling of being at home at the place where he was born. No one had to tell him, it happened. Norberg-Schulz describes Knut's experience – as articulated by the Norwegian author – as a sudden experience of belonging to a place, of being home and knowing a place.[26]

Another example of Norberg-Schulz's use of poetry in his architectural thinking is to be found in the caption of the very first photograph in *Genius Loci*. The caption to the depicted window reads 'a winter evening' and refers to a poem by George Trakl. The very same poem is quoted on the following page. The book also includes a series of other poems by poets such as Hölderlin and Rilke.

The reader of *Genius Loci* comes across Rilke early on: already on page 6, opposite of aforementioned photograph of a window at his house at Ris.[27] Here, Norberg-Schulz asks what the phenomena of place could be. 'Our everyday life-world consists of concrete "phenomena"',[28] he writes, and he explains that these could be as tangible as people, trees, wood, water, towns, windows, furniture, drifting clouds, changing seasons and the less concrete: feelings. To develop this thought, Norberg-Schulz turns to Rilke and writes: 'Thus, Rilke asks: "Are we perhaps *here* to say: house, bridge, fountain, gate, jug, fruit, tree, window, – at best: column, tower."'[29] This reference, taken from the Ninth Elegy of Rilke's *Duino Elegies*,[30] is not only mentioned on page 6 but again on page 15, 48 and 185. And Rilke not only reoccurs throughout *Genius Loci*, but again, and again, in several of Norberg-Schulz's other published works.[31]

A keyword search for 'Rilke' in the database at the Norberg-Schulz library at the National Museum of Arts, Architecture and Design in Oslo reveals 100 items. These books are either works by Rilke or secondary literature by other authors discussing Rilke's life and work. A compiled bibliography consists of ninety-seven titles by or about Rilke, as some of the titles are listed twice in the online search. The list is included as an appendix in this book and shows literature published between 1904 and 1987. The clear majority of the titles are authored by Rilke, most of which reprints, except for the first edition of

Die Sonnet an Orpheus (1922) and *Geschichten von lieben Gott* (1904).³² Some of the titles appear in several versions, or in several languages, as with *Duino Elegies*: one version in German from 1962; three English editions from 1961, 1963 and 1972; and one Italian copy from 1978. The overall list is dominated by the German language, except for three books in Norwegian, five books in English and two books in Italian. There are no titles in French. The titles also include many of Rilke's letters, as well as some biographies outlining the life of the poet. Also included in the library is Otto Bollnow's *Rilke* (1956), Else Buddenberg's *Denken und Dichten des Seins* (1956), Romano Guardini's *Rainer Maria Rilkes Deutung des Daseins* (1953) and J. F. Angelloz's *Rainer Maria Rilke* (1955). Paul Valéry's book on the Greek engineer Eupalinos as an architect becomes part of the bibliography, as the only title where Rilke does not appear as the principal theme or author.

A search for Heidegger in the same database reveals 107 items, but whereas Heidegger's importance for Norberg-Schulz's authorship is widely discussed by scholars, little attention has been given to his interest in Rilke. To my knowledge, the only scholarly attention the topic can be found in Raf de Saeger's chapter 'Stadier på livsveien mellom Norge og Flandern' ['Stages in a Life between Norway and Flanders'] in the book *Fellesskapets Arkitektur – Opprør! Christian Norberg-Schulz som arkitekt og stedstenker* (2020). Here, de Sager describes Norberg-Schulz's interest in travelling to the Dutch village Worpswede, where Rilke once had lived to get a sense of what the landscape might have looked like at his time.³³ In the two paragraphs dedicated to Rilke in his book chapter, he mentions Rilke's importance in Norberg-Schulz's library and links Rilke's poetry to Heidegger, but he does not go into detail.³⁴ To this day, two of Norberg-Schulz's good friends, de Sager and Kari Greve, celebrate Norberg-Schulz's birthday every 23 May by reading a poem by Rilke and drinking a glass of wine.³⁵ Portoghesi mentions Rilke with passion and explains that Norberg-Schulz was pivotal in introducing him to the poet. These accounts, and the extensive list of books in Norberg-Schulz's library, suggest that Rilke played an important role in Norberg-Schulz's life. Yet, so little attention has been awarded to Rilke's role in the work and thinking of these architects or others by architectural historians. What did Rilke say about architecture, place and space? How did Norberg-Schulz use Rilke in his work?

The Bohemian-Austrian poet was born in Prague in 1975 and travelled extensively through Europe before settling in Switzerland where he died in 1926. His lyrical and mystical authorship consists of poems, correspondence and one novel. These include the well-known ten elegies *Duino Elegien* [*Duino Elegies*], the fifty-five sonnets *Sonette an Orpheus* [*Sonnets to Orpheus*] (1923), the novel *Die Aufzeichnungen die Malte Laurid Brigge* [*The Notebooks of Malte Laurids Brigge*] (1910) and letters to contemporaries such as Nanny Wunderly-Volkhart, Lou Andreas-Salomé and the Fürstin Marie von Thurn und Taxis.³⁶ After Rilke moved to the French-speaking part of Switzerland, the poet – who had previously been writing in German

– wrote a series of poems in the French language, including a cycle of poems about windows: *Les Fenêtres* (1927).[37]

Coming from the field of architectural history, I take particular notice of references to architecture and place when reading Rilke. *Duino Elegies* is linked to Duino in Italy and includes references to architectural features such as towers and windows.[38] His novel about Malte is set in Paris and tells the story of the protagonist's struggles with the urban fabric of the city.[39] Other poems like *Der Panther* (1906) describe the animal being kept in a confined space, behind bars. *Les Fenêtres* is the cycle of poems dedicated to windows.[40]

Yet, scholars from the field of literature focusing on Rilke appear to have overlooked the role of architecture in the poets' work or his importance for architectural culture. Rüdiger Görner's claim that Rilke's use of spatial metaphors in his poetry and letter-writing is of relatively small importance has perhaps contributed to this lack of interest.[41] *The Cambridge Companion to Rilke* (2010) has dedicated chapters focusing on Rilke and the visual arts, or Rilke and philosophy, but does not discuss Rilke and architecture or space. Scholars such as John Sandford look at the importance of landscape in Rilke's poetry, and Ji-Ming Tang explores the window in the poet's authorship. Still, I wonder if perhaps more attention should be given to Rilke from the field of architecture and architectural history, particularly for those looking at the work of Norberg-Schulz and Portoghesi.[42]

I wish to challenge Görner's claim and argue that Rilke's spatial metaphors are of importance to Norberg-Schulz's phenomenology of architecture. I will approach this, initially, not by focusing directly on architecture in Rilke, but instead by exploring secondary literature discussing the link between phenomenology and Rilke, as was addressed by de Sager but not discussed in detail.[43] I will review the key terms *Dasein*, *Bezug* and particularly the 'I-world-relationship', in both phenomenology and Rilke, before returning to how I believe Norberg-Schulz read and used the poet.

Many scholars have drawn parallels between phenomenology and the work of Rilke. Andreas Kramer argues: 'Largely on account of his late work, Rilke has long been seen as a poet of "Being" (in the Heideggerian, existentialist sense).'[44] Here, Kramer suggests that Rilke's poetry articulates an understanding of being that could be considered similar to that of Heidegger.

Heidegger himself also made a similar link between his own thinking and the poetry of Rilke. Quoted in Angelloz and Bollnow, Heidegger once said in a lecture that his philosophical work was nothing but a philosophical account of what Rilke's poetry was expressing.[45]

Bollnow, himself a philosopher within the phenomenological tradition, goes into this question in detail. Despite being described as both an essential handbook to how Heidegger and Rilke met[46] and a 'well-known existentialist interpretation of Rilke',[47] Bollnow's *Rilke* (1951) has never been translated into English. Also, Buddenberg's *Denken und Dichten des Seins*, Guardini's *Rainer Maria Rilkes Deutung des Daseins* and Angelloz's *Rainer Maria Rilke* are not translated into English. They are, to my knowledge, only available in its original German. As a result, they might have fallen below the radar of some scholars.

Yet, all of these books discuss Rilke in the context of phenomenology. Kramer links Rilke's poetry to the Heideggerian notion of *Dasein*: 'being-in-the-world'.[48] This understanding of being-in sees being-not as isolated but formed and negotiated in relation to phenomena surrounding us. The Norwegian philosopher Guttorm Fløistad – who himself studied under Bollnow in Berlin – describes Heidegger's phenomenology as awarding a particular emphasis on the relationship between being and phenomena: being-in-the-world.[49]

Bollnow links Rilke to phenomenology through the poet's emphasis on *Bezug*: meaning relationship. *Bezug* is a *Grundwort* in Rilke's vocabulary, but instead of potentially being quite scientific and abstract, Rilke uses the term to describe human experience of the world.[50] Bollnow, thus, locates Rilke in the tradition of Husserl and Bretano due to the way that the poet considers being as constructed through a relationship with the world around – things and phenomena in it. Human beings are always related to, or in reference to, something else, as he writes:

> Here already, in the most simple and formal determinations of human existence it is shown how one cannot initially conceive man as a consciousness existing of itself, which afterwards sets itself in relation to the things of the external world, but, as consciousness, as such, in its very essence, is turned away from man and relates to something else which is not itself.[51]

Being related or in reference to that which is not human is what Bollnow here suggests determines our existence, a line of thought he sees as the precondition of phenomenology. Being-in-the-world, according to a phenomenologist, means that being is always relating to, and formed by, that which is external.

Literature discussing the window in Rilke's authorship outlines *Bezug* as a key trait of Rilke's windows. In his brief translator note to Rilke's poems, *Les Fenêtres*, Ulrich Fülleborn suggests how Rilke's poem *Les Fenêtres IV* (1927) particularly articulates Rilke's interest in 'Ich-Welt-Bezug': I-world-relationship.[52] The keyword *Bezug* also makes it into Ji-Ming Tang's study of the window in the work of the poet: underscoring *Bezug* as elemental in Rilke's windows.[53] Tang goes more into detail than Fülleborn's brief comment. According to Tang, Rilke's use of the window in his poetry and writing particularly addresses the notion of *Bezug*.

This secondary literature tells us that Rilke's work has been seen as a form of phenomenology, particularly in the way that the poet articulates the notion of *Bezug* and an I-world-relationship. In this literature also the window makes its appearance. Did Norberg-Schulz – a keen reader of Rilke – adopt Rilke's phenomenological approach to being-in-the-world?

Norberg-Schulz's library contains several books discussing Rilke's connection to phenomenology, including Bollnow's *Rilke* (1951) in which he had made notes in the margin: small dots and hyphens.[54] Since Norberg-Schulz's private library includes this book, alongside Buddenberg and Guardiani, I believe that Norberg-Schulz was well aware of scholars linking Rilke to phenomenology. But how then did Rilke's poetry and the poet's connection to phenomenology affect Norberg-Schulz's phenomenology of architecture?

In *Genius Loci*, Norberg-Schulz does not reference *Les Fenêtres*, neither does any other publications that link the poet to phenomenology. Instead, Norberg-Schulz turns to Rilke's *Duino Elegies*, quoting the Ninth Elegy again and again: 'Are we not *here* to say ... window'.[55]

Considered as the 'crowning achievements of a poet, and the last great poetic cycle of their kind in the German language',[56] the *Duino Elegies* addresses the loneliness of modern existence, beautifully and intensely. With Rilke's mystical and lyrical language, he approaches themes such as love, life and death. The very first elegy begins: 'Who, if I cried out would hear me',[57] Rilke cries out his despair and loneliness, searching for something out there.

The themes discussed earlier: being-in-the-world and how our being is formed in relationship with an external world are addressed in the elegies. *Duino Elegies* is the focus of Romano Guardini's book *Rainer Maria Rilkes Deutung des Daseins*.[58] Guardini's emphasis is on uncovering the concept of *Dasein* in Rilke's authorship, and he links the poet to phenomenologists such as Heidegger.[59] Each of his chapters is dedicated to one of Rilke's elegies, including the ninth. In the Ninth Elegy, being-in-the-world is turned outward towards a surrounding world, as the poet asks what it means to be here. Rilke sees being as something fleeting, as life comes and goes, but that existence can be grounded in experiences of here and now: 'Here is the time for the sayable; here is its home. Speak and bear witness!'[60]

This particular elegy is, according to Guardini, concerned with a new way of understanding what we see around us and how to *say* these *things*. To concretize the relationship between being and phenomena – as in being versus window – we articulate our being by articulating our relationship between ourselves and the things and world around us.[61] 'Then the thing gains a density and sense of being that it could never have reached on itself. As soon as such a word is spoken, the thing, "thinks". "Now I am really".'[62] Being is formed through the expression of language.

In his seminal work on language titled *Unterwegs zur Sprache* [*On the Way to Language*] (1959), Heidegger addresses the nature of language in relation to a thing and how poets experience this relationship. If a poet wishes to describe a thing, the word the poet uses to describe this thing becomes a process of experiencing the thing and allowing it to be. Language makes this happen:

> something *is* only where the appropriate and therefore competent word names a thing as being, and so established the given being as being. ...

> The being of anything that it resides in the word. Therefore this statement holds true: Language is the house of being.[63]

As such, being itself is reliant upon language and that this language is spoken. But further, what is being spoken is not something the poet makes up from thin air, but instead 'what has long been concealed and is essentially vouchsafed already'.[64] This means that through language, things come into being and that this being is already there, something concealed for us, and language, to discover. And to access this concealed being, Heidegger argues that the thing comes into being through language and that this coming-into-being is articulated through experience. He writes:

> To undergo an experience with something – be it a thing, a person, or a god – means that this something befalls us, strikes us, comes over us, overwhelms and transforms us. When we talk of 'undergoing' an experience, we mean specifically that the experience is not of our own making; to undergo here means that we endure it, suffer it, receive it as it strikes us and submits to it. It is this something itself that comes about, comes to pass, happens.[65]

As such, experience is something that comes over us, and happens suddenly, in a transformative manner.

I believe Heidegger's understanding of language could be a way to describe certain events that this book revolves around. For instance, the event of Helen Keller learning language, immediately and suddenly at the water fountain, when Norberg-Schulz had a Campari-moment at Piazza Navona or when he suddenly saw the connection between place and his own being when standing at the window of a train.[66] The immediacy evident in all of these experiences bears resonance with Heidegger's notion of language in his later work. To the later Heidegger, language speaks – immediately and so did language speak to Helen Keller at the water fountain and to Norberg-Schulz at the window of a train or while enjoying a drink at Piazza Navona.

'Are we not *here* to say . . . window',[67] Norberg-Schulz quotes Rilke in *Genius Loci*. I read this quote in the context of my previous discussion, where the poet Rilke expresses a need for beings to relate to an external world and to concretize their fleeting existence by *saying* the *things*. To Norberg-Schulz, a phenomenology of architecture could offer a theoretical framework for architects to design buildings that would allow human beings to be in contact with their surroundings. In his work, I see similar attention to the importance of *saying*.

'Places are hence designated by nouns',[68] Norberg-Schulz writes in *Genius Loci*, concluding his section on the phenomena of place and his initial reference to Rilke. To understand what place is, architects designate the place through nouns. The architect must *say*. But that does not necessarily mean that architects should write poetry. 'Architecture belongs to poetry, and its purpose is to help man dwell.'[69] This quote from Norberg-Schulz suggests that the architect should be *here* to *say* in a specific way: with design. Rilke appears in several of Norberg-Schulz's notes from the late 1970s and the 1980s, currently kept in the archive in Oslo. Among these references to the poet, I find the following note of particular interest: 'Rilke's "figures" are "expressive structures".'[70] Here, Rilke's poetry – or figures – is described as structures. But how could Rilke's poetry be used by architects?

'Architects draw their way forward',[71] architect Sverre Fehn once claimed: a quote Norberg-Schulz included in his editorial to a special issue of *Byggekunst* from 1978 themed 'Drawing and Reality'. The issue contains Norberg-Schulz's only reference to Rilke in *Byggekunst*, a journal he wrote for from 1951 to 1999 and was editor of between 1961 and 1978.[72] Norberg-Schulz references Rilke's *Sonette for Orpheus* (1922), here in the translation to Norwegian made by André Bjerke.[73] This Rilke poem forms a double spread with Rob Krier's drawings titled 'Notitzen am Rande'.[74] Opposite Norberg-Schulz's editorial, he has included another of Krier's drawings – a window.

In his editorial Norberg-Schulz mentions different types of drawings and their importance for architects: the travel sketch (*reiseskissen*), the idea sketch (*idéskissen*), the study sketch (*studieskissen*), the demonstration sketch (*demonstrasjonsskissen*) and the working drawing (*arbeidstegningene*). He describes drawing, in its various forms, as a vital tool for the architect to understand his or her surroundings, but also for the architectural historian to gain new insight into historical questions about authorship and location.

Norberg-Schulz was an architect, and he sketched. The grey cardboard folder from the Norberg-Schulz archive containing the material related to the 1980 Venice Architecture Biennale holds the aforementioned poem written in two languages. But the folder also contains a series of sketches. In comparison with other folders in the Norberg-Schulz archive which mainly contains text, the Venice folder is strikingly visual. With the exception of the poem, the folder contains mostly drawings. Norberg-Schulz sketched his ideas for the diorama by hand with a pen, occasionally using the colours brown, yellow, green and blue.

A human figure is drawn on a piece of paper with a black pen. This figure glances at a series of rectangular frames stretching across a wall. The figure's eye level is marked with a red line, drawn across the wall, forming a horizontal line separating the wall into two equal parts. The frames containing roughly sketched shapes and forms are of different proportions, located on different heights. The figure is immersed in the act of looking through these frames or window-like features, available in the Norberg-Schulz archive.[75]

'The window as a frame for the human figure is a discovery that belongs to the second half of my experience as an architect',[76] Paolo Portoghesi recalls when I asked him about Rilke's windows. And he continues:

It was back in my architecture after the theory of places, in connection with the postmodern and the Venice experience. The window was back precisely like a frame for the human figure, I mean, as an essential element of architecture, because all in all, it puts the human figure and the human dimension in relation with the architectural object.[77]

Portoghesi's discussion of the window as a frame for the human figure: a way that architecture measures the relation of human to the world where the window has a unique role becomes interesting next to Norberg-Schulz's drawings. The human figure is drawn next to a series of frames, window-like features, presenting the architecture between earth and sky. I wonder: if Norberg-Schulz adopted Rilke's notion of being *here* to *say*, did he share Portoghesi's understanding of the window or adopt Rilke's window's otherwise? That is a question for the next chapter.

Window 8
Sierre

Place

Sierre, Switzerland
Latitude: 46.294131
Longitude: 17.5333536
Language: French (Fenêtre)

Practice

Vinduene
Subtitles
Les Fenêtres IV (1927) by Rainer Maria Rilke. Translated into Norwegian by Anna Ulrikke Andersen
The practice-element of this chapter is not a film, but a set of subtitles that can be turned on for the film Calacata (2017), which was introduced in the previous chapter "Window 7 | Calacata"
https://vimeo.com/208204366
Password: anna

This is a textual response to the essay film in the form of subtitles offering a translation of Rainer Maria Rilke's *Les Fenêtres IV* (1927) into Norwegian. The subtitles are compatible with the film *Calcata* (2017). Language: English, French, German, Italian. Subtitles: Norwegian (Bokmål).

#	Start	End	CPS	Style	Text
1	0:07:30.05	0:07:36.94	3	Default	Vindu, du, som måler ventetiden,
2	0:07:37.22	0:07:45.99	1	Default	fyller seg så ofte
3	0:07:46.00	0:07:58.01	2	Default	når et liv vender seg utålmodig
4	0:07:58.19	0:08:02.86	2	Default	mot et annet liv.
5	0:08:13.08	0:08:23.25	2	Default	Du som skiller ad og som trekker til,
6	0:08:23.40	0:08:31.97	2	Default	foranderlig som havet,
7	0:08:32.02	0:08:45.02	2	Default	glasset, plutselig, speiler vår figur,
8	0:08:45.12	0:08:54.13	3	Default	blandet med det vi ser derigjennom,
9	0:09:03.57	0:09:17.61	1	Default	et forsøk å teste friheten,
10	0:09:17.78	0:09:25.00	4	Default	gjennom tilstedeværelsen av fare
11	0:09:25.28	0:09:36.51	2	Default	befinner seg i oss, og utjevner,
12	0:09:36.56	0:09:43.36	3	Default	det alt for store utendørs

FIGURE 8.1 *Vinduene*, translation of Rainer Maria Rilke's *Les Fenêtres IV* (1927), 2017. Anna Ulrikke Andersen.

Essay

Les Fenêtres – en norvégien

'With Chris, we had spoken of Rilke like a common friend',[1] Paolo Portoghesi explains when I interview him in Calcata, February 2016. I had asked about his friendship with Christian Norberg-Schulz and what they thought of Rainer Maria Rilke. Portoghesi continues:

> Rilke speaks about the tower, and therefore about an architectural typology. This mention of the tower is very important, then come the series of poems on windows and roses, which are part of a repertoire that I very much feel close to my interests. Once, in this garden where I built this staircase, I spent one evening reading the poems on roses. I have not spent any evenings reading those on windows yet, but maybe I will do that soon.[2] (Figure 8.2)

FIGURE 8.2 Paolo Portoghesi and Giovanna in their garden in Calcata, undated. Courtesy of Paolo Portoghesi.

In his garden, Portoghesi read Rilke's poems on the roses and knew Rilke's work on windows. This makes me wonder: When the two architects spoke of Rilke, did they also speak about the window? Was Norberg-Schulz's take on the window informed by Rilke's? Did Norberg-Schulz read *Les Fenêtres* (1927)?

* * *

Rilke was born in Prague, a city that at the time was part of the Austro-Hungarian Empire. His mother tongue was German, the language in which he wrote the great majority of his letters, poems and works. But towards the end of his life, Rilke turned to French. With this move, 'a gentle wind of polyglotism'[3] entered into his life and authorship. A frequent traveller, he eventually settled in the French-speaking Sierre, in Valais, Switzerland. Here he moved into a medieval tower by the name Muzot, where he lived from 1921 until he died in a nearby sanatorium on 29 December 1926 (Figure 8.3 and 8.4).

Making a move geographically, Rilke also moved from the German to the French language, first evident in 1924 with the cycle of poems titled *Vergers*.[4] After the move, he wrote in French, acquired a French-speaking

FIGURE 8.3 Rainer Maria Rilke in his garden at Muzot, in Sierre, 1924. Unknown photographer. Courtesy of AKG/NTB.

love interest – Balladine Klossowska – and adopted several geographical French names such as the French name for the town Sierre instead of the German Sieders.[5] According to Otto Bollnow, Rilke found poetic freedom in the melodic French language,[6] and Rilke himself claimed that when writing in French, it gave him the feeling of finally being able to breathe.[7] With ease and creative flow, and from his tower in the Alps, Rilke wrote his final poems, *Les Fenêtres*: a cycle of ten poems on windows, published posthumously in 1927 by Klossowska.[8]

Fenêtre IV

Fenêtre, toi, ô mesure d'attente,
tant de fois remplie,
quand une vie se verse et s'impatiente
vers une autre vie.

Toi qui sépares et qui attires,
changeante comme la mer, –
glace, soudain, où notre figure se mire
mêlée à ce qu'on voit à travers;

échantillon d'une liberté compromise
par la présence du sort;
prise par laquelle parmi nous s'égalise
le grand trop du dehors.⁹

* * *

During my fieldwork across Europe in February 2016, I visited Sierre and the Rainer Maria Rilke Foundation that is based in the town. Established in 1986, the foundation holds an archive and library, as well as a dual-language exhibition (French/German). Rilke's turn to French, his life in the

FIGURE 8.4 Muzot, Sierre, 2016, Anna Ulrikke Andersen.

medieval tower Muzot and poems and writings on windows are covered in this permanent exhibition.

As I walked through the rooms, looking at original artefacts – Rilke's books and belongings – I thought about how the poet moved to Sierre and adopted the French language. I remembered reading Bollnow, who stated that Rilke's French poems largely have been overlooked.[10] According to Karen Leeder and Robert Vilain, these poems have 'still not gained the critical attention [they] deserve'.[11] Written in French and not as widely discussed as Rilke's other work, *Les Fenêtres* falls within this category of poems. Perhaps this tendency of scholars prioritizing the poet's German work is why so few of them have looked at Rilke's windows and why no architectural historians have considered how Rilke – and his windows – has influenced architectural culture.

Whereas *Les Fenêtres* is the most explicit example of the window in Rilke's authorship, the window does figure in his earlier German work. The final room in this exhibition is dedicated to the window, where both his French poems and his German letters are included. The window is a recurrent motif in Rilke's authorship, and existing literature points to his novel *Die Aufzeichnungen des Malte Laurids Brigge* [*The Notebooks of Malte Laurids Brigge*] (1900) and the poems *Duino Elegien* [*Duino Elegies*] (1922).[12] In her book *Fenster-Geschichten: Die Bedeutung des Fensters bei Rilke und ausgewählten anderen Autoren* (2010), Ji-Ming Tang outlines the extensive occurrences of the window in Rilke's authorship, discussing how Rilke links windows to the themes of nature, love and death.[13]

In the exhibition, the following quote from Rilke's letter to Klossowska from 12 December 1920 is printed on the wall alongside *Les Fenêtres I* (1927), here translated into the English:

> Our dealing with distance is quite essentially dependent upon the mediation of the window, outside distance is only power, over-powering, without relation to us, while still immeasurably influential: the window, however, puts us in a relationship, it measures our part in the future, in the very instant that is space.[14]

Rilke had written this in a letter to Klossowska, but the same sequence, quoted in Tang,[15] reappears in a letter to another woman, his good friend Nanny Wunderly-Volkhart, on 27 August 1920.[16]

Tang quotes the latter letter without making any reference to the other and argues how the sequence shows Rilke's quite specific understanding of the window. Rilke's windows, according to Tang, put us in a relationship with the world. And in Rilke's poems, it is through the window, as a frame of our domestic being, that we can understand distance.[17] In my view, this quote sheds light on the discussion I raised in Window 7, where I referred to Bollnow's emphasis on *Bezug* – relations – as a keyword in Rilke's oeuvre and one that links the poet to phenomenology.

If the window puts us in a relationship to an external world and makes it possible for us to understand distance, as Tang claims, then the window appears to be a particularly important architectural element in articulating our being-in-the-world. This is further strengthened by accounts such as that of Wein, stating that 'Bollnow's image of Rilke . . . pervades overall in this motif [distance]'.[18] I build my argument on these scholars' work. As such, the discussion regarding *Bezug* relates to a specific understanding of distance.

But in his book on Rilke, Bollnow seems to overlook the window, as he focuses his attention on other aspects of the poet's authorship. Bollnow approaches the themes of *Bezug* and distance rather briefly and outlines how Rilke's use of symbols like the fountain, or ball, is particularly strong in the late Rilke but how his French poems do bring up a line of new symbols, including the window. But to Bollnow, the window is not important. He writes:

> In his late French poems, Rilke steps into a range of new images, such as the window, the garden and vine etc. But these new images will not be discussed further here, as I see them as evidence of a new stage of his authorship and not like the other images, which could be traced through his entire poetic development.[19]

Bollnow, thus, sees the window as evidence of a new stage in the poet's authorship, without linking it to Rilke's overall development, and because of this, Bollnow does not go into any detail. Failing to award the window any further attention, Bollnow fails to relate his discussion of *Bezug* in Rilke to the poet's work on windows.

But Tang, on the other hand, relates the discussion of windows to the notion of *Bezug*. She sees Rilke's use of the window as quite radical in a literary tradition, made apparent in the following passage by Tang, translated here from the German:

> [In existing literary research] the window has been considered as merely a mediating element between interior and exterior, or its role as a 'dividing wall' between interior and exterior has been emphasised in particular. In this way, the window is inevitably connected with a sense of duality. In the lyric poetry of Rilke, however, the window not only serves as a mediator or septum between interior and exterior. According to his conception of the 'unity of life and death', the original meaning of the window as a boundary line between interior and exterior is ultimately overcome. In the late Rilke, the window becomes the poetic 'figure' for the image of the unity of all opposites, and the figure of *Dasein*.[20]

In this passage, Tang outlines how Rilke breaks down what could be considered as a previous understanding of the window as only separating inside and outside, but instead suggests that the window creates both unity and separation between the two. In Rilke's poems and letters, inside and outside are no longer opposites only but unity *and* opposition. In Rilke, this thinking on a simultaneous unity and opposition also applies to other opposites, such as South and North, life and death. Tang sees this simultaneous separation and unity as central in Rilke's understanding of *Dasein*, as it creates a relationship between being and world.

I read Rilke's *Les Fenêtres* with Tang's understanding of Rilke in mind. My attention is drawn to the fourth poem in the cycle: *Les Fenêtres IV*. I think about the themes of relationship, between inside and outside, the world and I, those who came before and those who will come after. Translated here by A. Poulin, the poem reads:

> Windows, IV
>
> You, window, O waiting's measure,
> refilled so often
> when one life spills out and grows
> impatient for another.
>
> You who divides and attracts,
> as fickle as the sea –
> sudden mirror reflecting our face
> mingled with what we see in back;
>
> fraction of a freedom compromised
> by the presence of risk;
> trapped by whatever's in us
> that evens the odds of the loaded outside.[21]

In fact, *Les Fenêtres IV* stands as the poem which above all has been considered to articulate Rilke's interest in the I-world-relationship, as argued by Ulrich Fülleborn.[22] He writes: 'It [the window] is located between, on the exact boundary between inside and outside: we look out of a window, as it brings the world inside; it connects and separates at the same time (IV).'[23] According to Fülleborn's observation, the fourth poem of the window-cycle particularly articulates the I-world-relationship.

Following on from our previous discussion of Tang, the window in Rilke's authorship is central in articulating 'relationship' and understanding distance as both unity and separation, which Tang sees as quite unique about Rilke's approach to the window. Reading *Les Fenêtres IV* I take note of his mention of the 'loaded outside'. I read this as a potentially overwhelming outside, a distance which cannot be grasped unless framed by a window.

But I halt, also, at another sentence in the poem, which describes the window as changeable and fickle as the sea. If the window, in Rilke's work, sets us in a relationship with the distance and the overwhelming outside, then I read the poem as tackling this relationship as far from static. The relationship is fickle. I wish to consider this changeable understanding of the window, and the relationships it creates, in a larger context of Rilke's life and work.

Where Bollnow saw Rilke's windows as a new and late addition to the poet's repertoire, as mentioned earlier, Lutz Koepnick sees Rilke's windows as appearing much earlier. He traces the window back to *The Notebooks of Malte Laurids Brigge*. In Koepnick's article 'The Aesthetic of the Interface' in the exhibition catalogue to the temporary exhibition *Window | Interface* (2007) at Mildred Lane Kemper Art Museum, he draws attention to how Rilke's protagonist Malte attempts to sleep with his window open, outlined at the very beginning of the book. Struggling with insomnia, Malte is lying in darkness with his window open, experiencing the busy city street-life outside as if it is all taking place inside his room. To no longer be able to separate inside and outside can be one of the traumatic experiences of modernity, which here is experienced as a collapse of that very distinction. In the darkness, Malte experiences how the intrusive sound brings this outside to the very inside.

> Though his physical body might not move at all, his kinaesthetic, proprioceptive, and tactile modalities are in full motion and turn him into a thoroughly unsettled and seemingly boundless subject.[24]

In this article, Koepnick reads Rilke's passage from Malte as describing a very particular experience. Lying in bed, Malte's body is not moving, yet the protagonist experiences motion. This mobility, Koepnick links to an unsettled subject, one that I would argue is fickle and changeable. Malte's experience of being is one that is boundless, fluid and far from settled.

With Koepnick's discussion of Malte's unsettled subjectivity considered, I wish to return to Rilke's notion of the window as creating a relationship between being and the world. I suggest that Rilke's windows, as I discuss them in this chapter, could be described in relation to his concept of *beweglichen Daseins*. Building upon Curdin Ebneter's reading of Rilke, this concept, discussed in detail in Window 3 | Journey, suggests a being-in-the-world that is *beweglich:* mobile.[25] If Tang argues that Rilke's windows are creating unity and separation between different spaces, I read this experience as similarly *beweglich*.[26] Although having some static qualities, I see Rilke's windows as mobile.

Rilke described Italy as 'die Fibel meines beweglichen Daseins': the textbook of my mobile being,[27] a place he had known since childhood. Norberg-Schulz was older when he first visited Italy. Sometime between 1945 and 1949, he travelled by bike from Zürich with his friends from university. He first visited Rome in 1947 at the age of twenty-one.[28]

I think about Rilke's mobile windows: tactile, fickle and in constant flux. And I think about Norberg-Schulz as the 'flying Norwegian'[29] and his theory of place: how his theory of *genius loci* both describes a way to create meaning between being and world and suggests relationships between places. Ebneter's discussion of Rilke's *beweglisches Daseins* mentions the relationship between Rome and Paris.[30] In the context of this thesis and the life and work of Norberg-Schulz, perhaps the relationship between Italy and Norway is more relevant.

Norberg-Schulz read Rilke's poetry, letters and writings carefully. His library contains books discussing Rilke in a phenomenological context, including Bollnow and Guardini's work on Rilke's notion of *Bezug*. In Window 7 | Calcata, I argued that Norberg-Schulz adopted Rilke's understanding of a connection between being, place and language. I outline how Norberg-Schulz understood an architectural or poetic language as holding the promise of concretizing such a relationship.

But I wonder if Norberg-Schulz's concept of *Dasein* was as *beweglich* as he travelled and wrote about Norway and Italy? I had read Norberg-Schulz's claim that in the window, the *genius loci* was focused and explained.[31] Static or mobile? Rooted or restless? My discussion of Rilke's windows suggests the window can be both. Therefore, I wish to ask: Did Norberg-Schulz adopt Rilke's 'mobile' windows? Would this allow for rootlessness and rootedness to coexist within Norberg-Schulz's authorship?

> Norberg-Schulz interprets Heidegger in a fairly simplistic and instrumental way, by which the Spirit of the place and the organic relationship between man and house takes on a mythical character. Rootedness and authenticity are presented as being superior to mobility and the experience of rootlessness. What is more, he seems to be completely unaware of the violence that is implicit in concepts like this. It is no coincidence these words are part of the basic vocabulary of Nazi-ideology.[32]

In this quote already discussed in Window 4 | Basel to Hamburg, Hilde Heynen sees rootedness and authenticity as distinctly different to mobility and rootlessness. To Heynen, one cannot involve the other, and she places Norberg-Schulz in the side of rootedness and authenticity.

Rilke's windows, on the other hand, unite rootedness and mobility. When Norberg-Schulz's arguably obsessive interest in Rilke, and how aware he was of the literature connecting the poet with phenomenology, is taken into account, could it perhaps be that Heynen misinterprets the architectural theorist? Did Norberg-Schulz adopt Rilke's understanding of the window as flexible, fickle and mobile? Is perhaps the window not as rooted as firstly assumed?

An answer to these questions may be found in *Genius Loci: Towards a Phenomenology of Architecture* (1980). Here, Norberg-Schulz writes:

> Identification and orientation are primary aspects of man's being-in-the-world. Whereas identification is the basis for man's sense of belonging, orientation is the function which enables him to be that homo viator, which is part of his nature. It is characteristic for modern man that for a long time he gave the role as a wanderer pride of place. He wanted to be 'free' and

conquer the world. Today we start to realise that true freedom presupposes belonging, and that 'dwelling' means belonging to a concrete place.[33]

In this quote, Norberg-Schulz explicitly suggests that belonging and rootedness to one specific place is vital to any experience of dwelling and what I read as condemning travel and wandering the world. If Rilke's windows hold the promise of bridging and uniting rootedness and restlessness, it appears that Norberg-Schulz did not apply this general thinking to his authorship that was addressing themes of place and architecture.

Either Norberg-Schulz did not read Rilke's poems and writing on windows in the same way that Tang and I do, or he decided to overlook these fluid and flexible aspects of Rilke's window. Heynen's critique is, thus, poignant. Freedom in terms of belonging to one concrete place does not invite the experiences of people travelling, fleeing or being on the move. Although Norberg-Schulz travelled extensively, the quote from his book *Genius Loci* earlier suggests a rooted take on place.

According to feminist scholar Rosi Braidotti, movement and travel are integral to the mobile and transnational aspects of postmodern reality.[34] And interestingly enough: Braidotti links physical mobility and travel to linguistic mobility, evident in her discussion of the polyglot. Braidotti defines the polyglot as a linguistic nomad, who benefits from great mobility between different systems and is defined by a self that is settling in-between languages.[35] According to Braidotti, the nomadic subject is a suitable theoretical formation of contemporary subjectivity; and for her, nomadism is an ontological concept that defines a way of being. She writes: 'The polyglot becomes the prototype of the postmodern speaking subject, struck by the maddening, fulminating insight about the arbitrariness of linguistic meaning and yet resisting a free fall into cynicism.'[36]

This mobile identity of Braidotti's, beyond and in between borders could be used as a critical tool to break up binary oppositions, linear narratives and normative constructs, and hence allow for greater diversity and uncovering of layers. According to her, being a polyglot means having direct insight into a convoluted and diverse reality, where universal truths simply do not exist. [37]

Whereas polyglot and author Franz Kafka at times felt 'the multiplicity of languages to be a gag in his throat',[38] Rilke's move from German to French was described as one of liberation by Leeder and Vilain.[39] Norberg-Schulz himself seemed to thrive between languages: he was fluent in Norwegian, English, Italian and German. *Genius Loci*, was for instance, written in Italian and English simultaneously, while parts of the book were also published in German and Norwegian between 1975 and 1980.[40] He prepared the book in English and worked on the Italian translation with his wife Anna Maria. She remembers how they would constantly discuss terms, concepts and phrases, before agreeing on appropriate expressions.[41]

Norberg-Schulz's frequent travelling, as discussed throughout this book, was not only a set of journeys across geographical and national borders; they were also linguistic. My following of Norberg-Schulz from Norway to Italy and back again brought me through Swedish, Danish, German, Italian and eventually French. Not to forget the native language I share with Norberg-Schulz: Norwegian.

I cannot know if Norberg-Schulz read *Les Fenêtres* or how closely he read this cycle. The poems are not part of his library, and his French was not as good as his other foreign language skills.[42] The letters to Nanny Wunderly-Volkhart and a German version of *Die Duino Elegien Malte Laurids Brigge* (1963) are in his collection, but I do not know how closely he read them. In his writing, Norberg-Schulz does not refer to the two seminal works by Bollnow and Guardini that connect Rilke to Heidegger.

It is clear that Norberg-Schulz did have extensive knowledge about Rilke's work, and it would not be wrong to call him a Rilke-scholar of sorts. But did he read Rilke the way I do? I embrace the poet's understanding of how the window can articulate a relationship between being and the world as mobile and rooted at the very same time. I believe this understanding of the window could have opened up for an interest and attention to place that allows for rootless and rootedness to coexist in a fickle and intriguing way. Although I cannot find these mobilities in Norberg-Schulz's theory of *genius loci*, travelling and rootlessness were undoubtedly vital in the reality of his life, both linguistically and geographically.

To me, this stands as the most puzzling paradox of his oeuvre. Norberg-Schulz travelled extensively but argued that dwelling must be bound to a place. He was intensely interested in Rilke at large, but presumably not Rilke's mobile windows. If Norberg-Schulz had read Rilke's windows the way that I have, I believe it could have opened up for an attention to place that allowed for rootless and rootedness to coexist. As Rilke moved to Sierre, he left his German past behind and started writing in French. In doing so, did he perhaps lose his long-term reader: Christian Norberg-Schulz?

I do not shy away from the paradox described previously. Instead I wish to engage in the conversation. Portoghesi acknowledged Rilke's importance for architectural culture through his poems on towers, roses and windows. He did know about the poems concerning the windows but had not yet spent time reading them when I visited in 2016.[43] As I watch the photograph of the two men eating polenta, I am struck by how still, distant and enclosed the conversation is. Their eyes are not facing the camera, or meeting me: the follower. I wish I could enter into the discussion (Figure 8.5).

Calcata explores Portoghesi's interest in Rilke. In his house, the architect shows me original prints of Rilke's poems and passionately talks about Rilke's poems on windows. In the film, the sequence is only told by sound as the screen is black. Following this sequence is a long shot of my handwriting Rilke's *Les Fenêtres IV* in a notebook. It is a process of copying Rilke's

FIGURE 8.5 Paolo Portoghesi and Christian Norberg-Schulz eating polenta, undated. Courtesy of Paolo Portoghesi.

words that I include in full length. While I write, I read. While I write, the viewer reads. I wish Norberg-Schulz would read what I write.

I decide to send an *envois* to the dead theorist. I send him my reading of Rilke in the form of a translation, and this sending offers a critique of what I believe he missed out on. English and German translations already exist, but I decided instead to write it in his mother tongue: Norwegian.[44] My translation takes the form of a set of subtitles that can be turned on when watching my essay film *Calcata* offering a Norwegian translation of the poem *Les Fenêtres IV*. With it, I make my mark upon Norberg-Schulz's oeuvre. As I move from *Les Fenêtres* to *vinduene*, I translate Rilke's French and let it flow as a 'gentle wind of polyglotism' towards the north and into the Norwegian language.

Window 9
Oslo

Place

Oslo, Norway
Latitude: 59.913869
Longitude: 10.752245
Language: Norwegian Bokmål (Vindu), Norwegian Nynorsk (Vindauge)

Practice

The Window and I
2015
Anna Ulrikke Andersen
HD video
03:55
https://vimeo.com/161214958

The Window and I (2015) is an essay film taking the form of a self-portrait exploring what ways three sets of windows filter air, light and view and how they affect my body. The footage is shot with a Blackmagic Design Camera, and sound is recorded with a Zoom H4n and synchronized in post-production. This film was shot in my former home in London, UK; Reuma-sol in Alfaz del Pi, Spain; and my family's cabin in Budor, Norway. The film contains X-ray images of hands and the chest and excerpts of Claude Debussy's *Danseuse de Delphes* (1910), performed by Anna Ulrikke Andersen.

FIGURE 9.1 *The Window and I*, 2015. Anna Ulrikke Andersen.

Essay

Returned, X-rayed and exposed

Rubek: Are you happy to be home again, Maja?
Maja: Are *you*?
Rubek: I?
Maja: Yes. You've been abroad so much, much longer than I. Are you really happy to be home again?
Rubek: No, to be perfectly honest. Not really happy.
Maja: There you see. I knew it.
Rubek: Perhaps I have been abroad too long. This northern provincial life seems foreign to me.[1]

Rubek and Maja, the protagonists in Henrik Ibsen's play *When We Dead Awaken* (1899), return to Norway after time spent abroad. In this final play by the Norwegian playwright, the protagonists – the artist and his wife – struggle to re-adapt to their previous lifestyle, haunted by ghosts and love interests from the past as they settle into a spa hotel in rural Norway. Rubek finds the silence of provincial life difficult. This is something he noticed as soon as he arrived in Norway by train from the continent:

> I noticed how silent it was at all the little places we stopped at. I – heard the silence – like you Maja: And then I realized we had crossed the frontier. Now we were home. I knew it, because at every one of these little roadside halts, the train stopped, and stood quite still – though nothing happened.[2]

Arriving in Norway by train, the silence reminded Rubek that he was home. Home in a country where nothing happened.

Christian Norberg-Schulz similarly returned to Norway by train after having spent time on the continent, as depicted in the opening scene of *Livet finner sted* (1992). Standing by the window, he looks out and recalls a moment like Rubek's, crossing the frontier between Norway and Sweden – home and abroad. It was at this moment that he experienced a sudden feeling that the forest moving past quickly outside the window was part of him. 'This, I know! This is part of me!',[3] he exclaimed. Norberg-Schulz returned to Norway not once, not twice, but multiple times. Every departure for this 'flying Norwegian'[4] was followed by a return to his native Norway.

A later scene in *Livet finner sted* depicts another homecoming, this time by car. 'When I returned to Oslo 36 years ago, newly-wed, and with my Italian wife, we stopped here at Ekeberg to get a view of the city',[5] he explains directly to the camera. In contrast to the opening scene, set by the window of a train moving through a landscape, Norberg-Schulz is here arriving by car (Figure 9.2). In similar fashion to the scene on the train, he recalls a moment many years earlier, but here he speaks directly to the camera and not as a voice-over. The newly-wed couple stopped at Ekeberg, overlooking the city that was to become their home.

Ekeberg not only provided a view of the city where they were to live but also gave them a glimpse towards Vettakollen, where their house was awaiting them in Planetveien 14, which was designed by Norberg-Schulz and his more established colleague, architect Arne Korsmo (1900–69). The design and building of three houses at Planetveien 10–14 (1952–5) had begun just before the young Norberg-Schulz had headed off to the United States with a Fulbright scholarship. During his year at Harvard University, Norberg-Schulz met his wife, the Italian scholar of English literature, Anna Maria di Dominicis. On this stay abroad, he also met architect Ludwig Mies van der Rohe (1886–1969), a meeting which resulted in an interview in *Byggekunst* upon return.[6] While Norberg-Schulz was away in the United

FIGURE 9.2 *Livet finner sted*, 1992. Sven-Erik Helgesen and NRK. All rights reserved.

States, Korsmo continued the work on their shared design for Planetveien 10–14.

Senior to Norberg-Schulz, Korsmo was a much more established architect. Korsmo is commonly known as a pioneer of the international style within Norway. Adopting the architectural design principles of the modernist movement, including the open plan simply seen in buildings by Le Corbusier and Mies van der Rohe, Korsmo designed a series of buildings in Norway, including Villa Stenersen (1937–9) and Villa Dammann (1932).[7] His knowledge and interest in the international architectural scene led to him becoming the leader of PAGON (Progressive Architects Group Oslo, Norway), the Norwegian group of Congrès International d'Architecture Moderne (CIAM). Korsmo and his wife Grete Prytz-Kittelsen, who was a goldsmith, enamel artist and designer, had also received a Fulbright grant (1949–50) a couple of years before Norberg-Schulz. The two conducted research at the Institute of Design in Chicago.[8]

Here, Mies van der Rohe was the Head of the Architecture Department between 1943 and 1956. In Chicago, Korsmo and his wife befriended Edith Farnsworth, the medical doctor who commissioned Mies van der Rohe to design her house at Fox River, known in the modernist canon as Farnsworth House (1945–51) (Figure 9.3).[9] Farnsworth's apartment was close to where Korsmo and Prytz-Kittelsen were staying in Chicago, and as their friendship

FIGURE 9.3 The Farnsworth House at dusk, designed by Ludwig Mies van der Rohe, 1945–51, undated. Courtesy of The Farnsworth House, a sight of The National Trust for Historic Preservation.

developed, Farnsworth invited the couple as the first overnight guests to stay in the glasshouse before the furniture was moved in and curtains put up.

> The Korsmo's and Farnsworth slept on each side of the 'utility core' on temporary mattresses on the floor. During the evening, a dramatic storm raged outside, and the thousands of fireflies plastered by the rain to the glass wall created an effect like a foaming, glittering, and starry sky. The almost unlimited contact with nature offered by the walls of glass made an enduring impression on the couple.[10]

In her book *Planetveien 12: The Korsmo House, a Scandinavian Icon* (2014), Elisabeth Tostrup argues that the couple's stay at the Farnsworth House had a substantial effect on the Norwegian architect, and other scholars have discussed how the architecture of Mies van der Rohe influenced the design of Planetveien 10–14.[11]

Korsmo and his wife had stayed in the house before the curtains had been put up, but Farnsworth soon found that 'unlimited contact with nature offered by the walls of glass',[12] which had so impressed the Norwegians, to be a problem. Even with curtains, Farnsworth experienced living in the house as difficult due to the transparency of the glass walls, as Alice T. Friedman had discussed in detail in *Women and the Making of the Modern House: A Social and Architectural History* (2006). Here Friedman draws attention to the discrepancy between the actual house, with its large, glass walls, and the model of the house, where several walls were translucent rather than transparent.

The truth is that in this house with its four walls of glass, I feel like a prowling animal, always on the alert. I am always restless. Even in the evening, I feel like a sentinel on guard day and night. I can rarely stretch out and relax. . . . Mies talks about 'free space': but his space is very fixed. I can't even put a clothes hanger in my house without considering how it affects everything from the outside. Any arrangement of furniture becomes a major problem, because the house is transparent, like an X-ray.[13]

For Friedman, Farnsworth's experience of living in this 'X-ray'-house raises questions related to gender. Farnsworth's expectations and assumptions of power relationships between men and women, as well as the patron and the architect, affected her experiences in the house. This involved, for example, experiences of being watched and put on display, meant exposing her unconventional lifestyle. And her lifestyle – living as a single woman – was different from what was expected of a woman in the early 1950s. A man, in contrast, was more independent. For a woman to be X-rayed by her house made her more exposed and vulnerable than a man would have been.

In fact, scholars such as Lisa Cartwright, Jose van Dijck and Bettyann Kevles have discussed how the X-rayed woman has long been seen as a fetishized and erotic object. Before the dangers of exposure to the radioactivity of X-rays were known, women would have their hands X-rayed and give this image to their lovers as an intimate 'photograph'.[14]

Beatriz Colomina reconsiders the history of modern architecture as closely related to the early twentieth-century obsession with tuberculosis and the X-ray as a representation of the interior of the body. Colomina draws attention to Le Corbusier's interest in light, hygiene and whiteness in his architecture, and she considers this in relation to the health concerns of his contemporaries, such as the treatment of tuberculosis.[15] 'Modern buildings even started to look like medical images',[16] she argues. She draws attention to Mies's description of his work as skin and bone, underscoring how 'Books on modern architecture look like collections of chest X-rays. This is more than a dominant aesthetic. It is a symptom of a deep-seated philosophy of design derived from the medical discourse'.[17] Modern architecture, according to Colomina, is an X-ray architecture: 'Glass walls, like X-rays, are instruments of control. Just as the X-ray exposes the inside of the body to the public eye, the modern houses expose its interior. That which was previously private was now subject to public scrutiny.'[18]

For Farnsworth this rings true: Mies's transparent design exposed her to the eyes of curious strangers. Anne Maria Norberg-Schulz's life as a newly-wed in Oslo was not too dissimilar. The three attached houses at Planetveien 10-14 were designed with an open plan. Each of the houses is box-like and two-storey, with living quarters and upstairs bedrooms and bathroom, and a lower one-storey section with the kitchen adjoining. The individual houses have some variations. Norberg-Schulz's house in Planetveien 14 has only a railing – and no wall – separating the first floor to the open living room below. The interior of Korsmo and Prytz-Kittelsen's unit was colourful. Designed by Prytz-Kittlesen herself this colourful and iconic interior design remains in the house to date and is listed. Also, their house contains a staircase to the second floor that can be raised into the ceiling, freeing up more space at ground level. There are only a few windows towards the road, forming a closed, anonymous facade. The other side of the house is aimed towards the woods, where large windows open up towards the outside.

> And on Sundays, there were lots of people who came and looked through the glass. The walk on Sunday – the *tur*[19] – they came up and looked at the house and then they walked around and then . . . well, I had curtains.[20]

Hiding behind those thick, blue curtains in Planetveien 14,[21] Anna Maria Norberg-Schulz lived her life in Oslo, far away from her family in Rome. Norberg-Schulz once argued that windows in Nordic countries not only had to let light into the building but due to the long dark winters, the windows also let light out into the dark night.[22] At the same time, this exposed the habitants' private life to the external world. Living behind those large panes of glass, Anna Maria Norberg-Schulz was on display. The large windows facing the forest allowed people passing by not only to look into the living room and kitchen, but the open plan with the second-floor bedroom was separated by a railing and not the wall. The open plan

FIGURE 9.4 Planetveien 14, interior, still from film, 2016. Anna Ulrikke Andersen.

design did not shelter the bedroom by walls. Although people walking by would be walking metres below the first-floor bedroom and could not see the couple sleeping, the open plan and the large windows would not offer much protection. Without making the sleeping couple directly visible, the openness of the design could still be experienced as exposure to an outside world (Figure 9.4).

Anna Maria Norberg-Schulz did live in Norway until the end of her life, yet her first stay in Oslo was short. After a year in Planetveien, the couple sold the house as Norberg-Schulz received a research grant and they moved abroad.[23]

* * *

The first X-ray to be published was the X-rayed hand of Bertha Röntgen: a bony hand with her wedding ring clearly visible (Figure 9.5). On the ring-finger of my own hand, right not left, I wear a gold ring, which I have inherited from my maternal great-grandmother. Neither a wedding nor engagement ring, she received this as a gift for her confirmation, her coming of age in 1927, when she was fifteen years old. In the self-portrait *The Window and I* (2015), I spread out my fingers, with the ring, on a table. From the footage of my hands, the film cuts to an X-ray. But in contrast to Bertha Röntgen's hand, the X-ray of my hand does not contain my ring, as the doctors told me to remove all jewellery so that the X-ray could provide a good view of the bones in my body (Figure 9.6).

Thick green branches of trees are filmed from below. Moving slowly in the wind, rays of the sun cut through and let light into a garden. A cut to the interior of a flat, two large windows allow light into the otherwise dark interior. Leaves moving in the wind cast shadows on the wall. Then there is a table, with two hands on top: fingers spread to the sound of a piano, before the footage of the hands is replaced with an X-ray showing the bones below the skin (Figures 9.7 and 9.8).

'Death and the continuity of life convolute in the sign of the ringed X-rayed hand',[24] the scholar of media José van Dijck argues of Bertha Röntgen's X-rayed hand, the ring standing as a symbol of marriage and the fruitful reproduction of descendants. Her reading is feminist.

Feminist scholars Tess Cosslett, Celia Lury, Penny Summerfield suggest that 'Feminism is considerations of differences'.[25] To these authors, autobiography stands as a means of 'critical re-evaluation if its [feminism's] own long-standing concerns including subjectivity, knowledge and power, differences and collective identity'.[26] This means that the personal, subjective perspective offered by autobiographical work always offers different and important versions of knowledge, power and identity.

I think of differences, as I look at the ring on my right-hand finger in the footage. It tilts slightly to the right, as it always does. The fingers of my great-grandmother, who suffered from arthritis, were larger than mine. I have worn this ring almost every day for a decade but never had it adjusted

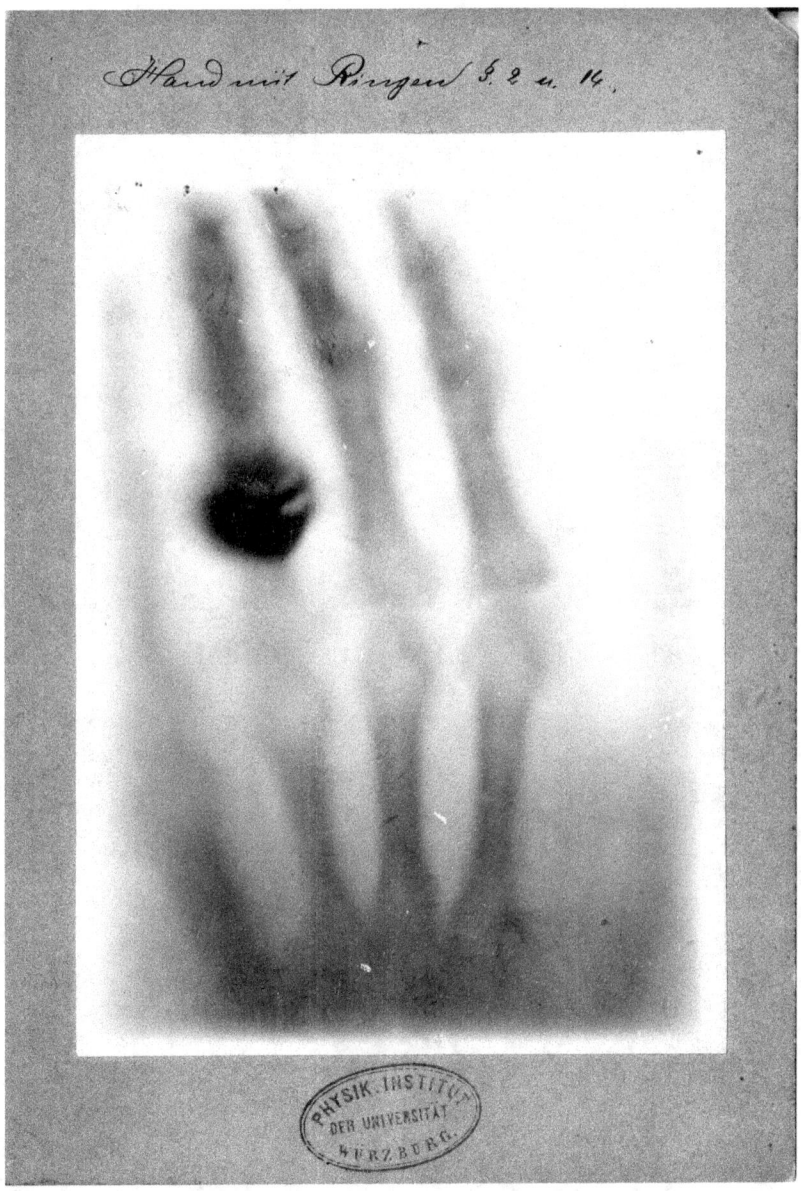

FIGURE 9.5 'Hand mit Ringen' [Hand with Rings], Bertha Röntgen's hand, one of the first X-rays by Wilhelm Röntgen printed, 22 December 1895, printed X-ray. H MS c1 [Hawes Collection] Courtesy of Countway Medical Library, Harvard University.

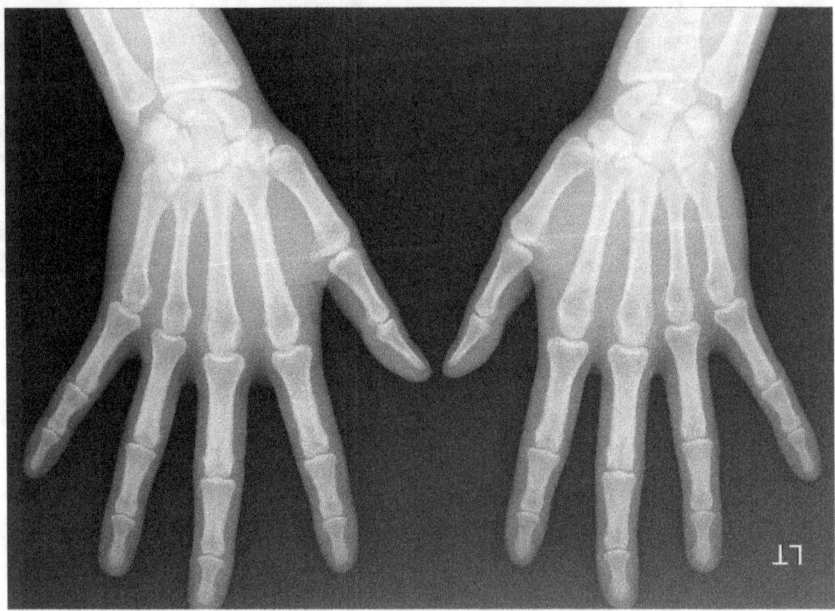

FIGURE 9.6 My hands X-rayed, 2014. Anna Ulrikke Andersen.

FIGURE 9.7 *The Window and I*, 2015. Anna Ulrikke Andersen.

to my size. Now, this misfit and the difference between me and her are captured on camera and depicted in my self-portrait, *The Window and I*.

Cinematic explorations of the self are also a defining feature of the essay film, as both Timothy Corrigan and Laura Rascaroli have argued.[27] As Corrigan argues, negotiating and exploring the self through public experience,

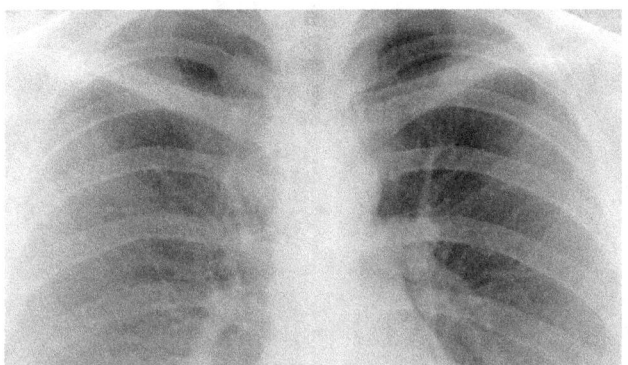

FIGURE 9.8 *The Window and I*, 2015. Anna Ulrikke Andersen.

the essay film becomes most important in pinpointing a practice that renegotiates assumptions about documentary objectivity, narrative epistemology, and authorial expressivity within the determining context of the unstable heterogeneity of time and place.[28]

Through cinematic explorations and experimentations with the self through the camera, the essay film allows larger themes to be addressed. For example, when Agnès Varda explores the act and history of gleaning in *The Gleaners and I* (2000), her own techniques of film-making using a lightweight digital camcorder allows her to film her own hand as she is picking up potatoes. Discussed in detail in Window 5 | Rome, Varda's film addresses wider societal concerns regarding waste and commerce, as she allows a focus on her own process and self as a film-maker, who with her own hand is picking up potatoes, references or a digital camera.

In a different film, a hand gently disturbs the water of a swimming pool, filmed and framed close-up. The water is fickle and moves, light reflecting on its surface. A pattern is created in the water: reflections of window sills. A shot of a large window that lets light into the swimming pool, in the background, a tall, yellow mountain. In blue, cold light, a chest X-ray melts into the footage of the chest. And again, with fragments of music played on a piano, a snow-covered branch slowly moves in the breeze. Two windows look onto a snow-covered landscape. Then an eye is seen focusing on the lens of a camera. This film, *The Window and I*, was shot in my home in London, UK; Reuma-sol in Alfaz del Pi, Spain; and my family's cabin at Budor, Norway. The film ventures from the exterior into the interior of the building through its window and eventually into the body of the film-maker herself: hands, and lungs, before focusing on the eye. I am the subject of my film and the film-maker.

Varda picks up a camcorder and films her own hand. Her own ageing hand reminds her that the end is near (Figure 9.9). To the blind and deaf

FIGURE 9.9 *The Gleaners and I*, 2000. Agnes Varda and Cine Tamaris.

American author Helen Keller her hands were also affected by ageing. Diana Fuss writes about Keller:

> But the most serious loss of all was her decreased sensitivity of her hands, crippled by arthritis. . . . Like sight and hearing, touch ages. Increasingly infirm, [Helen] Keller found herself unable to use a typewriter and uncomfortable reading Braille. By [1954] she needed to warm her hands continually in order to read a book.[29] (Figure 9.10)

With her ageing hand, Varda communicates through her film-making. With her camera and the film-making she produces with it, she gleans and gathers scattered material from around her. As Corrigan puts it: '*The Gleaners and I* is ultimately a moving sketch that gathers souvenirs of a self, extended through a disembodied hand, fractured through rapidly passing and dying images, and left to drift into the world of others.'[30]

Varda's hand, the hand of the film-maker, is located here in the film as subject matter rather than hidden behind the camera. *The Window and I* depicts my eye, and so exposes the *I* of the film-maker. In the film, I frame my body as it is affected by three set of windows, windows that filter and negotiate air, light and view. Rays of light lie across my hands; my eye is captured on camera.

FIGURE 9.10 Helen Keller, typing at her desk by the window, 1929. Photograph by Alfred Tennyson Beals. Courtesy of the American Foundation for the Blind, Helen Keller Archive.

Meeting Mies in Chicago, Anna Maria Norberg-Schulz recalls the architect's eyes:

> personally, he was frightening. Because he had some defect in the eye so that his eyes went wrongly. And you know, when you talk to a person with this defect, you don't know if he sees you. You know you are not talking to a blind person, but the eyes are not following you. So, (laughing) I remember it was quite tense. But he was a wise man, yes.[31]

Christian Norberg-Schulz did not make any notes about Mies's eyes when writing about the architect. In contrast to his wife's observations, he made a note of Mies's use of gestures and hand-movements: 'Mies spoke eagerly during our conversation, not at all as an oracle, but as an informal conversation. Like most people (perhaps with the exception of the Norwegians!) he gives his words emphasis with hand gestures and a smile.'[32] Mies used hand gestures, which was not unique internationally. But as Norberg-Schulz points out: it was unfamiliar for a Norwegian, as

FIGURE 9.11 Ludwig Mies van der Rohe, 1969. Courtesy of HB-35283-Z, Chicago History Museum, Hedrich-Blessing Collection.

he highlighted with an exclamation point (Figure 9.11) Non-Norwegian architects meeting Mies might not have taken any note of his hand gestures. But Norberg-Schulz did, and his note of the gestures says perhaps more about Norberg-Schulz's understanding of Norway than it says about Mies. Abroad, Norberg-Schulz realized that his own culture was different and did not use hand gestures. Leaving his native Norway, Norberg-Schulz understood what he had left in a new-found way.

'Ultimately, one must accept the risks, theoretical and otherwise, involved not only in leaving but in attempting to return',[33] Giuliana Bruno argues in *Atlas of Emotion: Journeys through Art, Architecture and Cinema* (2002). She underscores the difficulties one can experience upon a return after a journey. Having grown, changed, explored and learned, coming back can be difficult. For Norberg-Schulz, returning home to Norway on multiple occasions – from the United States or Italy – was not easy.

Norberg-Schulz's work was, as late as 1994, described and praised internationally but locally unknown.[34] Karl Otto Ellefsen, for one, discusses Norberg-Schulz's role as architectural theorist and educator in Norway. Ellefsen draws attention to how Norberg-Schulz must have found it difficult: divided between 'the role he had taken on within the Norwegian profession, and on the other, the intellectual and personal challenges of more profound theoretical work'.[35]

But even publishing his work proved difficult in Norway. *Intentions in Architecture* (1963) was originally his PhD dissertation conducted at the Norwegian University of Science and Technology, Trondheim. Written in

Norwegian and finished in 1960, Norberg-Schulz attempted to get this work published and contacted the Scandinavian University Press in Oslo. The publisher did not think the book would have a Norwegian audience and suggested an English version. Norberg-Schulz translated the manuscript into English, and the book was published in 1963, in cooperation with Allen Publishers, London. The Scandinavian University Press later contacted Norberg-Schulz to publish a Norwegian version in 1967. At that point, the original Norwegian manuscript had been lost, and he had to translate the English version back into Norwegian himself.[36]

Genius Loci: Towards a Phenomenology of Architecture (1980), on the other hand, was never translated for a Norwegian audience. Instead, *Mellom jord og himmel: en bok om steder og hus* from 1978 is considered to be the Norwegian popular version of *Genius Loci*.[37] *Mellom jord og himmel* is far from a literal translation of the book *Genius Loci* from 1979, as it is much shorter and has different illustrations. Written as part of a series, *Tankekors* (Considerations or Crux), its aim is to make philosophy more accessible to the Norwegian population.[38] In the book, Norberg-Schulz addresses contemporary challenges of national city planning and advocates a more careful treatment of the *genius loci* of each building task.

The fact that *Genius Loci* was never published in Norwegian, or in any other Scandinavian languages, might appear surprising to some. However, after speaking with Guttorm Fløistad, philosopher and editor of *Tankekors*, and Gordon Hølmebakk, editor of translation at Gyldendal publishing house, it seems that a Norwegian architectural audience was considered too small to get any profit from a Norwegian translation. Also, those who were interested in his phenomenological approach to architecture were considered likely to have the foreign language skills needed to read English. The short version, then, *Mellom jorg og himmel*, would instead reach a general, non-specialist Norwegian audience. As a result, *Mellom jord og himmel* became quite popular and was reprinted, with revised illustrations, in 1992 by Pax. Architect Anne Marit Vagstein defines the two publications as no more than related, in the sense that the theoretical core is the same, but the case studies and illustrations are different.[39] It appears that *Genius Loci* was too complex for the mainstream, and Norberg-Schulz had to write differently – and in a different language – to approach the general audience. Ellefsen argues: 'It seems symptomatic of the level of discourse and theory in Norwegian architecture that not even *Intentions* was an object of comprehensive theoretical discussion in Norway or the Nordic countries in general.'[40]

Simultaneously, Norberg-Schulz's approach did, however, not necessarily run in accord with political tendencies in Norway at the time. Ellefsen argues that the social democrats were seeking to institutionalize the country, forming the welfare state. Where the social democrats saw housing as highly political, did Norberg-Schulz's architectural thinking, in contrast, not explicitly address these political issues. Ellefsen describes Norberg-Schulz's writing as having 'a "professional" distance'[41] to politics, evident also in his editorship for *Byggekunst*.

Another way of considering why Norberg-Schulz's work was not read with interest in Norway is less about the lack of political or social content. Instead, could the difficulties he experienced in leaving and returning to his native Norway, which arguably changed his views and personality, mean that he had become too bold for the small nation? An instance is evident in the following event accounted for by Ellefsen. In an anniversary issue of *Byggekunst*, Norberg-Schulz critiqued the Oslo Town Hall designed by the well-established Norwegian architects Arnstein Arneberg and Magnus Poulsson, arguing that the city hall was 'characterised by a contradictory mixture of "styles", and the main impression is of a monumentality with embarrassing association'.[42] Arneberg received a copy of Norberg-Schulz's critique on his deathbed and read the younger theorist's critical words. Norberg-Schulz himself became harshly critiqued for his critique of Arneberg and Poulsson. Ellefsen describes the critique Norberg-Schulz received as abusive.[43] Norberg-Schulz had caused an uproar in the small Norwegian architectural scene: 'Many of his fellow professionals presumably ostracized him',[44] Ellefesen claims.

* * *

> It should be a task for the NRK to let the public know what our few internationally recognised thinkers stand for . . . Christian Norberg-Schulz has sharper than anyone described the defining meaning of place and warned against what now is occurring in our surroundings. A TV-film about Norberg-Schulz would, therefore, give an understanding of place, and underscore the anxiety many people experience as our world is torn into pieces.[45]

In this letter to NRK, Ulf Grønvold argued for the need to produce a TV documentary, celebrating the life and authorship of Norberg-Schulz. Because he was so widely known internationally it was important for the Norwegian public to know what the thinker stood for and get educated about an important theme, Grønvold argued. The project received funding, and the film was made. *Livet finner sted* was broadcast to the Norwegian public on 7 October 1992.

The film presented Norberg-Schulz's life, works, thoughts and ideas while relating these to local, well-known urban and architectural examples, taken from Oslo or the rural Seljord. The film was to be presented by the charismatic, slightly quirky, eloquent and engaging professor himself.

The sequences of the film from Seljord particularly intrigue me: wearing a pink shirt, Norberg-Schulz stands before a pink wall: a bank in the village. In the scene, Norberg-Schulz dismisses the architect's use of marble. Building and design, he says, involves many things: form, colour, materials.

As recent developments allow for new possibilities, the result can be quite eclectic.

> In this building, for instance, we have a wooden wall on the second floor,[46] windows in metal, aluminium, in fact, although it does not really look like it. And then we have this wall! From afar one might wonder, what kind of material is this? I first thought it was plastic when I looked at it from a distance, but then I got closer, and I realise it is marble! Marble is surely grand, but the question is: Does it belong in Seljord?'[47]

Dressed in pink, he stands in front of a pink wall. The still image from the sequence (Figure 9.12) resembles another photograph taken many years before, somewhere in Italy: where he is wearing beige. That older photograph was printed in Norberg-Schulz's book *Genius Loci: et opprinnelsens begrep* (1999)[48] and was used in an article about Norberg-Schulz's connection to Rome and Italy. Here, the photograph is used to highlight the importance that the city and its immediate surroundings had for his thinking, and so the similarity between the colour of his clothing and the colour of the architecture underscores his argument in which he supports how the *genius loci* of the Italian village and the city of Rome were the same, as discussed

FIGURE 9.12 *Livet finner sted*, 1992. Sven-Erik Helgesen and NRK. All rights reserved.

in detail in Window 6 | Piazza Navona. But the sequence from *Livet finner sted*, with the theorist wearing pink before the pink wall, reads differently. Although the colour of his clothing matches the architectural subject, in the film Norberg-Schulz opposes the architectural design before him and is critical to the architect's use of materials. Pointing to the marble, he asks: 'Does it belong in Seljord?'

To me, this opens up the question: To what extent Norberg-Schulz himself belonged in Seljord? If the material used by the architect is out of place, and not in keeping with *genius loci*, what about the man himself? In answering these questions, I am reading Norberg-Schulz's discussion of materials, and perhaps the making of the film *Livet finner sted* itself, as a variation on Ibsen's theme from 1899. 'Perhaps I have been abroad too long. This northern provincial life seems foreign to me.'[49]

By 1956 Norberg-Schulz had sold his house in Planetveien 14 and moved abroad. Years later, the family returned. This time, they moved into a wooden villa at Slemdal, Ris. Anna Maria Norberg-Schulz described the transition as moving to civilization: 'At Slemdal, we were very happy! It was a very normal house. A normal, white house, big house, in *Slemdalsveien*, the houses are all alike. And . . . very normal.'[50] Upon return to Oslo, the unconventional family – by Norwegian standards – blended into society to a greater degree.

Window 10

Trondheim

Place

Trondheim, Norway
Latitude: 63.44.6827
Longitude: 10.421906
Language: Norwegian Bokmål (Vindu), Norwegian Nynorsk (Vindauge)

Practice

The Death of the Chemist
Exhibition
Gamle Kjemi, NTNU, 23–25 May 2016
Kunstarken, Trondheim Academy of Fine Arts, NTNU, 23 May 2016
by Anna Ulrikke Andersen

Between 23 and 25 May 2016 the essay film *The Death of the Chemist* (2016) was installed in a staircase of Gamle Kjemi, NTNU (1910). The film was played on two iPads equipped with headphones. The iPads were attached to the wall in a metal frame and lettering on the wall introduced the visitors to the project, expanded upon in a printed leaflet. On 23 May 2016, I screened the film and gave a talk at Kunstarken, Trondheim Academy of Fine Arts, NTNU. The project ended on 26 May 2016 when I left the city by plane. Language: English, Norwegian.

FIGURE 10.1 Exhibition, *The Death of the Chemist*, Gamle Kjemi, 23–26 May 2016. Anna Ulrikke Andersen.

Essay

Reflections

Imagine a type of writing so hard to define its very name should be something like an effort, an attempt, a trial.[1]

An itinerary, a biographical note on the life and work of a Norwegian architectural theorist, a method; a chemist dying falling through a window, a passion for music, and a film filmed in February framing a building covered in snow; thinkers writing by the window, a house by the railway, and a shack made of plywood; an ageing man at the window of a train moving quickly through a densely forested landscape, journeys to Italy, and a film moving both through Europe and through the body; a young student watching the destructions of war through three, small windows of a military car, and feelings of disappointment; an architect ordering a window to be filled in with plaster, the end of a career in architecture and the dedication to writing, a camera on a roof terrace, filming, as I walk into the frame; a theorist drinking Campari at Piazza Navona, immediate experience at the water fountain, and re-enactments captured on camera; a drawing of a human figure looking at a series of window-like features, two friends sharing a passion for the poetry of Rilke, and a connection between the notion being and that of saying; a translation of a French poem into the Norwegian, a travelling poet writing about window, and the architectural theorist's failure to adopt the poet's notion; a glass-house in the woods, an internationally renowned theorist returning to his native Norway with his Italian wife, thoughts about being exposed and x-rayed; an installation of a film in a staircase, reflections on what lies beyond.

I had returned to Trondheim. It was May and the city was in bloom, and the air felt soft and warm. Time had passed since my last visit on 2 February 2016, when I filmed the old chemistry building Gamle Kjemi (2010) and visited the building with caretaker Stig Pallesen trying to find the exact site where Christian Norberg-Schulz's father had fallen into his death on 2 February 1926. When I last visited, snow had fallen in the night. White and thick, it covered the building and the square before it. I set up my camera and filmed the scene. Silently, I waited by my camera in the cold weather.

When I returned to Trondheim in May 2016, I brought with me the film *The Death of the Chemist*, ready to install and show in the building in question. The installation would bring the history of the chemist's death back into Gamle Kjemi (1910). The story would move into that very staircase where Stig Pallesen and I, months earlier, had concluded that the death of the twenty-eight-year-old most likely had taken place.

Norberg-Schulz was born on 23 May 1926, and the passing of time between the death and his birth, my first visit and my return become pivotal to my project. For the opening date of the exhibition with the installation, I decided on the ninetieth anniversary of Norberg-Schulz's birthday: 23 May 2016. At 12:00 I offered coffee and a short talk for an audience consisting of local artists, university staff based in the building and students from the university. After my talk, the visitors explored the installation and asked me questions about the project and the building. Later that night, I gave a talk discussing my project and the installation at Kunstarken at the Trondheim

Academy of Fine Arts/NTNU. Wearing a Campari-coloured dress, I asked what it means to be at a site where something had taken place and the fragmentary nature of archival research. The talk ended with the reading of *Les Fenêtres IV* (1927) by Rilke, and we toasted in white wine. I answered questions from the audience, and we watched *Livet finner sted* (1992), before continuing the discussion over wine (Figure 10.2).

The installation was open on the following days between 12:00 and 16:00. I was present and talked to people who came by to watch the work. When no one was there, unfolded the leaflet made for the exhibition and looked at the fragments of archival sources and references co-existing and forming a collection of material (Figure 10.3). I then folded it back in again, letting the large print still image of the building collapse and fold back into something as tangible as an informational blurb about my exhibition: when, where and who. I watched the film again and wearing the headphones I noticed how the soundtrack of the film blended with the sounds from the building: doors opening, people walking in stairs on their way to classes, libraries, lecture halls and reading rooms. The past intervened with the present.

My twenty-eighth birthday was 26 May 2016, and I wanted to leave Trondheim on that day and at the time that I was born – 06:05. That night, I stayed at a hotel close to the airport. I woke up early and checked in.

FIGURE 10.2 Lecture, Kunstarken, Trondheim Academy of Fine Arts/NTNU. 2016. Ellen Martine Andersen.

FIGURE 10.3 Leaflet, *The Death of the Chemist*, 2016. Anna Ulrikke Andersen.

The airport was empty, and only few people were flying. I sat in my seat at 06:05. The flight took off just before 06:10, scheduled to stop in Oslo before continuing to Heathrow, London. I looked out the window, ready for take-off and travel. Here, in Trondheim, my book would end (Figure 10.4).

* * *

This book has taken its reader and viewer on a journey through a history of architecture and cinema, Norberg-Schulz's life and work, and my own process of following the theorist. Composed as a list – which Brian Dillon in his book *Essayism* (2017) describes as potentially essayistic due to its fragmented nature[2] – the sequence gives a short summary of the journey, from Trondheim to Rome and back again. A series of essays, in film and writing, form a trial and an attempt to address the windows in Norberg-Schulz's life and work. Having embarked on and completed a journey, I eventually arrive at the final segment of my book.

What have I discovered?

The publication of this book marks the ten-year anniversary of when I first began my research and study of Norberg-Schulz. Throughout the year I have presented my work in seminars and conferences, and I was struck by the often passionate and lively discussions that followed any mentioning of his work. People seemed to have strong opinions on his work, as Rowan Wilken's brings forth in his article from 2013.[3] This landscape has been difficult to navigate, forcing me to think about my own position in relation to Norberg-Schulz's work. What do I think of his argument? Where do I stand?

Informed by these questions and fuelled by a growing interest in feminist scholarship and practitioners such as Jane Rendell, whose work

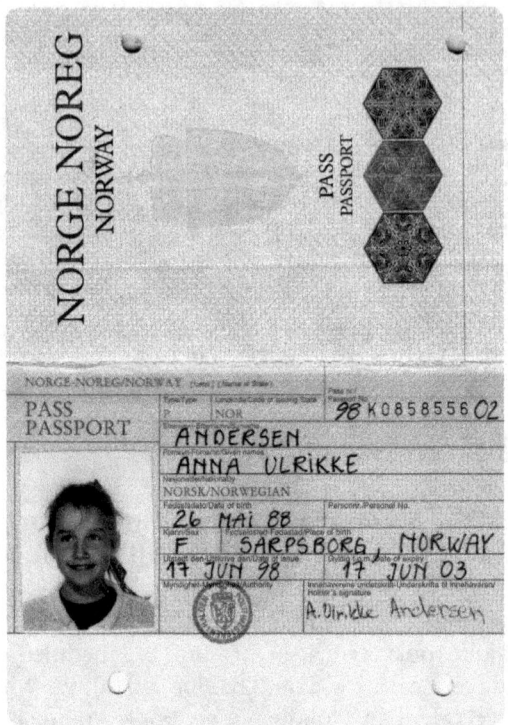

FIGURE 10.4 Passport, 1998. Anna Ulrikke Andersen.

places emphasis on the position of the speaking, writing subject, it became important to me to allow the *I* into my writing, my film-making and my travelling. The essay form proved incredibly fruitful in bringing this *I* into the frame and for me to navigate a wide range of references, and anecdotes, and create links between different aspects of architecture, windows, history, film-making, travel and the oeuvre of Norberg-Schulz. Including my first MRI (Figure 3.3) and my first passport from 1998 (Figure 10.4) became important to me as a way to position myself, both temporally in relation to Norberg-Schulz's lifespan and in the way I position my argument.

And thinking forward: I believe Norberg-Schulz's work can have a central role in the future of architecture. In a preface to one of Norberg-Schulz's publication, his dear friend Paolo Portoghesi writes: 'Norberg-Schulz "will be remembered in the history of our discipline as the most persuasive assertor of the fact that all works of architecture belongs to a place, and therefore first of all is local'.[4] If new sets of critical discourses, theories and perspectives are allowed into that framework, I believe that a set of new discourses can come forth. I am particularly intrigued by the mobile potential of Rilke's *Fensterblick* and how the poet understood windows, and its relevance for contemporary digital culture – as highlighted by Lutz Koepnick. I think film-making, and especially the essay film form, can play an intriguing role in pushing these questions further. These examples attempt to expose the uncertainties at play in the work of the historian, rather than smooth them over. Working with film, I have particularly played with the separation of sound and image as a way of destabilizing any notion of organic unity: one universal answer to the questions at hand. The essay form in film and writing has allowed me to do exactly this.

The essay as a form stands as an intriguing methodology to bridge the personal/reflexive with societal concerns, leaping between wide-ranging references. The essay is the core of my output and methodology – the way I write history – as both written essays and the fenestral essay films. I particularly embrace Laura Rascaroli's assertion that the essay film relies above all upon reframing. She writes:

> The essay film is performative inasmuch as it does not present its objects as stable given, as evidence of truth, but as the search for an object, which is itself mutating, incomplete, and perpetually elusive and thus deeply uncertain and problematized. What characterizes the object of the essay is not its being unique to the form – the essay is, in fact, eminently free in its choice of objects (Adorno 1984, 167) – but rather its 'arrangements', which is determined by a structure of gap. (Bensmaïa 1987, 17–18)[5]

To Rascaroli, one of the main features of the essay film lies in the way material is re-framed and arranged. Through gaps, elusiveness and uncertainty are brought into the light. In my written essays I take the reader on a journey through Europe, Norberg-Schulz's life, my own experiences, practice and the history of architecture, cinema, art and literature. In my fenestral essay films, I use cinematic means of editing, framing, sound and subtitling to reflect upon my position, sceptical towards how the historians approach the past.

My book, thus, makes a contribution to existing scholarship on the essay film and considers the genre as having the potential of writing architectural history. Through a focus on architecture, more specifically the window, where mobility, framing and self-reflection are features I consider as fenestral, my work underscores the importance of architecture and place in the genre of the essay film. Although Rascaroli's frequent use of spatialized language is a move towards considering space in the essay film, it is only Penelope Haralambidou who awards architecture full attention in 'The Architectural Essay Film' (2015),[6] and her objectives are aimed towards not architectural history but architectural design. My research has shown that architecture plays a role in the genre of the essay film, and the area invites further research. What role does the essay film play in writing architectural history?

In my approach to the window in Norberg-Schulz's life and work, I discover a man who is articulating a theory of place, and his personal experiences offer a very conflicted relationship between his own identity and the places where he lived, worked and travelled. Portoghesi's description of Norberg-Schulz as a 'flying Norwegian'[7] suitably refers to the legend of the 'Flying Dutchman': a ship doomed to sail, never settling in a port. Through extensive travel and visiting many places, Norberg-Schulz's attention to specific place as a series of tensions was moulded. For scholars looking into the work of Norberg-Schulz this has implications. In the context of his life, his theory appears less rigid and absolute than first assumed. The essay as a form allows for these contradictions, ambiguities and tensions to come forth, as they move, travel and venture through a series of landscapes, buildings, bodies, temporalities and ideas.

Appendix

Christian Norberg-Schulz's CV

Christian Norberg-Schulz. "CV" undated. Box: Diverse uregistrerte fra den svarte pulten. The Architectural Collections, the National Museum of Art, Architecture and Design.

Curriculum vitae

1926	Born in Oslo on May 23
1945–9	Studies at the Swiss Federal Polytechnic, Department of Architecture, under S. Gideon
1949	Diploma in architecture, Swiss Federal Polytechnic, Zürich
1951–6	Architectural practice in Oslo with Arne Korsmo
1951–6	Assistant professor at the State School of Arts and Crafts, Oslo
1952–3	Studies at Harvard University with Fulbright scholarship
1956	First prize, architectural competition for exhibition hall, Oslo
1956–8	Studies in Rome (history of architecture, building technology)
1958–66	Chairman of Oslo Architectural Association (OAF)
1963–78	Chief editor, *Byggekunst*, Oslo
1964	Doctor technique, Norwegian State Polytechnic, Trondheim
1964	Visiting critic, Yale University
1966	Visiting lecturer, Cambridge University
	Lectures in Liverpool, Graz
	Full professor, Oslo School of Architecture
1966–8	Board member, National Gallery, Oslo
1967	"Annual Discourse," Royal Institute of British Architects
	Lectures in Liverpool, Bristol, Edinburgh, Helsinki
	Lecture at Borromini Anniversary, Accademia di S. Luca, Rome
1968	Visiting lecturer, Cambridge University
	Lecture at Guarini Anniversary, Accademia delle Scienze, Turin
1968–9	Member of jury, Int.competition Lech am Arlberg, Austria
1969	Visiting lecturer, Cambridge University
	Lecture in Zürich

1969–73	"External examiner," Essex University
1970	Lecture at Vittone Anniversary, Accademia delle Scienze, Turin
1971	Lecture in Munich
1973	Visiting lecturer at the Massachusetts Institute of Technology
	Member of jury, National Theater competition, Oslo
1973–4	Research work in Rome ("Genius Loci")
1974	Visiting professor, Massachusetts Institute of Technology
	Lectures at Harvard University, Chicago, Pittsburg
	Member of board of directors, *LOTUS International*, Milan
1975	City planning consultant for the Sudanese government, Khartoum
	Lecture in Berlin
1976	Board member, int. Laboratory of Arch. and Urban Design, Urbino
	Lecture in Naples
1976–7	Dean, Oslo School of Architecture
1977	Lectures in Bruxelles, Cambridge, Bristol, Edinburgh, Munich, Venice, Florence, Rome, Urbino, Paris
	Board member, Museum of Modern Art in Oslo
1978	Doctor honoris causae, Hanover University, Germany
	Visiting professor, University of Dallas
	Lectures in Naples, London, Braunschweig, Karlsruhe, Stuttgart, Nürnberg
	Member of the Accademia Fiorentina delle Arti del Disegno
1979	Visiting professor, University of Dallas
	Lectures in Los Angeles, Berkeley, Lübeck, Florence, Rome
1980	Lectures in Naples, Rome, Hanover, Munich, Zürich
	Visiting lecturer, University of Cincinnati
	Exhibition on architectural theory, Biennale, Venice
	Member of jury, BDA-prize, Niedersachsen
1981	Lectures in Basel, Zürich, Aachen, Rome, Düsseldorf, Bonn, Dortmund (IBA)
1982	Lectures in Dublin, Chicago, Dallas, Lusanne, Siena (ILAUD), Stockholm, Genova
1983	Honorary award, American Institute of Architects
	Lectures in Linz, Genova, Barcelona, New York (Arch. League), San Francisco
	Member of exhibition committee Carlo Scarpa (Venice)
1984	Lectures in Rome, Siena, Stockholm
1985	Member of Icomos-commitae for the preservation of monuments (Paris)
	Member of jury, Oslo City Square Oslo
	Lectures in Århus, Stockholm, Barcelona, San Francisco, St. Lois, New York (Arch. League)
	Dean, Oslo School of Architecture

Books by or about Rainer Maria Rilke in Christian Norberg-Schulz's library

Books by or about Rilke in Norberg-Schulz's library, The Architectural Collection, The National Museum of Art, Architecture and Design, Oslo.

Albert-Lasard, Lou. *Wege mit Rilke*. Frankfurt am Main: Fischer, 1952.
Allemann, Beda. *Zeit und Figur beim späten Rilke*. Pfullingen: Neske, 1961.
Andreas-Salomé, Lou. *Rainer Maria Rilke*. Frankfurt am Main: Insel Verlag, 1988.
Angelloz, J.-F. *Rainer Maria Rilke*. Zürich: Verlag der Arche, 1955.
Betz, Maurice. *Rilke in Frankreich*. Wien: Herbert Riechner Verlag, 1938.
Boehm, Gottfried. *Rilke und die bildende Kunst*. Frankfurt am Main: Insel Verlag, 1985.
Bollnow, Otto Friedrich. *Rilke*. Stuttgart: Kohlhammer, 1956.
Buddenberg, Else. *Denken und Dichten des Seins*. Stuttgart: Metzler, 1956.
Buddenberg, Else. *Die Duineser Elegien Rainer Maria Rilkes*. Karlsruhe: Stahlberg, 1948.
Buddenberg, Else. *Rainer Maria Rilke*. Stuttgart: Metzlersche Verlagsbuchhandlung, 1954.
Fuerst, Norbert. *Rilke in seiner Zeit*. Frankfurt am Main: Insel Verlag, 1976.
Gebser, Jean. *Rilke und Spanien*. Frankfurt am Main: Suhrkamp, 1977.
Goth, Maja. *Rilke und Valéry*. Bern: Francke, 1981.
Guardini, Romano. *Rainer Maria Rilkes Deutung des Daseins*. München: Kösel-Verlag, 1953.
Hamburger, Käte. *Rilke*. Stuttgart: Klett, 1976.
Hamburger, Käte. *Rilke in neuer Sicht*. Stuttgart: Kohlhammer, 1971.
von Hattingberg, Magda. *Rilke und Benvenuta*. Wien: Andermann, 1947.
Hippe, Robert. *Erläuterungen zu ausgewählten Dichtungen Rainer Maria Rilkes*. Hollfeld: Bange, n.d., 1961.
Kassner, Rudolf. *Rilke*. Pfullingen: Neske, 1976.
Klippenberg, Katharina. *Rainer Maria Rilke*. Zürich: Niehans & Rokitansky, 1948.
Klippenberg, Katharina. *Rainer Maria Rilkes Duineser Elegien Und Sonette an Orpheus*. Frankfurt am Main: Insel Verlag, n.d.
Kramer-Lauf, Dietgard. *Tanz und Tänzerisches in Rilkes Lyrik*. München: Wilhelm Fink, 1969.
Leppmann, Wolfgang. *Rilke*. Bern: Scherz, 1981.
Mason, Eudo C. *Rainer Maria Rilke*. Göttingen: Vandenhoeck & Ruprecht, 1964.
Mövius, Ruth. *Rainer Maria Rilkes Stunden-Buch*. Leipzig: Insel Verlag, 1937.
Nevar, Elya Maria. *Freundschaft mit Rainer Maria Rilke*. Bern-Bümpliz: A.Züst, 1946.
Petzet, Heinrich Wiegand. *Das Bildnis des Dichters*. Frankfurt am Main: Insel Verlag, 1976.
Rilke, Rainer Maria. *Breife*. Wiesbaden: Insel Verlag, 1950.
Rilke, Rainer Maria. *Breife an einen jungen Dichter*. Frankfurt am Main: Insel Verlag, 1967.
Rilke, Rainer Maria. *Breifwechsel*. Wiesbaden: Insel Verlag, 1954.
Rilke, Rainer Maria. *Breifwechsel*. Frankfurt am Main: Insel Verlag, 1986.
Rilke, Rainer Maria. *Brev til en ung dikter*. Translated by Arild Batzer. Oslo: Dreyer, 1969.

Rilke, Rainer Maria. *Briefe an eine junge Frau*. Wiesbaden: Insel Verlag, 1949.
Rilke, Rainer Maria. *Briefe an Nanny Wunderly-Volkhart*. 2v vols. Frankfurt am Main: Insel Verlag, 1977.
Rilke, Rainer Maria. *Briefe über Cézanne*. Frankfurt am Main: Insel Verlag, 1983.
Rilke, Rainer Maria. *Briefwechsel in Gedichten mit Erika Mitterer*. Wiesbaden: Insel Verlag, 1950.
Rilke, Rainer Maria. *Das Florenzer Tagebuch*. Frankfurt am Main: Suhrkamp, 1982.
Rilke, Rainer Maria. *Das Marien-Leben*. Leipzig: Insel Verlag, n.d.
Rilke, Rainer Maria. *Das Studenbuch, enthaltend die drei Bücher*. Frankfurt am Main: Insel Verlag, 1962.
Rilke, Rainer Maria. *Das Testament*. Frankfurt am Main: Suhrkamp, 1975.
Rilke, Rainer Maria. *Der ausgewählten Gedichte*. Leipzig: Insel Verlag, 1946.
Rilke, Rainer Maria. *Der ausgewählten Gedichte*. Wiesbaden: Insel Verlag, 1951.
Rilke, Rainer Maria. *Der Brief des jungen Arbeiters*. Frankfurt am Main: Suhrkamp, 1974.
Rilke, Rainer Maria. *Die Apollosonette Rilkes und ihre plastischen Urbilden*. Berlin: Gebr. Mann, 1947.
Rilke, Rainer Maria. *Die Aufzeichnungen des Malte Laurids Brigge*. Frankfurt am Main: Insel Verlag, 1963.
Rilke, Rainer Maria. *Die Briefe an Gräfin Sizzo*. Frankfurt am Main: Insel Verlag, 1985.
Rilke, Rainer Maria. *Die Dame mit dem Einhorn*. Frankfurt am Main: Insel Verlag, 1978.
Rilke, Rainer Maria. *Die drei Liebenden*. Frankfurt am Main: Insel Verlag, 1979.
Rilke, Rainer Maria. *Die Sonette an Orpheus*. Wiesbaden: Insel Verlag, 1922.
Rilke, Rainer Maria. *Die Sonette an Orpheus*. Frankfurt am Main: Suhrkamp, 1985.
Rilke, Rainer Maria. *Die Weise von Liebe und Tod des Cornets Christoph Rilke*. Leipzig: Insel Verlag, 1930.
Rilke, Rainer Maria. *Die Weise von Liebe und Tod des Cornets Christoph Rilke*. Leipzig: Insel Verlag, 1978.
Rilke, Rainer Maria. *Duineser Elegien*. Frankfurt am Main: Insel Verlag, 1962.
Rilke, Rainer Maria. *Duino Elegies*. Berkley: University of California Press, 1961.
Rilke, Rainer Maria. *Duino Elegies*. London: Chatto and Windus, 1963.
Rilke, Rainer Maria. *Elegie Duinesi*. Torino: Einaudi, 1978.
Rilke, Rainer Maria. *Gedichte*. Stuttgart: Reclam, 1973.
Rilke, Rainer Maria. *Gedichte an die Nacht*. Frankfurt am Main: Suhrkamp, 1976.
Rilke, Rainer Maria. *Geschichten vom lieben Gott*. Leipzig: Insel Verlag, 1904.
Rilke, Rainer Maria. *Geschichten vom lieben Gott*. Frankfurt am Main: Insel Verlag, 1978.
Rilke, Rainer Maria. *Jeg klinger ved timens berøring*. Translated by Andre Bjerke. Oslo: Aschehoug, 1964.
Rilke, Rainer Maria. *Lettre a un'amica veneziana*. Milano: Rosellina Archinto, 1986.
Rilke, Rainer Maria. *Lettre su Cézanne*. Milano: Electa editrice, 1984.
Rilke, Rainer Maria. *Malte Laurids Brigges Opptegnelser (1910)*. Oslo: Aschehoug, 1965.
Rilke, Rainer Maria. *Nacht, Mensch und Engel*. Frankfurt am Main: Insel Verlag, 1975.

Rilke, Rainer Maria. *Neue Gedichte*. Frankfurt am Main: Insel Verlag, 1975.
Rilke, Rainer Maria. *Poems 1906 to 1926*. London: The Hogarth Press, 1976.
Rilke, Rainer Maria. *Poems from the Book of Hours*. New York: New Directions Books, 1975.
Rilke, Rainer Maria. *Rainer Maria Rilke 1875–1975*. München: Kösel, 1975.
Rilke, Rainer Maria. *Rainer Maria Rilke, Anita Forrer*. Frankfurt am Main: Insel Verlag, 1982.
Rilke, Rainer Maria. *Rainer Maria Rilke; Lou Andreas-Salomé*. Frankfurt am Main: Insel Verlag, 1979.
Rilke, Rainer Maria. *Rainer Maria Rilke und Stefan Zweig in Briefen und Dokumenten*. Frankfurt am Main: Insel Verlag, 1987.
Rilke, Rainer Maria. *Requiem*. Frankfurt am Main: Insel Verlag, 1959.
Rilke, Rainer Maria. *Rilkes Landschaft*. Frankfurt am Main: Insel Verlag, 1981.
Rilke, Rainer Maria. *Sämtliche Werke*. Frankfurt am Main: Insel Verlag, 1955.
Rilke, Rainer Maria. *Schweizer Vortragsreise 1919*. Frankfurt am Main: Insel Verlag, 1986.
Rilke, Rainer Maria. *Sonnets to Orpheus*. Translated by C. F. MacIntyre. Berkeley: University of California Press, 1971.
Rilke, Rainer Maria. *Tagebücher aus der Frühzeit*. Frankfurt am Main: Insel Verlag, 1973.
Rilke, Rainer Maria. *The Duino Elegies*. Translated by Stephen Garmey and Jay Wilson. New York: Harper & Row, 1972.
Rilke, Rainer Maria. *Über den jungen Dichter*. Frankfurt am Main: Insel Verlag, 1966.
Rilke, Rainer Maria. *Über Dichtung und Kunst*. Frankfurt am Main: Suhrkamp, 1974.
Rilke, Rainer Maria. *Übertragungen*. Frankfurt am Main: Insel Verlag, 1975.
Rilke, Rainer Maria. *Werke in drei Bänden*. Zürich: Buchclub Ex Libris, 1966.
Rilke, Rainer Maria. *Worpswede*. Bremen: Schünemann, 1976.
Rilke, Rainer Maria. *Zwei Prager Geschichten*. Frankfurt am Main: Insel Verlag, 1978.
Salis, Jean Rudolf von. *Rainer Maria Rilke Schweizer Jahre*. Frankfurt am Main: Suhrkamp, 1952.
Schnack, Ingeborg. *Rainer Maria Rilke*. Frankfurt am Main: Insel Verlag, 1977.
Schnack, Ingeborg. *Rainer Maria Rilke*. Frankfurt am Main: Insel Verlag, 1990.
Steiner, Jacob. *Rilkes Duineser Elegien*. Bern: Francke, 1962.
Stephens, Anthony R. *Rilkes Malte Laurids Brigge: Strukturanalyse des erzählerischen Bewusstseins*. Bern: Herbert Lang, 1974.
Storck, Joachim W and Ingeborg H. Solbrig. *Rilke heute*. Frankfurt am Main: Suhrkamp, 1975.
Thurn und Taxis-Hohenlohe, Marie von. *Erinnerungen an Rainer Maria Rilke*. München: Oldenbourg, 1937.
Unknown, *Rilkes Duineser Elegien*. Frankfurt am Main: Suhrkamp, 1980.
Unseld, Siegfried. *"Das Tagebuch" Goethes Und Rilkes "Sieben Gedichte."* Frankfurt am Main: Insel Verlag, 1978.
Valéry, Paul. *Eupalinos oder Der Architekt*. Frankfurt am Main: Erste Verlag, 1973.
Wolff, Joachim. *Rilkes Grabschrift*. Heidelberg: Lothar Stiehm, 1983.

References to Rainer Maria Rilke in Christian Norberg-Schulz's authorship

Norberg-Schulz's use of Rilke in published work

References to Rilke's Ninth Elegy

Norberg-Schulz, Christian. *Architecture: Meaning and Place*. New York: Electa/Rizzoli, 1988. 7, 11, 16.

Norberg-Schulz, Christian. *Architecture: Presence, Language Place*. Milano: Skira, 2000. 56–7, 134, 157, 328.

Norberg-Schulz, Christian. 'Den europeiske arkitekturens opphav og mangfold', in *Øye og hånd: Essays og artikler: ny rekke*. Ed. Gordon Hølmebakk. 91–6. Oslo: Gyldendal, 1997. 94.

Norberg-Schulz, Christian. 'Fra sted til sted', in *Øye og hånd: Essays og artikler: ny rekke*. Ed. Gordon Hølmebakk. 231–245. Oslo: Gyldendal, 1997. 233.

Norberg-Schulz, Christian. *Genius Loci: Towards a Phenomenology of Architecture*. London: Academy Editions, 1980. 6, 15, 48, 185.

Norberg-Schulz, Christian. *Nattlandene: Om byggekunst i Norden*. Oslo: Gyldendal Norsk Forlag, 1993. 19, 21.

Norberg-Schulz, Christian. *Nightlands: Nordic Building*. Translated by Thomas McQuillan. *Nattlandene: Om byggekunst i Norden*. Oslo: Gyldendal Norsk Forlag/Cambridge, MA: MIT Press, 1997. 13.

Norberg-Schulz, Christian. *Mellom jord og himmel: En bok om steder og hus*. Oslo: Universitetsforlaget, 1978. 33.

Norberg-Schulz, Christian. *Principles of Modern Architecture*. London: Andreas Papadakis Publisher, 2000. 114.

Norberg-Schulz, Christian. *Roots of Modern Architecture*. Tokyo: A.D.A. Edita, 1988. 177.

Norberg-Schulz, Christian. *The Concept of Dwelling: On the Way to Figurative Architecture*. New York: Electa/Rizzoli, 1985. 153.

References to Rilke's Sonnet for Orpheus

Krier, Rob 'Notizen am Rande', ed. Christian Norberg-Schulz. *Byggekunst*, no. 1 (1978), 16–17.

Norberg-Schulz, Christian. *Architecture: Presence, Language Place*. Milano: Skira, 2000. 134, 159.

Other references

'Rilke's poems about fruits'

I assume that this reference is to the poem *III Frukt* in the Norwegian translation ny André Bjerke of the *Sonnet for Orpheus*, in *Jeg klinger ved timens berøring: dikt i utvalg*. Oslo: Aschehoug, 1964. 51.
Norberg-Schulz, Christian. 'Tegning og virkelighet', *Byggekunst*, no. 1 (1978), 1.

NOTES

Framework

1 Sven-Erik Helgesen, *Livet finner sted* (1992), NRK, https://tv.nrk.no/program/fkur30002291/livet-finner-sted.
2 Betzy Sølvberg and Frid Weld, 'Christian Norberg-Schulz: en selektiv bibliografi', in *Christian Norberg-Schulz: et festskrift til 70årsdagen*, eds Guttorm Fløistad, Ketil Moe and Thomas Thiis-Evensen, 226–37 (Oslo: 1996) 237.
3 Helgesen, *Livet finner sted*.
4 Christian Norberg-Schulz, 'Kina og den moderne arkitekturen', *Byggekunst*, 11 (1951) 177–82.
5 Christian Norberg-Schulz, *Intentions in Architecture* (Cambridge MA: MIT Press, 1963) 24.
6 Ibid., 42.
7 Jean Piaget and Bärbel Inheder, *The Child's Conception of Space* (London: Routledge & K. Paul, 1956), 388, quoted in Norberg-Schulz, *Intentions in Architecture*, 42.
8 Rudolf Arnheim, 'The Gestalt Theory of Expression', *Psychological Review*, 56:3 (May 1949), 156–71.
9 Norberg-Schulz, *Intentions in Architecture*, 34.
10 Christian Norberg-Schulz, *Existence, Space & Architecture* (New York: Praeger, 1971).
11 Christian Norberg-Schulz, *Genius Loci: Paesaggio Ambiente Architettura*, translated by Anna Maria Norberg-Schulz (Milano: Electa Editrice, 1979).
12 Christian Norberg-Schulz, *Genius Loci: Towards a Phenomenology of Architecture* (London: Academy Editions, 1980), 6.
13 Ibid., 189.
14 Ibid., 201.
15 Ibid.
16 Ibid., 202.
17 Christian Norberg-Schulz, *Mellom jord og himmel: en bok om steder og hus* (Oslo: Universitetsforlaget, 1978).
18 Christian Norberg-Schulz, *The Concept of Dwelling: On the Way to Figurative Architecture* (Milan: Electa editrice, 1985); Christian Norberg-Schulz, *Stedskunst* (Oslo: Gyldendal, 1996).

19 Christian Norberg-Schulz, *Modern Norwegian Architecture* (Oslo: Norwegian University Press, 1986); Christian Norberg-Schulz, *Nightlands: Nordic Building*, translated by Thomas McQuillan (Cambridge, MA; London: MIT Press, 1996).

20 Christian Norberg-Schulz, *Øye og hånd: essays og artikler: ny rekke*, ed. Gordon Hølmebakk (Oslo: Gyldendal, 1997); Christian Norberg-Schulz, *Et sted å være: essays og artikler*, ed. Gordon Hølmebakk (Oslo: Gyldendal, 1986).

21 David Seamon and Robert Mugerauer, *Dwelling, Place, and Environment: Towards a Phenomenology of Person and World* (Malabar, Fla.: Krieger, 2000); David Seamon, *Life Takes Place: Phenomenology, Lifeworlds, and Place Making* (London: Routledge, 2018); Gro Lauvland, 'Verk og vilkår: Christian Norberg-Schulz' stedsteori i et arkitekturfilosofisk perspektiv' (PhD Dissertation, Oslo: Arkitektur- og Designhøyskolen, 2007); Anne Marit Vagstein, 'Stedet det stemte rom: Sammenhengen mellom sted og arkitektur' (PhD dissertation, Oslo: Arkitekthøgskolen, 1999); Léa-Catherine Szacka and Kirsten Hammer, eds. *Understanding Postmodern Architecture: A Norwegian Perspective* (Oslo: Arkitektur- og designhøgskolen i Oslo, 2015); Jorge Otero-Pailos, *Architecture's Historical Turn: Phenomenology and the Rise of the Postmodern* (Minneapolis: University of Minnesota Press, 2010); Jorge Otero-Pailos, 'Photo[historio]graphy', in *An Eye for Place: Christian Norberg-Schulz; Architect, Historian, Editor*, eds Gro Lauvland, Karl Otto Ellefsen and Mari Hvattum, 62–94 (Oslo: Akademisk Publisering, 2009); Jorge Otero-Pailos, 'Norberg-Schulz' hus: En moderne søken etter hjemmets visuelle mønstre', *Byggekunst*, 88:7 (2006), 10–17.

22 Gro Lauvland, Karl Otto Ellefsen and Mari Hvattum, eds, *An Eye for Place: Christian Norberg-Schulz; Architect, Historian, Editor* (Oslo: Akademisk Publisering, 2009).

23 Otero-Pailos, *Architecture's Historical Turn*.

24 Hendrik Auret, *Christian Norberg-Schulz's Interpretation of Heidegger's Philosophy: Care, Place and Architecture* (London: Routledge, 2018); Gro Lauvland, ed., *Fellesskapets arkitektur – opprør! Christian Norberg-Schulz som arkitekt og stedstenker* (Oslo: Abstrakt forlag, 2019).

25 See *Byggekunst*, 8 (1986); Jan Carlsen, 'Christian Norberg-Schulz: Bader i fontenen på st. Olavs plass' in *Norsk Arkitekturmuseum: Årbok 1995*, ed. Ulf Grønvold, 118–24 (Oslo: Norsk Arkitekturmuseum, 1995); Guttorm Fløistad et al. eds, *Christian Norberg-Schulz: Et festskrift til 70-årdagen* (Oslo: Norsk arkitekturforlag, 1996); Arne Gunnarsjaa, 'Christian Norberg-Schulz – den skrivende hustegner', in *Fellesskapets arkitektur – opprør! Christian Norberg-Schulz som arkitekt og stedstenker*, ed. Gro Lauvland, 13–100 (Oslo: Abstrakt forlag, 2019); Pauline Gjøsteen, 'Le jeune Christian Norberg-Schulz: esquisse de biographie intellectuelle', Diploma thesis, Genève: Institut d'architecture – Université de Genève, 2002 ; Pauline Gjøsteen, 'Italiesin comme "expérience": une biographie intellectuelle de Christian Norberg-Schulz, de 1945 à 1963' Université de Genève. PhD thesis, 2014; Raf de Sager, 'Stadier på livsveien mellom Norge og Flanderen', in *Fellesskapets arkitektur – opprør! Christian Norberg-Schulz som arkitekt og stedstenker*, ed. Gro Lauvland, 101–16 (Oslo:

Abstrakt forlag, 2019); Lauvland, 'Verk og vilkår'; Paolo Portoghesi 1986. 'To Christian: From Paolo Portoghesi', in *Byggekunst*, 8 (1986), 333; Lauvland, *Fellesskapets arkitektur – opprør!*.

26 Otero-Pailos, *Architecture's Historical Turn*, 146.
27 Gunila Jivén and Peter J. Larkham, 'Sense of Place, Authenticity and Character: A Commentary', *Journal of Urban Design*, 8:1 (2003), 70.
28 Hilde Heynen, 'Worthy of Question: Heidegger's Role in Architectural Theory', *Archis*, 12 (1993), 42–9.
29 Hlde Heynen, *Architecture and Modernity* (Cambridge, Mass: MIT Press, 1999), 22–3.
30 Alberto Pérez-Gómez, 'The Place Is Not a Postcard: The Problem with Genius Loci', in *An Eye for Place: Christian Norberg-Schulz: Architect, Historian and Editor*, ed. Karl Otto Ellefsen, Mari Hvattum, and Gro Lauvland, 26–34 (Oslo: Akademisk Publisering, 2009), 33.
31 Rowan Wilken, 'The Critical Reception of Christian Norberg-Schulz's Writings on Heidegger and Place', in *Architectural Theory Review*, 18:3 (2013), 340–55, 352.
32 Arnfinn Bø-Rygg, 'Arkitektur og filosofi: om Christian Norberg-Schulz' bruk av Heidegger's senfilosofi', *Norsk Filosofisk Tidsskrift*, 2 (1986), 37–54.
33 Elie Haddad, 'Christian Norberg-Schulz's Phenomenological Project in Architecture', *Architectural Theory Review*, 15:1 (2010), 88–101.
34 Ibid., 98.
35 Wilken 'The Critical Reception of Christian Norberg-Schulz's Writings on Heidegger and Place', 350.
36 Ibid, 352.
37 Auret, *Christian Norberg-Schulz's Interpretation of Heidegger's Philosophy*.
38 These films were made in response to Jane Rendell's module *Theorising Practices, Practicing Theories*, at the Bartlett School of Architecture Spring 2013. The films were shown and exhibited as part of *Site-Writing Site-Reading* at the exhibition *Cities Methodologies* April 2013. *The Spirit of the [Natural] Place* (2013), directed by Anna Ulrikke Andersen. https://vimeo.com/64596951; *The Spirit of the [Natural] Place: Commentary* (2013), directed by Anna Ulrikke Andersen. https://vimeo.com/65017738.
39 Anna Ulrikke Andersen, 'Translation in the Architectural Phenomenology of Christian Norberg-Schulz', *Architectural Research Quarterly*, 22:1 (2018), 81–90.
40 Jane Rendell, 'A Place between Art, Architecture and Critical Theory', proceedings to *Place and Location* (Tallinn, Estonia, 2003) 221–33.
41 Jane Rendell, *Art and Architecture: A Place Between* (London: I.B. Tauris, 2006).
42 Rendell, *Site-Writing*, 12.
43 Ibid., 18.

44 Leslie Fiedler, '1: The Discovery of the Self', in *The Art of the Essay*, ed. Leslie Fiedler, 1–5 (New York: Thomas Y. Crowell Company, 1958), 1.
45 Michel de Montaigne, 'Of Presumptions', in *The Art of the Essay*, ed. Leslie Fiedler, 5–29 (New York: Thomas Y. Crowell Company, 1958), 5.
46 Montaigne, 'Of Presumptions', 27.
47 Brian Dillon, *Essayism* (London: Fitzcarraldo Editions, 2017), 20.
48 Ibid., 20–2.
49 Ibid., 56.
50 Ibid., 33.
51 Ibid., 124.
52 Ibid., 67.
53 Ibid., 80.
54 Ibid., 85.
55 Ibid., 53.
56 Theodor Adorno, 'The Essay as Form' originally printed in 1958, in *Essays on the Essay Film*, eds Nora M. Alter and Timothy Corrigan (New York: Columbia University Press) 62.
57 Ibid., 61.
58 Ibid., 70.
59 Ibid.
60 Nora M. Alter, *The Essay Film after Fact and Fiction* (Columbia University Press, 2018); Nora M. Alter and Timothy Corrigan, eds, *Essays on the Essay Film* (New York: Columbia University Press, 2017); Timothy Corrigan, *The Essay Film : From Montaigne, After Marker* (New York: Oxford University Press, 2011); Laura Rascaroli, *How the Essay Film Thinks* (New York: Oxford University Press, 2017); Laura Rascaroli, *The Personal Camera : Subjective Cinema and the Essay Film* (London: Wallflower, 2009); Laura Rascaroli, 'The Essay Film: Problems, Definitions, Textual Commitments', *Framework; Detroit, Mich*, 49:2 (Fall 2008): 24–47.
61 Hans Richter, 'Der Filmessay: eine neue Form des Dokumentarfilms' ['The Film Essay: A New Form of Documentary Film'], in *Schreiben Bilder Sprechen: Texte zum essayistischen Film*, eds Christa Blümlinger and Constatin Wuldd, translated by Richard Langston, 195–8 (Wien: Sonderzahl, 1992).
62 Hans Richter, 'Der Filmessay: eine neue Form des Dokumentarfilms' ['The Film Essay: A New Form of Documentary Film'], in *Essays on the Essay Film*, eds Nora M. Alter and Timothy Corrigan, 89–92 (New York: Columbia University Press, 2017), 89.
63 Richter, 'The Film Essay', 89.
64 Ibid., 91.
65 Rascaroli, *How the Essay Film Thinks*, 189.
66 Ibid., 169.
67 Corrigan, *The Essay Film*, 105.

68 Ibid., 6.
69 Rascaroli, *The Personal Camera*, 190.
70 Norberg-Schulz, *Genius Loci: Paesaggio Ambiente Architettura*.
71 Michel Chion, *The Voice in Cinema* (New York: Columbia University Press, 1999); Mary Ann Doane, 'The Voice of Cinema: The Articulation of Body and Space', in *Film Sound: Theory and Practice*, eds Elisabeth Weis and John Belton, 162–76 (New York ; Chichester: Columbia University Press, 1985).
72 Ebneter Curdin, ed., *Rilke: Les Jours d'Italie/Die Italienischen Tage* (Sierre: Foundation R.M. Rilke, 2009); T. Jefferson Kline, ed., *Agnès Varda: Interviews* (University Press of Mississippi, 2014); Adam Sharr, *Heidegger's Hut* (Cambridge, MA; London: MIT Press, 2006).
73 Giuliana Bruno, *Atlas of Emotion: Journeys in Art, Architecture, and Film* (New York; London: Verso, 2002); Peter Wilson, *Some Reasons for Travelling to Italy* (London: Architectural Association, 2016).
74 Victor Burgin, *The Remembered Film* (London: Reaktion, 2004); Sharon Kivland, *Freud on Holiday: Volume 1, Freud Dreams of Rome* (York: Information as Material, 2006).
75 Mireille Ariel and Agnès Varda, 'Agnès Varda Talks about Cinema', in *Agnès Varda: Interviews*, translated by T. Jefferson Kline, 64–77 (Jackson, Mississippi: University Press of Mississippi, 2015).
76 Jaques Derrida, *La carte postale: de Socrate à Freud et au-delà* (Paris: Flammarion, 1985).
77 Christian Norberg-Schulz, 'Vann', in *Øye og hånd: essays og artikler*, ed. Gordon Hølmebakk, 27–32 (Oslo: Gyldendal, 1997).
78 Sophie Calle, 'Suite Vénitienne', in *Sophie Calle: Suite Vénitienne. Jean Baudrillard. Please Follow Me*, translated by Danny Barash and Danny Hatfield, 1–74 (Seattle, Wash.: Bay Press, 1988); Sven Lütticken, ed., *Life, Once More: Forms of Reenactment in Contemporary Art* (Rotterdam: Witte de With, 2005).
79 Ji-Ming Tang, *Fenster-Geschichten: Die Bedeutung des Fensters bei Rilke und ausgewählten anderen Autoren* (Kassel: Kassel University Press GmbH, 2009); Rainer Maria Rilke, *Les Fenêtres, dix poèmes de Rainer Maria Rilke, illustrés d'eaux-fortes de Baladine* (Paris: Librairie de France, 1927).
80 Beatriz Colomina, 'X-Ray Architecture: Illness as Metaphor', in *Positions* (2008) 30–5; Alice T. Friedman, *Women and the Making of the Modern House: A Social and Architectural History* (New Haven, Conn.; London: Yale University Press, 2006); Elisabeth Tostrup, *Planetveien 12: The Korsmo House, a Scandinavian Icon* (London: Artifice Books on Architecture, 2014).

Window 1

1 'En trist ulykke ved Den tekniske Høiskole', in *Aftenposten morgen*, 3 February 1926, and 'Ulykke paa Høiskolen' in *Dagsposten*, 3 February 1926.

2   The first hymn is a Norwegian translation of the German *Mein G'müt ist mir verirret* (1601) by Paul Gerhard. The second hymn's title translates to 'When we once will gather again'. 'Docent Norberg-Schulz' begravelse' in *Trondhjem Adresseavis*, 10 February 1926.
3   Michel Chion, *The Voice of Cinema* [*Voix au cinema* 1947], translated by Claudia Gorbman (New York: Columbia University Press, 1999) 27.
4   Ibid., 18.
5   *Gamle Kjemi* (1919), Box: PBE, Gøshaugen, NTH, Tegninger fra 1905–20, Trondheim City Archive *Gamle Kjemi* (1908), Box: PBE, Gløshaugen, NTH, Tegninger fra 1905–20, Trondheim City Archive.
6   'Ulykke paa Høiskolen' in *Dagsposten*, 3 February 1926.
7   Walter Benjamin, 'Theses on the Philosophy of History' ['Über den Begriff der Geschichte' 1940], in *Illuminations: Essays and Reflections*, ed. Hannah Arendt, translated by Harry Zorn, 255–66 (New York: Harcourt Brace Janovich, 1968), 256.
8   Rainer Maria Rilke, *The Notebooks of Malte Laurids Brigge* [1910], translated by Michael Huse (London: Penguin Random House UK, 2009) 1–2.
9   Lutz Koepnick, 'The Aesthetic of the Interface', in *Window|Interface*, eds Lutz Koepnick and Sabine Eckmann, 15–49 (St. Louis, Mo.: Mildred Lane Kemper Art Museum, 2007) 40.
10 Rendell, *Art and Architecture*, 150.
11 Ibid., 184.
12 Doane, 'The Voice in the Cinema'.
13 Ibid., 162.
14 Ibid., 163.
15 Annette Kuhn and Guy Westwell, eds, 'Essay Film', in *A Dictionary of Film Studies* (Oxford University Press, 2012), http://www.oxfordreference.com/view/10.1093/acref/9780199587261.001.0001/acref-9780199587261-e-0238.
16 Rascaroli, *How the Essay Film Thinks*, 116.
17 Gilles Deleuze, *Cinema 2: The Time Image* [1985], translated by Hugh Tomlinson and Robert Galeta (Minneapolis: University of Minnesota Press, 1989), quoted in Rascaroli, *How the Essay Film Thinks*, 117.
18 Rascaroli, *How the Essay Film Thinks*, 141.
19 Rendell, *Art and Architecture*, 143.
20 Ibid.
21 Keith Jenkins, *Re-Thinking History* (London: Routledge, 1991), 10.
22 Ibid., 68.
23 Ibid., 69.
24 'Ulykke paa Høiskolen' in *Dagsposten*, 3 February 1926.
25 Joseph Perricone, ' . . . And the Ship Sails On: A Reviewing of Fellini', in *Literature/Film Quarterly*, 15:2 (1987) 78–84.

26 'Standing-Room Crowd Attends Fellini Funeral', in *The New York Times*, 4 November 1993. http://www.nytimes.com/1993/11/04/arts/standing-room-crowd-attends-fellini-funeral.html (accessed 13 August 2017).

27 'Il me semblait avoir besoin de forces qui puissent avoir l'air, avec vraisemblance, de celles de personnes qui n'existent plus, disparues dans le temps.' My translation of Blanchard Gérard, 'Images de la musique de cinema', in *Communication et langages*, 60:2 (1984) 66–76, 73.

28 'Tout le film de Fellini apparaît comme un film de mémoire, le film du souvenir, le film "rétro" par excellence: hommage au cinéma muet. Les premières minutes du film sont d'ailleurs muettes. Un quai du port de Naples est reconstitué à Rome, dans une ancienne usine de pâtes désaffectée. Le silence est le lieu mythique des premières images de cinema.' My translation of Gérard, 'Images de la musique de cinema', 75.

29 Chion, *The Voice of Cinema*, 6.

30 Elizabeth Weiss and John Belton, *Film Sound: Theory and Practice* (New York, Chichester: Columbia University Press, 1985) 3–4.

31 Grigori Alexandrov, Sergei Eisenstein and Vesevolod Pudovkin, 'Statement of Sound', in *Film Sound*, eds Belton and Weis, 83–5. First published in *Leningrad Magazine*, August 1928. 83.

32 Alexandrov, Eisenstein and Pudovkin, 'Statement of Sound', 84.

33 Vesevolod Pudovkin, 'Asyncronism as a Principle of Sound Film', in *Film Sound*, eds Elizabeth Weiss and John Belton, 86–91 (New York, Chichester: Columbia University Press, 1985), 86–91.

34 Øivind Hanche, Gunnar Iversen and Nils Klevjer Aas, *Bedre enn sitt rykte: en liten norsk filmhistorie* (Oslo: Norsk Filminstitutt, 2004) 23.

35 Carol O'Sullivan, *Translating Popular Film* (New York: Palgrave Macmillan, 2011) 10.

36 H. Harlan Kennedy, 'Fellini's Ship Sails into Venice', in *Film Comment*, 19:6 (1983) 2–6, 2.

37 Anders Eggen, 'Elizabeth Norberg Schulz', in *Norsk biografisk leksikon*, 2009. https://nbl.snl.no/Elizabeth_Norberg-Schulz (accessed 24 May 2017).

38 Interview with Anna Maria Norberg-Schulz, Oslo, 7 September 2014.

39 Interview with Anna Maria Norberg-Schulz, Oslo, 7 September 2014.

40 Christian Norberg-Schulz, 'Frossen Musikk', in *Øye og hånd: essays og artikler*, ed. Gordon Hølmebakk, 40–8 (Oslo: Gyldendal Norsk Forlag, 1997).

41 Léa-Catherine Szacka, *Exhibiting the Postmodern: The 1980 Venice Architecture Biennale* (Venice: Marsilio Editori, 2016) 120.

42 Christian Norberg-Schulz, *Nightlands: Nordic Building* (Cambridge, Mass: MIT Press, 1997) 10, 44.

43 Norberg-Schulz, *Genius Loci: Towards a Phenomenology of Architecture*, 21.

44 'Opplevelsen på toget lærte meg at det vi er, er det vi er blitt kjent med fra barnsbena. Vi Nordmenn *er* den tette skogen og den myke skogbunnen. Derfor skifter alltid folkearkitekturen uttrykk, selv om funksjonen er den samme. For

det å bo betyr å respektere omgivelsene. En kan ikke bo i Norge uten å være venner med sneen. Uten å like å gå på ski, eller like lyden av snøen som knirker under føttene.' My translation, Sven-Erik Helgesen, *Livet finner sted*, 1992, NRK, 10:38–11:19.

45 Mari Hvattum, 'Genius Historie', in *An Eye for Place: Christian Norberg-Schulz: Architect, Historian and Editor*, eds Gro Lauvland, Mari Hvattum and Karl Otto Ellefsen, 108–15 (Oslo: Akademisk Publisering, 2009) 108.

46 'Nordens lys, rom, ting og menneske', my translation. Christian Norberg-Schulz, 'NRK Skisse til disposisjon' ['NRK Sketch for Disposition'], 29 September 1990. Box: Korrespondanse, klipp og annet diverse. The National Museum of Art, Architecture and Design, Oslo.

47 Norberg-Schulz, 'NRK Skisse til disposisjon'.

48 Norberg-Schulz, *Genius Loci: Towards a Phenomenology of Architecture*, 21.

Window 2

1 Jorge Otero-Pailos, 'Norberg-Schulz' hus: *en moderne søken etter hjemmets visuelle mønstre*'. In *Arkitektur N*, published 21. februar 2017, originally published in Arkitektur N 7 (2006) https://arkitektur-n.no/artikler/norberg-schulz-hus (accessed 17.03.2017); Raf de Sager, 'Stadier på livsveien mellom Norge og Flandern' in *Fellesskapets arkitektur – opprør! Christian Norberg-Schulz som arkitekt og stedstenker*, ed. Gro Lauvland, 101–15 (Oslo: Abstrakt Forlag, 2020) 114.

2 De Sager, 'Stadier på livsveien mellom Norge og Flandern', 113.

3 Hendrik Andries Auret, 'Appendix C', in 'Care, Place and Architecture: A Critical Reading of Christian Norberg-Schulz's Architectural Interpretation of Martin Heidegger's Philosophy', University of the Free State, 2015, 433.

4 De Sager's text is translated from English to Norwegian. In the text, he writes that the room was located at *førte etasje*, which translates into first floor. However, in Norway we use *første etasje* to describe the ground floor. After visiting the villa myself in 2014, it is clear to me that the photograph was taken from a window at *andre etasje*, which translates into second floor but is equivalent to the English first floor. De Sager, 'Stadier på livsveien mellom Norge og Flandern', 115.

5 Anna Ulrikke Andersen, 'Listening with Christian Norberg-Schulz: Sonic experience and music theory in his writings', in *The Sound of Architecture: Acoustic Atmospheres in Place*, eds Angeliki Sioli and Elisavet Kiourtsoglou (Leuven: University of Leuven Press, 2022).

6 Karen Hellmann, *The Window in Photographs* (Los Angeles, CA: The J. Paul Getty Museum, 2013) 7.

7 Hentie Loew, 'The Development of the Window', in *Windows: History, Repair and Conservation,* eds Michael Tutton, Elizabeth Hirst and Jill Pearce, 7–96 (Shaftesbury: Donhead Pub, 2007) 7.

8 Anne Friedberg, *The Virtual Window: From Alberti to Microsoft* (Cambridge, Mass: MIT Press, 2006).

9   Ibid., 12.
10 Koepnick, 'The Aesthetics of the Interface', 18.
11 Diana Fuss, *The Sense of an Interior: Four Writers and the Rooms That Shaped Them* (New York: Routledge, 2004) 3.
12 Ibid., 4.
13 Ibid., 142.
14 Ibid., 5.
15 Michael Schreyach, 'The Recovery of Criticism', in *The State of Art Criticism*, eds James Elkins and Michael Newman, 3–25 (London: Routledge, 2008) Discussed in Jane Rendell, *Site-Writing: The Architecture of Art Criticism* (London: I.B. Tauris, 2010) 6.
16 Rendell, *Site-Writing*, 12.
17 Norberg-Schulz, *Genius Loci: Towards a Phenomenology of Architecture*, 7.
18 Ibid., 179.
19 Ibid., 176.
20 Martin Heidegger, 'Das Ding', in *Vorträge und Aufsätze*, 11th ed., 157–75 (Stuttgart: Klett-Cotta, 2009).
21 Martin Heidegger, 'Bauen Wohnen Denken', in *Vorträge und Aufsätze*, 11th ed., 139–56 (Stuttgart: Klett-Cotta, 2009); Martin Heidegger, 'Building Dwelling Thinking', in *Basic Writings from 'Being and Time' (1927) to 'The Task of Thinking' (1964)*, ed. D. F. Krell, 347–63 (London: Routledge, 1993) 347.
22 Norberg-Schulz, *Genius Loci: Towards a Phenomenology of Architecture*, 176.
23 Sharr, *Heidegger's Hut*, 42.
24 Ibid., 76.
25 The poem was never published by Friedrich Hölderlin, but Heidegger published and discussed the poem in his book *Hölderlin's Hymne 'Der Ister'* (Frankfurt am Main: Vottorio Klostermans Verlag, 1984); Martin Heidegger, *Hölderlin's Hymn 'The Ister'*, translated by William McNeil and Julia Davis (Bloomington, Indiana: Indiana University Press, 1996) 2.
26 Sharr, *Heidegger's Hut*, 63.
27 Ibid., 103.
28 Auret, 'Care, Place and Architecture', 440.
29 Norberg-Schulz, *Genius Loci: Towards a Phenomenology of Architecture*, 21.
30 Ibid., 19.
31 Ibid., 179.
32 'Meine Fenster sin groß; ich sehe den Park sich aufbauen und viel Himmel, also auch viel Nacht. Vor dem einen steht der Schreibtisch, und das Stehpult, an dem ich meistens bin, hat seinen Platz in der Mitte des Zimmers so, daß es sich beider Fenster erfreut.' My translation of Rainer Maria Rilke and Lou Andreas-Salomé, *Briefwechsel*, v. Ernst Pfeiffer (Frankfurt a.M.: Insel Verlag, 1975). Quoted in Tang, *Fenster-Geschichten*, 8–9.

33 'Wenn ich am Morgen aufwache, so leigt vor meinem offenen Fenster im reinen Raum, ausgeruht, das Gebirg; [. . .] und jetzt sitz ich da und schau und schau bis mir die Augen wehthun, und zeig mir und sag mir vor als sollt ich auswendig lernen, und habs doch nicht und bin recht einer, dems nicht gedeiht.' My translation of Maria Rilke and Andreas-Salomé, *Briefwechsel*. Quoted in Tang, *Fenster-Geschichten*, 8.

34 'Der Fensterblick ist seine Methode, mit den "Riesen", also der Außenwelt, zu ringen'. My translation. Tang, *Fenster-Geschichten*, 9.

35 'Diese Äußerungen und auch die vielen überlieferten Fotos, die Rilke am Fenster arbeitend zeigen, lassen vermuten, dass Rilke die Stoffe für seine Gedichte möglicherweise auch dem Fenster verdankte und das Fenster eine wichtige Inspirationsquelle für sein Dichten war.' My translation. Tang, *Fenster-Geschichten*, 9.

36 I will discuss these poems in detail in Window 7 | Calcata and Window 8 | Sierre.

37 Portoghesi, 'To Christian: From Paolo Portoghesi'.

38 Ariel and Varda, 'Agnès Varda Talks about the Cinema', 65.

39 Ibid., 45.

40 Ibid., 65.

41 Ibid..

42 Andersen, 'Listening with Christian Norberg-Schulz'.

43 Interview with Anna Maria Norberg-Schulz, 7 September 2014.

44 Emily Kramer, 'The House that Agnès Built: Angès Varda at LACMA', in *Droste Effect Mag* (2014). http://www.drosteeffectmag.com/house-agnes-built-agnes-varda-lacma/ (accessed 14 December 2017).

45 *Toute Varda: L'intégrale Agnès Varda*, twenty-two DVD box set, ARTE Boutique and Ciné-Tamaris, 2012.

46 Francoise Wera and Agnés Varda, 'Interview with Agnès Varda', in *Agnés Varda: Interviews*, ed. T. Jefferson Kline, 118–25 (Jackson, Mississippi: University Press of Mississippi, 2014) 118.

Window 3

1 Bruno, *Atlas of Emotion*, 404.

2 Ibid., 397.

3 Ibid.

4 'Hvis et slikt program skal bli godt fjernsyn, og yte CNS rettferdighet, må programmet beskrive en reise i tid og rom, en sirkel fra Hjartdal til Roma – og tilbake til bygdenorge med sine tradisjoner – og sin "samvirkelagsarkitektur". Det blir derfor et kostbart program.' My translation of Sven-Erik Helgesen, 'Livet finner sted: Et program om Christian Norberg-Schulz' 14 June 1990. Box: Korrespondanse, klipp og annet diverse. The Norberg-Schulz Archive,

the Architectural Collections, the National Museum of Art, Architecture and Design, Oslo.

5   Sven-Erik Helgesen produced the film *Det sakrale rom*, dir. Arvid Esperød, NRK, 1998. He directed: *Diktet om breen*, NRK, 1994.
6   Norberg-Schulz, *Genius Loci: Towards a Phenomenology of Architecture*.
7   Ibid.
8   Christian Norberg-Schulz, 'Et sted å være: for NRK', (1990) Box: Korrespondanse, klipp og annet diverse. The Norberg-Schulz Archive, the Architectural Collections, the National Museum of Art, Architecture and Design, Oslo.
9   Conversation with Sven-Erik Helgesen, 21 May 2013.
10 The voice-over used in the opening scene of *Livet finner sted* appears to be an excerpt of the essay 'Et sted å være: for NRK'. Christian Norberg-Schulz, 'Et sted å være: for NRK', (1990) Box: Korrespondanse, klipp og annet diverse. The Norberg-Schulz Archive, the Architectural Collections, the National Museum of Art, Architecture and Design, Oslo.
11 My translation, Helgesen, *Livet finner sted*.
12 Portoghesi, 'To Christian: From Paolo Portoghesi'.
13 'The Flying Dutchman', Wikipedia. https://en.wikipedia.org/wiki/Flying_Dutchman (accessed 4 May 2018).
14 Christian Norberg-Schulz, CV. Box Diverse uregistrerte fra den sorte pulten. The Norberg Schulz Archive. The Architectural Collections. The National Museum of Art, Architecture and Design, Oslo.
15 Norberg-Schulz, CV.
16 Interview with Anna Maria Norberg-Schulz, 7 September 2014.
17 Christian Norberg-Schulz, *Travel Journal*. Box 2002:15 Arkivstykke 2F notatbøker/notater, The Christian Norberg-Schulz Archive, the Architectural Collections, the National Museum of Art, Architecture and Design, Oslo.
18 Private photographs kept by the Norberg-Schulz family and interview with Anna Maria Norberg-Schulz, 7 September 2014.
19 Interviews with Anna Maria Norberg-Schulz, 7 September 2014.
20 Ibid.
21 Ibid.
22 Otero-Pailos, *Architecture's Historical Turn*, 160.
23 The literature covering the grand tour and its importance for the field of architecture, art and thinking is large. A few suggestions would be Christopher Hibbert, *The Grand Tour* (London: Thames Methuen, 1987); Harry Siedler, *The Grand Tour: Travelling the World with an Architect's Eye* (Köln, London: Taschen, 2004); Jeremy Black, *Italy and the Grand Tour* (New Haven, London: Yale University Press, 2003); Johann Wolfgang von Goethe, *Italienische Reise [Italian Journey]*, translated by W. H. Auden and Elizabeth Mayer (London: Collins, 1962). For literature specifically

discussing Norwegian travelling to Italy, see Giuliano D'Amico and Elettra Carbone, *Lyset kommer fra sør: Italias frigjøringskamp sett fra datidens norske forfattere* (Oslo: Gyldendal, 2011); Elettra Carbone, *Nordic Italies: Representations of Italy in Nordic Literature from the 1830s to the 1910s* (Rome: Edizioni Nuova Cultura, 2016).

24 Anne Hultzsch, *Architecture, Travelers and Writers: Constructing Histories of Perception 1640-1950* (Oxford: Legenda, 2014) 54.
25 Rendell, *Art and Architecture*, 190.
26 Ibid., 188.
27 Ibid., 185.
28 Rebecca Solnit, *Wanderlust: A History of Walking* (London: Verso, 2011).
29 Rebecca Solnit, *A Field Guide to Getting Lost* (Edinburg: Canongate, 2006).
30 Ibid., 4–5.
31 Joachim W. Stock, 'Venedig, Mimi Romanelli und Rilkes Liebestheorie', in *Rilke: Les jours d'Italie/Die italienischen Tage*, ed. Curdin Ebneter, 299–319 (Sierre: Foundation R. M. Rilke) 299.
32 Ebneter draws attention to the work of Rudolf Kasher, who suggested that Rilke's travelling was not of interest. Ebneter's work is aimed at drawing attention to this aspect of Rilke's life and work. Curdin Ebneter, 'Rilkes italienische Tage', in *Rilke: Les jours d'Italie/Die italienischen Tage*, ed. Curdin Ebneter, 13–68 (Sierre: Foundation R. M. Rilke, 2009) 67.
33 Rüdiger Görner, 'Rilke: A Biographical Exploration', in *The Cambridge Companion to Rilke*, eds Karen Leeder and Robert Vilain, 9–26 (Cambridge: Cambridge University Press, 2010), 16.
34 Ebneter, 'Rilkes italienische Tage', 13.
35 Ibid., 61.
36 Jo Catling, 'Rilke auf Capri', in *Rilke: Les jours d'Italie/Die italienischen Tage*, ed. Curdin Ebneter, 187–227 (Sierre: Foundation R. M. Rilke, 2009).
37 Rita Rios, 'Rilkes florenzer Tagebuch, beobachtungen zum lyrischen Umgang mit der Renaissance', in *Rilke: Les jours d'Italie/Die italienischen Tage*, ed. Curdin Ebneter, 117–33 (Sierre: Foundation R. M. Rilke, 2009).
38 'Italia kannte und liebte ich seit meinem achten Jahr, - es war in seiner deutlichen Vielfalt und Formfülle, sozusagen, die Fibel meines beweglichen Daseins.' My translation, Rainer Maria Rilke, 'An eine junge Freundin', 17 March 1926, in *BII*, 427 (Frankfurt M/Leipzig: Insel, 1991). Quoted in Ebneter, 'Rilkes italienische Tage', 66.
39 In his schematic representation of the antagonistic forces in Rilke, Ebneter mentions Rilke's references to artworks such as Russian Icons, or culturally specific ideologies, such as an optimistic attention to the future. Other forces relate to natural conditions, such as climate or landscapes, or include the opposition between subjective experience and the common experiences shaped by books such as Baedeker. Ebneter, 'Rilkes italienische Tage', 66.
40 Rilke's notion of *beweglichen Daseins* will be discussed in greater detail in Window 8 | Sierre.

41 'Gewiss scheint mir, dass in Rilkes 'beweglichem Dasein' auch Bezüge zu Ländern, Landschaften und Orten etwas Schwebendes und Wandelbares an sich hatten.' My translation, Ebneter, 'Rilkes italienische Tage', 67.
42 Norberg-Schulz, CV.
43 Norberg-Schulz, *Travel Journal*.
44 Norberg-Schulz also travelled beyond Italy. In the spring of 1974, he went to Boston, before again returning to Rome. He later visited Jordan and Paris, and at the end of his research stay he drove north from Rome, through Germany towards Norway.
45 Norberg-Schulz, *Travel Journal*, 20 May 1974.
46 Norberg-Schulz, *Genius Loci: Towards a Phenomenology of Architecture*, 138–66.
47 Norberg-Schulz, CV. Norberg-Schulz, *Travel Journal*, 20 May 1974.
48 Edmund Husserl, *Logical Investigations*, translated by J. N. Findlay (Oxon: Routledge, 2001) 1:168.
49 Guttorm Fløistad, *Filosofi og vitenskap fra renessansen til vår egen tid* (Oslo: Universitetsforlaget, 1983) 423.
50 Heidegger, 'Building Dwelling Thinking'.
51 Norberg-Schulz, *Travel Journal*, 23 May 1974.
52 Norberg-Schulz, *Genius Loci: Towards a Phenomenology of Architecture*, 22.
53 David Woodruff Smith, 'Phenomenology', *The Stanford Encyclopedia of Philosophy* (Winter 2016 Edition), Edward N. Zalta (ed.), https://plato.stanford.edu/archives/win2016/entries/phenomenology/.
54 Norberg-Schulz, *Travel Journal*, 8 August 1974.
55 Interview with Anna Maria Norberg-Schulz, 7 September 2014.
56 Gunnar Bugge and Christian Norberg-Schulz, *Stav og laft i Norge* (Oslo: Norsk arkitekturforlag, 1969) 4.
57 Norberg-Schulz, *Genius Loci: Towards a Phenomenology of Architecture*.
58 Interview with Paolo Portoghesi, 17 February 2016.
59 Corrigan, *The Essay Film: From Montaigne after Marker*, 104.
60 Ibid., 104.
61 Wolfgang Schivelbusch, *The Railway Journey: The Industrialization of Time and Space in the Nineteenth Century* (Oakland, California: University of California Press) 62.
62 Bruno, *Atlas of Emotion*, 17.
63 Ibid.
64 Schivelbusch, *The Railway Journey*, 16–17.
65 Ibid., 61.
66 Federico Fellini, *Ragazza in Treno*, 1984, Campari.
67 Celluloid Liberation Front 'Fellini's commercials' *Sight and Sound*, http://www.bfi.org.uk/news-opinion/sight-sound-magazine/reviews-recommendations/bytes/fellini-s-commercials (accessed 13 October 2016).

68 Bruno, *Atlas of Emotion*, 62.
69 Ibid., 6.
70 Ibid., 4.
71 Elizabeth Legge, 'Not Getting There Is Half of the Fun: Holiday with Freud', *Art Journal*, 74:1 (2015) 92–5, 92.
72 Conversation with Sven-Erik Helgesen, 21 May 2013.
73 Ibid.
74 'Når jeg tenker tilbake så gikk stedets betydning opp for meg en tidlig morgen da jeg stod i togkorridoren på vei mot Oslo, etter å ha tilbragt et helt år i Italia. Skogene i Østfold fór forbi, med ganske alminnelig grantrær, og skogbunn med lyng og mose. Plutselig følte jeg på hele kroppen: dette kjenner jeg, dette er en del av meg selv.' My translation, Helgesen, *Livet finner sted*.
75 As with the scenes from the desert, taken from a film about Sverre Fehn's journeys to Morocco from 1988. Stein Andersen and Bjørn Engvik, *Rommet og lyset*, NRK, 1988. https://tv.nrk.no/serie/arkitektur-i-norden/FSAM04000185/29-12-1988.
76 Ibid.
77 Bettyann Holtzmann Kevles, 'A Subtler Slice: Magnetic Resonance Imaging', in *Naked to the Bone: Medical Imaging in the Twentieth Century*, 173–200 (New Brunswick, NJ: Rutgers University Press, 1997).
78 Justine Cooper, *RAPT I* (1998), video, 5:06, available online http://justinecooper.com.
79 Robyn Donohue, 'Justine Cooper: Rapt', http://justinecooper.com/donohue.html (accessed 19 October 2017).
80 Donohue, 'Justine Cooper: Rapt'.
81 Bruno, *Atlas of Emotion*, 5.
82 Ibid., 24.
83 Ibid.
84 I will discuss Rilke's understanding of *beweglichen Dasein* in reference to Norberg-Schulz's discussion of architecture, dwelling and place in Window 8 | Sierre.
85 *Fensterblick* is a reference to a discussion of Rilke working by the window in Tang, discussed in detail in Window 2 | Oslo. Tang, *Fenster-Geschichten*, 9.

Window 4

1 For a more in-depth discussion of architecture on post-war Norway, see Espen Johnsen, ed., *Brytninger: Norsk arkitektur 1945-1965* (Oslo: Nasjonalmuseet, 2010).
2 Karl Otto Ellefsen claims there were 150 students in 'Works and Environments: Christian Norberg-Schulz as Communicator and Participant

in the Development of Norwegian Architecture in the 1950s, the 1960s and the 1970s' in Gro Lauvland, Karl Otto Ellefsen and Mari Hvattum, eds, *An Eye for Place*, 116–53 (Oslo: Akademisk Forlag, 2009), 119. The journey is also discussed in the recent publication: Arne Gunnarsjaa, 'Christan Norberg-Schulz: den skrivende hustegner', in *Fellesskapets arkitektur – opprør! Christian Norberg-Schulz som arkitekt og stedstenker*, ed. Gro Lauvland, 13–100 (Oslo: Abstrakt forlag, 2020).

3 Although the details are the same, Gunnarsjaa's 2020 discussion of Norberg-Schulz's journey to Switzerland in 1945, and experiences from Basel, uses alternative references to mine: Jan Carlsen, 'Stedskunst', *Arkitektnytt*, 11 (1995), 206–7; Jan Carlsen, 'Modernismen sto ikke stille', *Arkitekturnytt*, 8 (1995), 154–5, 154; Christian Norberg-Schulz, 'Antikvariske Verdier', *Byggekunst*, 5 (1960), 113–23, 113. Referenced in Gunnersjaa, 'Christian Norberg-Schulz: den skrivende hustegner'.

4 'Tidligere brukt til å repatriere fanger fra konsentrasjonsleirene', Jan Carlsen, 'Den standhaftige arkitekturfilosofen: en fagbiografisk skisse', in *Christian Norberg-Schulz: et festskrift til 70-årsdagen*, eds Guttorm Fløistad, Ketil Moe and Thomas Thiis-Evensen, 16–27 (Oslo: Norsk arkitekturforlag, 1996), 18.

5 Carlsen, 'Christian Norberg-Schulz: bader i fontenen på St. Olavs plass'; Ellefsen, 'Works and Environments'; Helgesen, *Livet finner sted*, 41:00; Christian Norberg-Schulz, 'Faglig Forfatterskap', Forelesning på Skrivekurset, AHO 14 September 1999. Box: 1, Diverse. The Architectural Collections, The National Museum of Art, Architecture and Design, Oslo.

6 Norberg-Schulz, 'Faglig Forfatterskap'.

7 George Friedrich Händel, Samson (HWV 57), 1743. http://opera.stanford.edu/iu/libretti/samson.htm.

8 Roland Barthes, *Camera Lucida: Reflections on Photography [La Chambre Claire*, 1980] (London: Penguin Random House, 1993), 115.

9 Ibid., 57.

10 Ibid., 64.

11 Discussed in detail in Ursel Berger and Thomas Pavel, *Barcelona Pavilion: Mies van der Rohe and Kolbe: Architecture & Sculpture* (Berlin: Jovis, 2006); Ignasi Rubio, *Mies van der Rohe: Barcelona Pavilion*. (New York: Watson Guptill Publications, 1993).

12 Alan Colquhuon, *Modern Architecture* (Oxford: Oxford University Press, 2002), 176.

13 Burgin, *The Remembered Film*.

14 Ibid., 74.

15 Ibid., 57.

16 David Lowenthal, *The Past Is a Foreign Country* (Cambridge: Cambridge University Press, 1985), xvi.

17 Craig Saper, 'A Disturbance of Memory', in Introduction to *Freud on Holiday: Volume 2: A Disturbance of Memory*, Sharon Kivland, 9–12 (York: Information as Material, 2006), 10.

18 Sharon Kivland, 'A Resourceful Woman', in *Volume 2: A Disturbance of Memory*, 13–83 (York: Information as Material, 2006), 75.
19 Ibid., 39.
20 Leopold von Ranke and Fritz Richard Stern, 'Preface: Histories of the Latin and Germanic Nations from 1494–1514', in *The Varieties of History: From Voltaire to the Present*, trans. and ed. Fritz Richard Stern (London: Meridian Books, 1957), 53.
21 Tony Horwitz, *Confederates in the Attic: Dispatches from the Unfinished Civil War* (New York: Vintage, 1998).
22 Sven Lütticken, 'An Arena in Which to Reenact', in *Life Once More: Forms of Reenactment in Contemporary Art*, ed. Sven Lütticken, 17–60 (Rotterdam: Witte de with Center for Contemporary Art, 2005), 29.
23 Rebecca Schneider, *Performing Remains: Art and War in Times of Theatrical Reenactment* (London: Routledge, 2011), 30.
24 Ibid., 31.
25 Burgin, *The Remembered Film*, 86.
26 Ibid., 77.
27 Corrigan, *The Essay Film: From Montaigne after Marker*, 111.
28 Helgsen, *Livet finner sted*.
29 Norberg-Schulz, 'Faglig Forfatterskap'.
30 Mari Hvattum, 'Genius Historiae: Christian Norberg-Schulz in a Historiographic Perspective', in *An Eye for Place – Christian Norberg-Schulz: Architect, Historian, Editor,* eds Karl Otto Ellefsen, Mari Hvattum and Gro Lauvland, 108–15 (Oslo: Akademisk Publisering, 2009), 108.
31 Ibid., 110.
32 Jenkins, *Re-Thinking History*, 14.
33 Norberg-Schulz, 'Faglig Forfatterskap'.
34 Norberg-Schulz, *Genius Loci: Towards a Phenomenology of Architecture*.
35 Otero-Pailos, *Architecture's Historical Turn*.
36 Ibid.
37 Norberg-Schulz, *Genius Loci: Towards a Phenomenology of Architecture*, 5.
38 Martin Heidegger, *Sein und Zeit*, 19th Edition (Tübingen, Max Niemeyer, 2006); Martin Heidegger, *Being and Time,* translated by Joan Stambaugh, foreword by Dennis J. Schmidt (Albany: State University of New York Press, 2010).
39 Heynen, 'Worthy of Question: Heidegger's Role in Architectural Theory', 42–9.
40 Hide Heynen, *Architecture and Modernity: A Critique* (Cambridge, MA: MIT Press, 1999), 22–3.
41 Norberg-Schulz, *Genius loci: Towards a Phenomenology of Architecture*, 22.
42 I will return to this discussion again in Window 8 | Sierre.

Window 5

1 Letter from Christian Norberg-Schulz to the building committee, 31 January 1962. Box: DNIR, 1959–2002: 003; 4; Romainstituttet: eget hus på Gianicolo. Istituto di Norvegia in Roma.

2 Note, 25 August 1958. Box: DNIR, 1959–2002, 003.4; Romainsituttet, diverse, avisutklipp, opprettelse. Istituto di Norvegia in Roma.

3 'Norge må ha et romersk institutt for forskere, kunstnere, og arkitekter'. My translation of Hans Petter L'Orange and Rolf Andersen. 1955. Box: DNIR, 1959–2002: 003; 4; Istituto di Norvegia in Roma.

4 Box: 1959–2002, 003.4. Diverse, Avisklipp, Opprettelse. Istituto di Norvegia in Roma.

5 Letter from Christian Norberg-Schulz to Hans Petter L'Orange, 5 March 1961. Box: DNIR, 1959–2002, 003.4; Romainsituttet, diverse, avisutklipp, opprettelse. Istituto di Norvegia in Roma.

6 Telegram from Prebensen to L'Orange, 9 March 1961. Box: DNIR, 1959–2002, 003.4; Romainsituttet, diverse, avisutklipp, opprettelse. Istituto di Norvegia in Roma.

7 'Møter i byggekommiteen for den norske stiftelsen Gianocolo – hus og møter angående arbeidets gang under byggeperioden', until 7 October 1961. Box: DNIR, 1959–2002: 003; 4; Romainsituttet: eget hus på Gianicolo. Istituto di Norvegia in Roma.

8 Letter from Christian Norberg-Schulz to Hans Petter L'Orange, 19 October 1961. Box: DNIR, 1959–2002: 003; 4; Romainsituttet: eget hus på Gianicolo. Istituto di Norvegia in Roma:

9 'Møter i byggekommiteen for den norske stiftelsen Gianocolo – hus og møter angående arbeidets gang under byggeperioden', until 7 October 1961. Box: DNIR, 1959–2002: 003; 4; Romainsituttet: eget hus på Gianicolo. Istituto di Norvegia in Roma:

10 Letter from Christian Norberg-Schulz to Hans Petter L'Orange, 27 October 1961; Letter from Christian Norberg-Schulz to Hans Petter L'Orange, 14 November 1961. Box: DNIR, 1959–2002: 003; 4; Romainsituttet: eget hus på Gianicolo. Istituto di Norvegia in Roma:

11 Jorge Otero-Pailos, 'Photo[historio]graphy: Christian Norberg-Schulz's Demotion of Textual History', *Journal of the Society of Architectural Historians*, 66:2 (June 2007) 220–41, 223.

12 Harriet Eide 'Nordens lys er vår identitet'. Unknown Newspaper. 15 September 1993. Box: Diverse uregistrerte fra skuffen i den svarte pulten. CNS. The Architectural Collections, the National Museum of Art, Architecture and Design.

13 Norberg-Schulz. 'CV', undated. Box: Diverse uregistrerte fra den svarte pulten. The Architectural Collections, the National Museum of Art, Architecture and Design.

14 Harriet Eide, 'Nordens lys er vår identitet'. Unknown Newspaper. 15 September 1993. Box: Diverse uregistrerte fra skuffen i den svarte pulten. CNS. The Architectural Collections, the National Museum.

15 Pauline Gjøsteen, '"Italiesin" som utprøvende teori?: Christian Norberg Schulz' sommerhus i Porto Ercole, Toscana (1959–62)', in *Brytninger: norsk arkitektur 1945-65*, ed. Espen Johnsen, 172–83 (Oslo: Nasjonalmuseet, 2010); Pauline Gjøsteen, 'Weidemanns hus av Norberg-Schulz og Hovig: arkitekturen som optisk "linse"', *Kunst og Kultur*, 97:4 (2014) 230–9.

16 Gjøsteen, 'Weidemanns hus av Norberg-Schulz og Hovig', 230.

17 Jacques Derrida, *The Postcards: From Socrates to Freud and Beyond* [*La carte postale: De Socrate à Freud et au-delà* 1980], translated by Alan Bass (Chicago: University of Chicago Press, 1987) 28.

18 Ibid.

19 Ibid.

20 Ibid, 9.

21 Ibid., 28.

22 Ibid., 20.

23 Delphine Bénézet, *The Cinema of Agnès Varda: Resistance and Eclecticism* (London: Wallflower Press, 2014) 5.

24 Wera and Varda. 'Interview with Agnès Varda'.

25 *Lions Love (. . . and Lies)* (1969) Agnès Varda.

26 *Daguerréotypes* (1976), Agnès Varda.

27 *The Beaches of Agnès* (2008), Agnès Varda.

28 Kate Ince, 'Feminist Phenomenology and the Film World of Agnès Varda', *Hypatia*, 28:3 (2013) 601–17, 613.

29 Ibid., 607.

30 Ibid.

31 'Når vi kommer frem til tjernet, setter vi oss ned og faller til ro. Vi husker skogen vi har gått igjennom og stien vi har fulgt, og vi opplever tjernet som et mål. Nå er vi fremme; det er ikke nødvendig å gå videre, iallefall ikke med det samme. Først vil vi oppleve dette stedet, vite hva tjernet forteller oss, og skjønne hvorfor nettopp dét innbyr til opphold. 'Vi er fremme' sier vi.' My translation of Christian Norberg-Schulz, 'Båntjern', in *Et sted å være: Essays og artikler*, ed. Gordon Hølmebakk, 25–30 (Oslo: Gyldendal Norsk Forlag, 1986) 28.

32 Norberg-Schulz uses his own experience in many of his books and articles. Examples could be found in Norberg-Schulz, 'Båntjern'; Norberg-Schulz, *Genius Loci: Towards a Phenomenology of Architecture*.

33 Norberg-Schulz. 'Båntjern', 28.

34 Jivén and Larkham, 'Sense of Place, Authenticity and Character', 70.

35 Heynen, 'Worthy of Question: Heidegger's Role in Architectural Theory', 42–9.

36 Wilken, 'The Critical Reception of Christian Norberg-Schulz's Writings on Heidegger and Place'.

37 Pérez-Gómez, 'The Place Is Not a Postcard', 31.

38 Ibid.

39 Hannah Arendt, *The Human Condition* (Chicago, Ill: Chicago University Press, 1958).

40 Lauvland, 'Verk og vilkår', 95–7.
41 'Nordmenn er glad i naturen', my translation, Norberg-Schulz, 'Båntjern', 25.

Window 6

1. 'Etter en av turene til tuffdalene og etruskergravene satt jeg en ettermiddag på Piazza Navona med et glass *campari* og gledet meg over folkelivet. Med ett hadde jeg følelsen av at jeg fremdeles var i en tuffdal; dette er jo det *samme* (selv om det ikke er likedan!) Slik begynte mitt studium av *genius loci*. Det skyldtes altså en plutselig inspirasjon, og slett ikke en logisk tankerekke.' My translation of Christian Norberg-Schulz 'Genius Loci: et opprinnelsens begrep', in *På klassisk grunn: Det norske institutt gjennom 40år*, eds K. B. Aavitsland and R. T. Eriksen, 100–9 (Oslo: Andresen og Butenschøn, 1999) 102.
2. Christian Norberg-Schulz, *Michelangelo som arkitekt* (Oslo: Gyldendahl, 1958).
3. Norberg-Schulz, *Genius Loci: Towards a Phenomenology of Architecture*, 152.
4. Christian Norberg-Schulz, *Baroque Architecture* (Milan: Electa, 1979) 14.
5. Ibid., 8.
6. Ibid., 26.
7. Ibid., 12.
8. Ibid., 18.
9. Norberg-Schulz, *Genius Loci: Towards a Phenomenology of Architecture*, 140–2.
10. Ibid., 143.
11. Ibid.
12. Ibid.
13. Ibid., 164.
14. Ibid.
15. Ibid.
16. Norberg-Schulz, 'Genius Loci: et opprinnelsens begrep', 102.
17. Fuss, *The Sense of an Interior*, VII.
18. Peggy Phelan, 'Hickley and Ronald Reagan: Reenactment and the Ethics of the Real', in *Life Once More: Forms of Reenactment in Contemporary Art*, ed. Sven Lütticken, 147–68 (Rotterdam: Witte de with Center for Contemporary Art, 2005), 163.
19. Jean Baudrillard, 'Follow Me', in *Sophie Calle. Suite Venitienne. Jean Baudrillard. Please Follow Me*, translated by Dany Barash and Danny Hatfield, 75–87 (Seattle: Bay Press, 1988) 82.
20. Calle, 'Suite Venitienne', 57.
21. Rainer Maria Rilke, *The Roses; & The Windows*, translated by A. Poulin, Jr.; Foreword by W. D. Snodgrass (Port Townsend, Wash.: Graywolf, 1979) 76–77.

22 Koepnick, 'The Aesthetic of the Interface'.
23 Helen Keller, *The Story of My Life* (New York: Bantam Classics, 2005), 15–16.
24 Helen Keller, *Midstream: My Later Life* (New York: Doubleday, Doran & Company, 1930), 316–17.
25 Keller, *The Story of My Life*, 15–16.
26 'Husk generelt: Bergman's Jordbærstedet. Huset som "åpner" seg i sommernatten'. Husk kvinnene i Lipari om aftenen som kom ut på sine svulmende balkonger under et "segl" omgitt av en ornamentert "ramme". Husk Helen Keller 'Water'. My translation of Norberg-Schulz, *Travel Journal, 1973–74*.
27 Keller, 'Enchanted Windows', 316–17.
28 Maurice Merleau-Ponty, *Phenomenology of Perception* (London: Routledge, 2013) 267.
29 Fuss, *The Sense of an Interior*, 118–19.
30 'I *The Story of my Life* forteller den døvbilde amerikanske forfatterinnen Helen Keller om hvordan verden åpnet seg for henne. Det skjedde da hun var syv år gammel, og hun sier selv at det var forståelsen av at alle ting har et *navn* som frigjorde henne'. Norberg-Schulz, 'Vann', 27.
31 'Som det mest bevegelige av alle elementer, har det alltid grepet menneskene, og i gamle kosmologier er vannet alle tings opphav'. Norberg-Schulz, 'Vann', 27.
32 'Fenomenologi betyr derfor fremfor alt, å avdekke de sammenhenger som skjuler seg i språket. Ved at fenomenologisk forklare alle tings væren i verden, er den utgangspunkt for enhver vitenskap. For, som Heidegger sier, "vitenskap åpner ingen verden, men undersøker det som allerede er åpnet". Vi må med andre ord forstå vannet fenomenologisk før iv kan definere det som H2O.' My translation of Norberg-Schulz, 'Vann', 28.
33 Helgesen, *Livet finner sted*.
34 Norberg-Schulz, *Genius Loci: Towards a Phenomenology of Architecture*, 179.

Window 7

1 Interview with Paolo Portoghesi, Calcata, 17 February 2016.
2 Ibid.
3 Ibid.
4 Ibid.
5 Ibid.
6 Ibid.
7 Léa-Catherine Szacka, *Exhibiting the Postmodern: The 1980 Venice Architecture Biennale* (Venice: Marsilio Editori, 2016).
8 Ibid., 120.

9. Ibid., 119.
10. A few reviews of the Biennale mention the critic's section: *Corriere delle sera*, 25 July 1980, 3; *Diario*, 17 July 1980, 5; Lorenzo Berni, in *Panorama*, 25 August 1980; *L'Ordine*, 24 July 1980, 3; *La republica*, 12 Uagust 1980; *La Nazione*, 21 July 1980; *El Pais*, 20 September 1980, 3; *Domus*, October 1980; *Bauwelt*, 15 August 1980.
11. Håvard Mørkved Bohne, Ulrikke Dreyer, Ingrid Engøy Henriksen and Øyvind Anker Ljosland, 'Christian Norberg-Schulz at the Venice Biennale', in *Understanding Postmodern Architecture: A Norwegian Perspective*, eds Léa-Catherine Szacka and Kristian Hammer, 42–53 (Oslo: Arkitektur- og designhøgskolen i Oslo, 2015).
12. 'Venice 1980', Christian Norberg-Schulz, 1980. Box: Korrespondanse, klipp og annet diverse. The Christian Norberg-Schulz Archive, the Architectural Collections, the National Museum Architecture, Oslo.
13. Paolo Portoghesi et al., *The Presence of the Past: First International Exhibition of Architecture* (Milan: Electa/Venice: Edizione La Biennale di Venezie, 1980).
14. Szacka, *Exhibiting the Postmodern*, 120.
15. Ibid.
16. *Drawing of diorama with Norwegian text, 1980 Biennale, Christian Norberg-Schulz*, photograph of archival material. By Christian Norberg-Schulz. Box: Korrespondanse, klipp og annet diverse. The Christian Norberg-Schulz Archive, the Architectural Collections, the National Museum Architecture, Oslo.
17. Szacka, *Exhibiting the Postmodern*, 119.
18. 'Life Place Architecture', Christian Norberg-Schulz, 1980, Box: Korrespondanse, klipp og annet diverse. The Christian Norberg-Schulz Archive, the Architectural Collections, the National Museum Architecture, Oslo.
19. Norberg-Schulz, *Genius Loci: Towards a Phenomenology of Architecture*.
20. Christian Norberg-Schulz, *Minnesjord* (Oslo: Gyldendal Norsk Forlag, 1991).
21. 'En vesentlig kontakt med tingene kreves'. My translation of Christian Norberg-Schulz, 'Den Poetiske Forståelsesform', in *Øye og hånd: essays og artikler*, ed. Gordon Hølmebakk, 15–23 (Oslo: Gyldendal, 1997), 22.
22. 'Et dikt er hverken teori eller praksis, det verken beskriver eller handler. Snarere *fremstiller* det tingene på en måte som tolker deres tinglighet eller vesen.' My translation of Norberg-Schulz, 'Den Poetiske Forståelsesform', 16.
23. Norberg-Schulz, 'Den Poetiske Forståelsesform', 22.
24. Norberg-Schulz, *Mellom jord og himmel*.
25. 'Her er du heime, Knut. Kva? – Det var ingen som sa dette. Men det er detta som er på ferd i dag. Her er du heime. Ei herleg og sann og enkel verd opnar seg for han på den staden han er fødd.' My translation of Tarjei Vesaas, *Vindanen* (Oslo: Gyldendal, 1952), 102, quoted in Norberg-Schulz, *Mellom jord og himmel*, 11.
26. 'Knut opplever plutselig hva det vil si å høre til et sted, å kjenne et sted', Norberg-Schulz, *Mellom jord og himmel*, 12.

27 Discussed in detail in Window 2 | Oslo.
28 Norberg-Schulz, *Genius Loci: Towards a Phenomenology of Architecture*, 6.
29 Ibid.
30 Rainer Maria Rilke, *Duino Elegies/Duineser Elegien: Rainer Maria Rilke*, translated by David Oswald (Einsiedeln: Daimon Verlag, 1992).
31 Norberg-Schulz recurrently quoted Rilke's work on his theory of architecture. Added as an appendix to this book, this includes quotes of 'Ninth Elegy' from *Duino Elegies* (1922), *Sonnet for Orpheus* (1922) and a reference to Rilke's poems about fruits. I do not know what poem he refers to here.
32 Some of Norberg-Schulz's books were purchased by the Getty Institute in Los Angeles, California. Getty was primarily interested in Norberg-Schulz's most valuable books, which might include originals of Rilke's poems. The Architectural Collections and the National Museum of Art, Architecture and Art in Oslo have list of which books are at Getty.
33 De Sager, 'Stadier på livsveien mellom Norge og Flandern', 111.
34 Ibid.
35 Conversation with Kari Greve, Oslo, 23 May 2013.
36 Rainer Maria Rilke, *Duino Elegies* (London: Chatto and Windus, 1963); Rainer Maria Rilke, *Die Sonette an Orpheus* (Frankfurt am Main: Suhrkamp, 1985); Rainer Maria Rilke, *The Notebooks of Malte Laurids Brigge*, translated by and ed. Michael Hulse (Ann Arbor, Mich.: Proquest LLC, 2011); Rainer Maria Rilke, *Briefe an Nanny Wunderly-Volkhart*, 2 vols. (Frankfurt am Main: Insel Verlag, 1977); Rilke and Andreas-Salomé, *Briefwechsel*; Marie von Thurn und Taxis-Hohenlohe, *Erinnerungen an Rainer Maria Rilke* (München: Oldenbourg, 1937).
37 Rainer Maria Rilke, *Les Fenêtres, dix poèmes de Rainer Maria Rilke, illustrés d'eaux-fortes de Baladine* (Paris: Librairie de France, 1927).
38 Rilke, *Duino Elegies*, 84–5.
39 Rilke, *The Notebooks of Malte Laurids Brigge*.
40 Rainer Maria Rilke, *Neue Gedichte* (Frankfurt am Main: Insel Verlag, 1974) 33.
41 Rüdiger Görner, 'Rilke: A Biographical Exploration', in *The Cambridge Companion to Rilke*, eds Karen Leeder and Rob Vilain, 9–26 (Cambridge: Cambridge University Press, 2010), 16.
42 John Sandford, *Landscape and Landscape Imagery in R.M. Rilke* (London: Institute of Germanic Studies University of London, 1980).
43 De Sager, 'Stadier på livsveien mellom Norge og Flandern', 111.
44 Andreas Kramer, 'Rilke and Modernism', in *The Cambridge Companion to Rilke*, eds Karen Leeder and Rob Vilain, 113–30 (Cambridge: Cambridge University Press, 2010) 129.
45 My translation of J. F. Angelloz, *Rainer Maria Rilke* (Zürich: Verlag der Arche, 1955), quoted in Otto Friedrich Bollnow, *Rilke* (Stuttgart: Kohlhammer, 1956), 18.

46 '... unetbehrlich als Handbuch'. My translation of Hermann Mörchen. 'Bollnow: Rilke (Book Review)', *Zeitschrift für Religions – und Geistesgeschichte* 3:1 (1951), 381–2, 382.

47 Jack M. Stein. 'Rainer Maria Rilke. Otto Friedrich Bollnow, Rilke Orbis Litterarum', *Germanic Review*, 33:1 (1 February, 1958), 58.

48 Not to say that Rilke was a philosopher, Bollnow makes it clear how the poet was 'wonderful but unphilosophical poet, which was Rilke', my translation of Stein. 'Rainer Maria Rilke. Otto Friedrich Bollnow, Rilke Orbis Litterarum', 58. Philosophers like Heidegger and Bollnow were intrigued by Rilke's poetry, seeing the poets work as part of a larger cultural thought focused around being.

49 Fløistad, *Filosofi og vitenskap fra renessansen til vår egen tid*, 426.

50 'Das Grundwort, mit dem Rilke den Zustand bezeichnet, wo der Mensch, vom falschen Eigenwesen gereinigt, nur noch der zu ihm sprechenden Forderung gehorcht und seine Aufgaben hingeben lebt, ist bei Rilke das Wort Bezug'. Bollnow, *Rilke*, 190.

51 'Schon hier, bei den einfachsten und formalsten Bestimmungen des menschlichen Daseins wird gezeigt, wie man den Menschen nicht als ein zunächst für sich bestehendes Bewusstsein fassen kann, das hinterher dann zu den Dingen der Außenwelt in Beziehung tritt sondern wie der Bewusstsein schon als solches, seinem eigensten Wesen nach von dem Menschen fortgerichtet und auf etwas andres bezogen ist, was nicht es selbst ist.' My translation in collaboration with Kimon Krenz of Bollnow, *Rilke*, 194.

52 Ulrich Fülleborn, 'Translator's Note', in *Les Roses – Die Rosen: Gedichte Französisch – Deutsch*, ed. Rainer Maria Rilke, translated by Yvonne Goetzfried, 2nd edn (Cadolzburg: Ars Vivendi Verlag, 2012), 88.

53 Tang, *Fenster-Geschichten*, 11.

54 Bollnow, *Rilke*, in Norberg-Schulz's library, the National Museum of Art, Architecture and Design, Oslo.

55 Rilke, 'Ninth Elegy', quoted in Norberg-Schulz, *Genius Loci: Towards a Phenomenology of Architecture*, 6.

56 Roger Paulin and Peter Hutchinson, 'Preface', in *Rilke's Duino Elegies: Cambridge Readings*, eds Roger Paulin and Peter Hutchinson (London: Riverside, CA: Duckworth; Ariadne, 1996), vii.

57 Rainer Maria Rilke, *Duino Elegies* (London: Chatto and Windus, 1963), 25.

58 Romano Guardini, *Rainer Maria Rilkes Deutung des Daseins: Eine Interpretation der Duineser Elegien*, 5th edn (Ostfildern/Paderborn: Grünewald/Schöningh, 1996), 2.

59 Guardini, *Rainer Maria Rilkes Deutung des Daseins*, 2.

60 Rilke, 'Ninth Elegy'.

61 '[Wir sind hier] zu erfahren, was man wirklich halten, sehen und dann auch sagen kann'. '[We are here] to experience what we really can hold, see, and then also say'. My translation of Guardini, *Rainer Maria Rilkes Deutung des Daseins*, 304.

62 'Dann gewinnt das Ding eine Dichte und einen Sinn des Seins, die es aus sich selbst heraus nie erreichen könnte. Sobald ein solches Wort gesprochen wird

"meint" das Ding. "Jetzt erst bin ich wirklich."' In Guardini, *Rainer Maria Rilkes Deutung des Daseins*, 304–5.

63 Martin Heidegger, 'The Nature of Language', in *On the Way to Language*, translated by Pieter D. Hertz, 57–109 (New York: Harper & Row Publishers, 1982) 63.

64 Ibid., 66.

65 Ibid., 57.

66 Discussed in detail in Window 6.

67 Rilke, *Duino Elegies*.

68 Norberg-Schulz, *Genius Loci: Towards a Phenomenology of Architecture*, 15–16.

69 Ibid., 23.

70 Christian Norberg-Schulz, 'Note', 1980. Box: 60, 70, 80-tall, the Architectural Collections, the National Museum of Art, Architecture and Design, Oslo.

71 'Som foreksempel gengir vi noen av luxembourgeren Rob Kriers fabelaktige skisser, der tingene er sett i sin essens: broen, vinduet, buen står frem som arketypiske former som "speiler" virkeligheten. Slik blir vår verden igjen en verden av bilder. Arkitekten tegner seg frem'. My translation of Christian Norberg-Schulz, 'Tegning og virkelighet', *Byggekunst*, editorial, 60:1 (1978) 1.

72 Norberg-Schulz wrote for this Norwegian journal of architecture throughout his career. His first article titled 'Kina og den moderne arkitekturen', which translates into 'China and Modern Architecture', discusses what he considers to be evident parallels between traditional Chinese architecture and Western modernist architecture. Since then, he wrote articles, editorials, book reviews and presentations of his buildings for the journal, and between 1961 and 1978 he was the editor. His latest published article was from 1999, titled 'Skuffelsenes århundre – et tilbakeblikk', which translates into 'A Century of Disappointments – Looking Back', where he argues that twentieth-century modernist architecture was a disappointment.

73 I have not been able to determine the exact publication, but I assume it might be printed in Rainer Maria Rilke, *Jeg klinger ved timens berøring: dikt i utvalg; i gjendiktning ved Andre Bjerke*, translated by Andre Bjerke (Oslo: Aschehoug, 1964).

74 Rob Krier, 'Notitzen am Rande', *Byggekunst*, 60:1 (1978) 16–17.

75 Christian Norberg-Schulz, 'Note' 1980. Box: 60, 70, 80-tall, the Architectural Collections, the National Museum of Art, Architecture and Design, Oslo.

76 Interview with Paolo Portoghesi. Calcata, 17 February 2016.

77 Ibid.

Window 8

1 Interview with Paolo Portoghesi, 17 February 2016.

2 Ibid.

3 'Doux vent polyglotte.' My translation of wall text, permanent exhibition, Foundation Rainer Maria Rilke, Sierre, Switzerland. Visited 7 February 2016.
4 Rainer Maria Rilke, *Vergers: Suivi de Quatrains Valaisans, Les Roses, Les Fenêtres et de Tendres Impôts à La France* (Paris: Gallimard, 1978).
5 Wall text, permanent exhibition, Foundation Rainer Maria Rilke, Sierre, Switzerland. Visited 7 February 2016.
6 Bollnow, *Rilke*, 36.
7 'Lieber Freund, jetzt erst werd ich athmen und, gefasst, an Handliches gehen'. My translation of wall text, permanent exhibition, Foundation Rainer Maria Rilke, Sierre, Switzerland. 7 February 2016.
8 *Les Fenêtres* (1927) is part of Rilke's French poems. *Les Roses* (1927) is a cycle of twenty-four poems with Rilke's own illustrations written in French in Lusanne in 1924 but only published after his death in 1927. *Les Fenêtres* consist of ten poems, dedicated to his last love interest Balladine Klossowska, most likely written in Muzot in 1924, with the exception of number III and IV that was written in Ragaz. The remaining poems were written in Val-Mont Sanatorium in April and May 1926, where Rilke died that same year on 29. December.
9 Rilke, *Les Fenêtres*.
10 'Man hat die Bedeutung dieser französischen Gedichte lange nicht richtig erkannt. Die damals in Frankreich veröffentlichten Bändchen sind bis zu ihrer Veröffentlichung im Insel-Verlag wenig in Deutschland bekannt geworden und haben darum auf das Rilkebild kaum einen Einfluß ausgeübt.' Bollnow, *Rilke*, 335.
11 Karen Leeder and Rob Vilain, 'Introduction', in *The Cambridge Companion to Rilke*, eds Karen Leeder and Rob Vilain, 1–6 (Cambridge: Cambridge University Press, 2010) 2.
12 Ulrich Fülleborn suggests the window was discovered by the late Rilke, first apparent in his Tenth Elegy from 1922. Lutz Koepnick, on the other hand, would argue otherwise, and quotes *The Notebooks of Malte Laurids Brigge* (1910) when describing Rilke's radical understanding of the window drawing lines from this to the interactive nature of interface design seen in contemporary screen culture. It would be difficult to argue that the window did not have an importance to Rilke before his later French poems. Ulrich Fülleborn, 'Nachwort', in *Les Roses – Die Rosen. Les Fenêtres – Die Fenster*, by Rainer Maria Rilke, 80–94 (Cadolzburg: Ars Vivendi Verlag, 2001), 89; Koepnick, 'The Aesthetic of the Interface', 47–9.
13 Tang, *Fenster-Geschichten*, 11.
14 'Unser Umgang mit der Weite ist recht eigentlich auf die Vermittlung des Fensters angewiesen, draußen ist sie nur noch Macht, Übermacht, ohne Verhältnis auf und, wenn auch ungeheuer im Einfluß -; das Fenster aber setzt uns in einen Bezug, elle nous mesure notre part de cet avenir dans l'instant-mème qu'est l'espace.' My translation of wall text, permanent exhibition, Foundation Rainer Maria Rilke, Sierre, Switzerland. Visted 7 February 2016.
15 Tang, *Fenster-Geschichten*, 10.

16 'Wer doch einmal die Geschichte des Fensters schriebe – dieses wunderlichen Rahmens unseres häuslichen Daseins, vielleicht sein eigentliches Maaß, ein Fenster voll, immer wieder ein vollgeschöpftes Fenster, mehr haben wir nicht von der Welt; und wie bestimmt die Form unseres jeweiligen Fensters die Art unseres Gemüths: das Fenster des Gefangenen, die croisée eines Palastes, die Schiffsluke, die Mansarde, die Fensterrose der Kathedrale -: sind das nicht ebensoviel Hoffnungen, Aussichten, Erhebungen und Zukünfte unseres Wesens? Unser Umgang mit der Weite ist recht eigentlich auf die Vermittelung des Fensters angewiesen, draußen ist sie nur noch Macht, Übermacht, ohne Verhältnis auf uns, wenn auch ungeheuer im Einfluß -: das Fenster aber setzt uns in einen Bezug, *elle nous mesure notre part de cet avenir dans l'instant-même qu'est l'espace* ... /Von allen Fenstern der Welt werden mir die des "Stübli", an die sie mich führen, für immer unvergeßlich sein; damals standen die roten Geranien davor, und es war über sie hinweg eine Beweglichkeit des Gefühls zur Ferne, eine Hingabe des Stübchens hinaus und ein Erwiderung weither, ganz als wärst ein Fenster, durch das man fliegen könnte. Und doch auch das sah ich ihm an, diesem Stübli-Fenster, daß es sich zuzustließen vermag als eine Wehr, eine Sicherung, daß es sein kann wie eine Hand über den Augen, d.h. eigenes Blut über eigenes Blut gelegt, ein Schutz des Wesens mit sich selbst, eine Bestärkung, Schließen, Verdichtung und Einkehr.' Rainer Maria Rilke, *Breife an Nanny Wunderly-Volkhart*, vol 2 (Frankfurt A.M: Insel Verlag, 1977) 315.

17 Tang, *Fenster-Geschichten*, 10.

18 'Bollnows Rilkebild, das vom reifen Rilke ausgeht, ist überall von diesem Motiv [Distanz] durch drungen.' My translation of Hermann Wein, 'Philosophische Anthropologie Und Rilke: Zu Otto Friedrich Bollnow, Rilke (W. Kohlhammer Verlag, Stuttgart 1951, 355 Seiten)', *Zeitschrift Für Philosophische Forschung*, 7:3 (1953) 386–91, 390.

19 'Die Neigung zu einem solchen Symbolgebrauch verstärkt sich beim späten Rilke. Zumal in den französischen Gedichten der letzten Jahre tritt eine ganze Reihe neue Sinnbilder hinzu, wie das Fenster, der Garten, der Weinstock uzw., doch sollen diese neuen Bilder hier nicht besonders verfolgt werden, weil sie nur für die neue Stufe bezeichnend sind und nicht wie die anderen die samt dichterische Entwicklung durchziehen.'

Bollnow, *Rilke*, 241.

20 '[In literarischen Forschung ist bis heute] das Fenster entweder nur als ein Element Flur die Vermittlung zwischen Innen und Außen wahrgenommen worden, oder seine Rolle als "Scheidewand" zwischen Innen und Außen wurde besonders stark hervorgehoben. Auf diese Weise ist das Fenster unausweichlich mit dem Sinn der Dualität verbunden. In der Lyrik Rilkes dient das Fenster aber nicht nur als Vermittler oder als Scheidewand zwischen Innen und Außen, sondern, seincr Auffassung der "Einheit vom Leben und Tod", entsprechend, wird der ursprüngliche Sinn des Fensters als Grenzlinie zwischen Innen und Außen letztendlich auch überwunden. Das Fenster wird beim späten Rilke zur poetischen "Figur" für das Bild der Einheit von allen Gegensätzlichen und zur Daseinsfigur.' My translation of Tang, *Fenster-Geschichten*, 6.

21 Rainer Maria Rilke, *The Roses; & The Windows*, translated by A. Poulin, Jr.; Foreword by W. D. Snodgrass (Port Townsend, Wash.: Graywolf, 1979) 77.

22 Ulrich Fülleborn, 'Nachwort', in *Les Roses – Die Rosen: Gedichte Fransösisch – Deutsch*, ed. Rainer Maria Rilke, translated by Yvonne Goetzfried, 2nd edn, 80–94 (Cadolzburg: Ars Vivendi Verlag, 2012) 88.

23 'Es [das Fenster] befindet sich genau ab der Grenze zwischen Innen und Außen: Durch Fenster sehen wir hinaus, kommt die Welt zu uns herein; sie verbinden und trennen zugleich (IV).' My translation of Fülleborn, 'Nachword', 89.

24 Koepnick, 'The Aesthetic of the Interface', 48.

25 Ebneter, 'Rilkes italienische Tage'. This is discussed in greater detail in Window 3 | Journey.

26 Tang, *Fenster-Geschichten*, 6.

27 'Italien kannte und liebte ich seit meinem achten Jahr, – es war in seiner deutlichen Vielfalt und Formfülle, sozusagen, die Fibel meines beweglichen Daseins'. My translation of Rilke, 'An eine junge Freundin'. Quoted in Ebneter, 'Rilkes Italienische Tage', 66.

28 Interview with Anna Maria Norberg-Schulz, 7 September 2014.

29 Portoghesi, 'To Christian: From Paolo Portoghesi'.

30 Ebneter, 'Rilkes italienische Tage'. This is discussed in greater detail in Window 3 | Journey.

31 Norberg-Schulz, *Genius Loci: Towards a Phenomenology of Architecture*, 179.

32 Heynen, *Architecture and Modernity*, 22–3.

33 Norberg-Schulz, *Genius Loci: Towards a Phenomenology of Architecture*, 22.

34 Rosi Braidotti, *Nomadic Subjects: Embodiment and Sexual Difference in Contemporary Feminist Theory*, 2nd edn (New York: Columbia University Press, 2011).

35 Ibid., 21.

36 Ibid., 41.

37 Ibid.

38 George Steiner, *After Babel: Aspects of Language and Translation* (London: Oxford University Press, 1975) 71.

39 Leeder and Vilain, 'Introduction', 2.

40 Examples include Christian Norberg-Schulz, 'Genius Loci', in *Entwerfen Der Historischen Strasse*, ed. Martina Schneider, 12–19 (Berlin: Abakon-Verlag, Edition Lichterfelde, 1976); Norberg-Schulz, *Genius Loci: Paesaggio, Ambiente, Architettura*; Norberg-Schulz, *Mellom jord og himmel: en bok om steder og hus*.

41 Conversation with Anna Maria Norberg-Schulz, 2013.

42 Arne Gunnarsjaa, 'Christian Norberg-Schulz: den skrivende hustegner', 16.

43 Interview with Paolo Portoghesi, 17 February 2016.

44 Norwegian has two written standards: Norwegian Bokmål and Norwegian Nynorsk. The history surrounding these standards is complex, raising various geographical, political and linguistic implications. I have not decided to go into detail regarding Norwegian Nynorsk, as this would bring up a set of questions, which lies outside of the scope of this thesis. Instead, I have decided to translate Rilke into Norwegian Bokmål: the standard both Norberg-Schulz and I use.

Window 9

1. Henrik Ibsen, *When We Dead Awaken*, translated by Michael Meyer (London: Rubert Hart-Davis, 1960), 18.
2. Ibid.
3. Helgesen, *Livet finner sted*.
4. Portoghesi, 'To Christian: From Paolo Portoghesi'.
5. 'Da jeg kom tilbake til Oslo for seks-og-tredve år siden, nygift og med italiensk kone, stoppet vi her på Ekeberg for å se utsikten over byen'. My translation, *Livet finner sted*, 27:36-27:47.
6. Arne Korsmo and Christian Norberg-Schulz, 'Mies van der Rohe', *Byggekunst* 5 (1952), 85–91.
7. For more about Korsmo's architecture, see Christian Norberg-Schulz, *The Functionalist Arne Korsmo* (Oslo: Universitetsforlaget, 1986); Jon Brænne, Eirik T. Bøe and Astrid Skjerven, *Arne Korsmo: arkitektur og design* (Oslo: Universitetsforlaget, 2004).
8. Tostrup, *Planetveien 12*, 62.
9. Ibid., 63.
10. Ibid., 64.
11. Ibid.; Jorge Otero-Pailos, 'Norberg-Schulz' hus.
12. Tostrup, *Planetveien 12*, 64.
13. Joseph A. Barry, 'Report on the American Battle between Good and Bad Modern Houses', *House Beautiful*, 95 (May 1953), 172–3, 266–72, 270. Quoted in Friedman, *Women and the Making of the Modern House*, 141.
14. Discussed in José van Dijck, *The Transparent Body: A Cultural Analysis of Medical Imaging* (Seattle, Wash.: University of Washington Press, 2005), 89; Bettyann Holtzmann Kevles, *Naked to the Bone: Medical Imaging in the Twentieth Century* (New Brunswick: Rutgers University Press, 1997).
15. Colomina, 'X-ray Architecture: Illness as Metaphor', 31.
16. Ibid., 33.
17. Ibid.
18. Ibid.
19. *Tur* translates to hike, walk or tour; traditionally, Norwegians would go on a hike in the woods on Sundays.
20. Interview with Anna Maria Norberg-Schulz, 7 September 2014.
21. Ibid.
22. Norberg-Schulz, 'Genius Loci', 8.
23. Interview with Anna Maria Norberg-Schulz, 7 September 2014; Christian Norberg-Schulz, 'CV', undated. Box: Diverse uregistrerte fra den svarte pulten. The Architectural Collections, the National Museum of Art, Architecture and Design.
24. van Dijck, *The Transparent Body*, 94.

25 Tess Cosslett, Celia Lury and Penny Summerfield, eds, *Feminism and Autobiography: Texts, Theories, Methods* (London: Routledge, 2000), 3.
26 Ibid., 2.
27 Rascaroli, *The Personal Camera*, 3.
28 Corrigan, *The Essay Film: From Montaigne, after Marker*, 6.
29 Fuss, *The Sense of an Interior*, 145.
30 Corrigan, *The Essay Film: From Montaigne, after Marker*, 73.
31 Interview with Anna Maria Norberg-Schulz, 7 September 2014.
32 'Under samtalen hadde Mies snakket ivrig, og slett ikke som et orakel, men i grei muntlig tale. Som andre mennesker (kanskje med unntagelse av nordmennene!) understreker han ordenen med håndbevegelser og et lite smil. Ennå var det mange ting å spørre om og Mies foreslo å fortsette samtalen hjemme hos seg selv over en drink. Mies bor i en gammeldags (!) leilighet. Den store stuen har helt hvite vegger og møblene er enkle, kubiske og sorte. På veggen gløder det mystisk i store Klee-bilder. Hushjelpen som serverer, plasserer tingene på det lave kinesiske bordet så omhyggelig som om hun skulle være i ferd med å løse planen i et Mies-hus' My translation of Christian Norberg-Schulz, 'Samtaler med Mies', in *Et sted å være: essays og artikler*, 215–20 (Oslo: Gyldendahl Norsk Forlag, 1986) 219.
33 Bruno, *Atlas of Emotion*, 410.
34 'I lokalmiljøet er han ukjent. Ute i verden er han lovprist'. My translation unknown author, in *Aftenposten*, 20 May 1994, 8. Kept in: Diverse uregistrerte fra den sorte pulten. The Architectural Collections. The National Museum of Art, Architecture and Design.
35 Ellefsen, 'Works and Environments', 118.
36 Jan Carlsen, 'Den standhaftige arkitekturfilosof: en fagbiografisk skisse', in *Christian Norberg-Schulz: Et festskrift til 70års dagen*, eds Guttorm Fløistad, Ketil Moe and Thomas Thiis-Evensen, 20–1 (Oslo: Norsk akitekturforlag, 1999).
37 Norberg-Schulz himself described *Mellom jord og himmel* as the populist version of *Genius Loci*. Christian Norberg-Schulz, 'Et faglig testamente', in *Øye og hånd: essays og artikler: ny rekke*, ed. Gordon Hølmebakk (Oslo: Gyldendal, 1997), 86.
38 Guttorm Fløistad (philosopher and editor of *Tankekors*), Interview 22 May 2013.
39 Anne Marit Vagstein, 'Helhetens navn er et sted', in *Christian Norberg-Schulz: Et festskrift på 70års dagen*, eds Guttorm Fløistad, Ketil Moe and Thomas Thiis-Evensen, 138 (Oslo: Norsk arkitektforlag, 1996).
40 Ellefsen, 'Works and Environments', 147.
41 Ibid., 128.
42 *Byggekunst*, 3:90 (1961). Quoted in Ellefsen, 'Works and Environments', 131.
43 Ellefsen, 'Works and Environments', 131.
44 Ibid.

45 'Det bør være en oppgave for NRK å la allmenheten få kjennskap til hva våre få internasjonalt anerkjente tenkere star for ... Christian Norberg-Schulz har skarpere enn noen annen forklart stedets avgjørende betydning og advart mot det som nå skjer i våre omgivelser. I et TV-program om Norberg-Schulz vil det derfor kunne gi en forståelse av stedet, og underbygge den uro som svært mange føler ved at vår omverden rives istykker'. Grønvold, undated. 'Christian Norberg-Schulz: Vår største humanistiske tenker idag'. Box: Korrespondanse, klipp og gannet diverse. The Norberg-Schulz Archive, the Architectural Collections, the National Museum of Art, Architecture and Design, Oslo.

46 In UK this would be first floor, as what is considered ground floor in the UK would be first floor in Norway.

47 'Byggeskikk har med mange ting å gjøre, former, farger og materialer. Fra gammelt av bygget vi stort sett alt i tre, men i våre dager har det kommet igjen veldig mange nye muligheter, og det er jo ikke så lett å bruke disse på en måte som passer til stedet. Svært ofte blandes materialene hulter i bulter. I dette huset har vi for eksempel en tre-vegg oppe i annen etasje, også har vi metall-vinduer, aluminium er det egentlig, selv om det ikke ser ut som aluminium. Også har vi disse veggene her! På avstand så lurer man på, hva er vel dette for et materiale? Jeg trodde kanskje det var plast da jeg så det på avstand, også kommer jeg borttil også ser jeg at det faktisk er marmor! Og det jo egentlig litt flott, men spørsmålet er om marmor hører hjemme i Seljord?' My translation of Helgesen, *Livet finner sted*, 17:51–18:52.

48 Norberg-Schulz 'Genius Loci: et opprinnelsens begrep', 102.

49 Ibsen, *When We Dead Awaken*, 18.

50 Interview with Anna Maria Norberg-Schulz, 7 September 2014.

Window 10

1 Dillon, *Essayism*, 12.

2 Dillon, *Essayism*, 11.

3 Rowan Wilken, 'The Critical Reception of Christian Norberg-Schulz's Writings on Heidegger and Place'.

4 Paolo Portoghesi, 'Preface', in *Architecture: Meaning and Place: Selected Essays*, ed. Christian Norberg-Schulz, 7–8 (Milano: Electa editrice, 1988).

5 Rascaroli, *How the Essay Film Thinks*, 187–8.

6 Penelope Haralambidou, 'The Architectural Essay Film', *Arq: Architectural Research Quarterly* 19:3 (September 2015): 234–48.

7 Portoghesi, 'To Christian: From Paolo Portoghesi'.

INDEX

Page numbers followed with "n" refer to endnotes.

1980 Venice Architectural
    Biennale   111–13, 121

acousmêtre   11, 19, 23
Adorno, Theodor   7
Alexandrov, Grigori   25
antagonistic forces   55, 65,
    181 n.39
architecture   34, 37, 120–1, 161
    phenomenology of   5, 56, 57,
    119–20
Arendt, Hannah   93
Arneberg, Arnstein   152
Arnheim, Rudolf   3
Atlas of Emotion (2002, Bruno)   12,
    51, 60, 63, 150
Auret, Hendrik Andries   4–6, 39

'Båntjern' (1986)   92, 93
Baroque architecture   97–8
Barthes, Roland   70
Basel   12, 69, 76, 100
Baudrillard, Jean   101
being-in-the-world   3, 36, 38, 56, 65,
    118, 119, 129, 131, 132
Benjamin, Walter   7, 20
Bernini, Gian Lorenzo   97, 99–101, 107
Between Earth and Sky   151
beweglichen Dasein   55, 131, 132
Bezug   117, 118, 128–9, 132
blut und boden   5, 78, 79
Bollnow, Otto   116–20, 126–9, 131, 134
Braidotti, Rosi   133
Bruno, Giuliana   50–1, 58–60, 63,
    65, 150
Burgin, Victor   70, 71, 74–5

Calcata   13–14, 110, 112
Calcata (2017, Andersen)   109, 111,
    134, 135
Calle, Sophie   13, 101–2
campagna   98–9
Campari   13, 59, 97, 99–101
Campari, Gaspare   97
Campari-moment   13, 96–107, 120
I: Campari-Moment (2014,
    Andersen)   96, 103
II: Campari-Moment (2016,
    Andersen)   96, 103
Carlsen, Jan   69
Catling, Jo   55
Chion, Michel   25
    acousmêtre   19, 23
Colomina, Beatriz   142
Cooper, Justine   12, 62–3
Corrigan, Timothy   8, 58, 75–6, 146
critical spatial practice   6, 23

Daguerréotypes (1976, Varda)   11, 42, 44
Dasein   3, 117, 118, 129, 130, 132
The Death of the Chemist (2016,
    Andersen)   9, 15, 18, 22, 24, 26,
    29, 103, 155, 157
Deleuze, Gilles   23
Derrida, Jacques   88–90
de Saeger, Raf   116
Dickinson, Emily   100
Dillon, Brian   7, 159
Doane, Mary Anne   22
Donohue, Robyn   62
Duino Elegien (*Duino Elegies*, 1922,
    Rilke)   55, 111, 115–17, 119
Düsseldorf   75

INDEX

Ebneter, Curdin   54–5, 131, 181 n.39
Eisenstein, Sergei   25
Ekeberg   139
E la nave va (and the Ship Sails On, 1983, Fellini)   11, 24, 26
Ellefsen, Karl Otto   150, 151
enchanted windows   104
'The Essay as Form' (1984, Adorno)   7
the essay film   8, 23, 161
The essay form   6–9, 161
essayism   7
Essayism (2017, Dillon)   159

Farias, Victor   78
Farnsworth, Edith   74–5, 140–2
Farnsworth House (1945–51)   21, 74–5, 140–2
Fehn, Sverre   121
Feidler, Leslie   7
Fellini, Federico   24, 26, 59
feminism   91, 144
Fløistad, Guttorm   118, 151
Fontana dei Quattro Fiumi (1651)   97
forre   98–9
frame   35, 36
Freud, Sigmund   72–3, 88–9, 100
Freud on Holiday (2006, Kivland)   12, 60, 72
Friedberg, Anne   34
Friedman, Alice T.   15, 141, 142
Fülleborn, Ulrich   118, 130, 194 n.12
Fuss, Diana   34–5, 100, 105, 148

Gamle Kjemi (1910)   9, 18, 19, 155, 157
genius loci   3, 13, 14, 28, 29, 36, 39, 51, 55–7, 78, 97, 99, 107, 131, 132, 134, 151, 153, 154
Genius Loci: Towards a Phenomenology of Architecture (1980, Norberg-Schulz)   3, 4, 9, 11, 27, 31, 32, 36, 39, 40, 51, 56, 77, 98, 107, 113–15, 119, 120, 132, 133, 151, 153
Gérard, Blanchard   25

Gestalt-Psychology   3
The Gleaners and I (2000, Varda)   90–1, 147, 148
Gløshaugen   9
Görner, Rüdiger   54, 117
Grønvold, Ulf   51, 60, 152
Guardini, Romano   116, 117, 119, 132, 134

Haddad, Eli   5
Hamburg   12, 69–73, 77, 100
hand gestures   149–50
Hardwick, Elizabeth   7
Heidegger, Martin   3–5, 36–40, 56, 77–9, 111, 113, 117, 119, 132, 134
   fourfold concept   36–7, 56–7
   keyword search for   116
   notion of *Dasein*   3, 118
   notion of language   119–20
   phenomenology   5, 36–8, 56, 93, 106, 118
Helgesen, Sven-Erik   51–2, 60, 61
Heynen, Hilde   78–9, 132
Hinckley, John W. Jr.   101
history/historiography   76–7
Hitler   75, 78
Hölderlin, Friedrich   38–9, 111
Hølmebakk, Gordon   151
Hultzsch, Anne   53–4
Husserl, Edmund   56
Hvattum, Mari   28, 76

Ibsen, Henrik   139, 154
Ince, Kate   90
Intentions in Architecture (1963, Norberg-Schulz)   150–1
involuntary memories   74
Italy   50–61, 65, 86, 131, 132, 134

James, William   105
The Jazz Singer (1927, Crosland)   25
Jencks, Charles   112
Jenkins, Keith   24, 77
Journey to Italy (2016, Andersen)   12, 49, 60

Kafka, Franz 133
Keller, Helen 13, 34–5, 100, 103–7, 120, 148
Kivland, Sharon 60, 72–3
Klossowska, Balladine 126–8
Koepnick, Lutz 21, 34, 103, 131, 161
Korsmo, Arne 27, 140–1
Kramer, Andreas 117, 118
Kramer, Emily 43

language 119–20
Lauvland, Gro 93
Le Corbusier 140, 142
Leeder, Karen 128
Les Fenêtres (1927, Rilke) 14, 41, 103, 117–19, 123–35, 159
Livet finner sted (1992, Helgesen) 1–2, 5, 8, 28, 52, 57–9, 61, 68, 76, 107, 139, 152, 154, 159
Loewenthal, David 72
L'Orange, Else 13, 81, 82, 86, 87, 89, 103
L'Orange, Hans Petter 84–6
Lütticken, Sven 73

magnetic resonance imaging (MRI) 12, 49, 60–3, 65
Manglano-Ovalle, Iñigo 21–2
Merleau-Ponty, Maurice 105
Mies van der Rohe, Ludwig 70–1, 139–42, 149–50
Minnesjord (1991, Norberg-Schulz) 114
The Miracle Worker (1962, Penn) 104–5
mobility 41, 43, 79, 131–3
modern architecture 142
Montaigne, Michel de 7
MRI. *See* magnetic resonance imaging (MRI)
Municipality of Rome 84, 85
Muzot 125, 127–8
My Shack of Cinema (1968–2013, Varda) 31, 43–4

Nazi ideology 78–9, 132
Nazi Party 78, 79
Nightlands: Nordic Building (1997, Norberg-Schulz) 27

nomadism 133
Norberg-Schulz, Anna Maria 27, 43, 53, 57, 68, 70, 133, 139, 142–4, 149, 154
Norberg-Schulz, Christian 1–2, 27–9, 32–3, 36–7, 39–40, 42–3, 51, 83–9, 91–3, 96, 100–1, 105–7, 110, 113–14, 131–4, 149–54, 158
  architectural theory 114
  articles 193 n.72
  Baroque architecture 98
  Campari-moment 13, 100, 107, 120
  'Den poetiske forståelsesform' (1996) 114
  domestic reality 42
  drawings 121–2
  as flying Norwegian 42, 52, 57, 131, 139, 162
  forre and *campagna* landscape 98–9
  Genius Loci 3–5
  Intentions in Architecture (1963) 150–1
  library 115–16, 119
  life and work 1–2, 5, 6, 8–9, 15, 28, 51, 132, 157, 159, 161
  'Map of Norway' 57–8
  Minnesjord (1991) 114
  Nightlands: Nordic Building (1997) 27
  phenomenology of architecture 5, 56, 117, 119, 120
  Portoghesi and 112
  returned to Norway 139, 150
  Rilke and 116
  theory of architecture 3
  theory of place 3–6, 40, 51, 57, 77, 98, 114, 120, 131
  use of poetry in architectural thinking 114–15
Norberg-Schulz, Christian Wilhelm 18–19
Norberg-Schulz, Elizabeth 27
Norway 51, 53, 57–8, 60–1, 65, 69, 132, 134
The Norwegian Institute in Rome 13, 81–6, 89

The Norwegian Institute in Rome (2016, Andersen)   81, 86–7, 103
Norwegians love nature   93
NRK (The Norwegian Broadcasting Corporation)   1, 51, 61–2, 152
NTNU (Norwegian University of Science and Technology)   9, 18, 155, 158
Nymoen, Anne Lie   68

Oslo   11, 14–15, 32, 40, 51–2, 57–8, 61–2, 68–70, 92, 113, 121, 139, 142–4, 154, 160
Østfold   12, 52, 61, 69
Otero-Pailos, Jorge   77–8, 85

Pallesen, Stig   18, 157
pancarte   88–90
past and history   24, 77
Pérez-Gómez, Alberto   5, 92–3
Perricone, Joseph   25
Phelan, Peggy   13, 101
phenomenology   4, 114, 117–19, 132
  of architecture   5, 56–7, 119, 120
  defined   57
  Heidegger's   5, 36–8, 56, 93, 106, 118
Photograph, defined   70
Piaget, Jean   3
Piazza Navona   13, 56–7, 61, 96–101, 103, 120, 154, 157
Planetveien 10–14 (1952–55)   14, 27, 139–44, 154
Plato   88
poetry/poem   114
polyglot   133
Portoghesi, Paolo   13–14, 42, 52–3, 56, 58, 109–12, 116, 121–2, 124, 125, 134, 160, 162
positive reflexive skepticism   24
The Postcards: From Socrates to Freud and Beyond (1987, Derrida)   13, 88
postmodern architecture   112, 113, 142
Poulsson, Magnus   152
Proust, Marcel   100
Prytz-Kittelsen, Grete   140, 143

Ragazza in Treno (*Girl on the Train*, 1984, Fellini)   59
Rainaldi, Girolamo   97
Rainer Maria Rilke Foundation   127
Ranke, Leopold von   73, 76
RAPT I (1998, Cooper)   62, 65
RAPT II (1998, Cooper)   62
Rascaroli, Laura   8, 23, 161
re-enactment   73–4, 100, 101
Rendell, Jane   6, 22–3, 35–6, 46, 54, 65, 159–60
Richter, Hans   8
Rilke (1951, Bollnow)   117, 119
Rilke, Rainer Maria   8, 11, 13–14, 21, 40–2, 54, 65, 103, 109, 111, 115–18, 120–2, 125–35, 159, 160, 181 n.39, 194 n.12
  Duino Elegien (*Duino Elegies*, 1922)   55, 111, 115–17, 119
  Fensterblick   41–2, 65, 160
  Italian journey   54–5
  keyword search for   115–16
  Les Fenêtres (1927)   14, 41, 103, 117–19, 123–35, 159
  notion of *Bezug*   117, 118, 132
  phenomenology and   117–19
  writing in French   125–6
Ris   11, 32, 39, 40, 47, 115, 154
Rome   12–13, 53, 55–6, 58, 81, 98–100, 131, 143, 159
Röntgen, Bertha   144
Rosselini, Roberto   50

Sandford, John   117
Schivelbusch, Wolfgang   59
Schneider, Rebecca   73–4
Schreyach, Michael   35
Scorcese, Martin   101
Scully, Vincent   112
self-reflective criticism   35
Sharr, Adam   38, 39
Sierre   14, 125–7, 134
silent film   26
The Singing Fool (1929, Bacon)   26
site-writing   23
Slemdal   154
Socrates   88
Solnit, Rebecca   54

sound and image   21–9, 52, 65, 103, 106, 161
sound film   26
The Spirit of the Place   27, 36, 39, 51, 57, 61, 78, 98, 132
Sterten, Raymond   18
The Story of My Life (1903, Keller)   103–5
Suite Venitienne (1980, Calle)   13, 101
Szacka, Léa-Catherine   113

Tang, Ji-Ming   14, 40–1, 117, 118, 128–31, 133
Taxi-Driver (1976, Scorcese)   101
Three Windows on Europe: September 1945 (2018, Andersen)   12, 68, 76
Torp, Hjalmar   84, 85
Tostrup, Elisabeth   141
Tout(e) Varda (2012)   43, 44
travelling   54, 57, 60
   by train   59, 75
Trondheim   9, 11, 15, 19, 25, 57–8, 60, 150, 157, 159–60
Trondheim Academy of Fine Arts   158–9
tufa-valley   97

Unterwegs zur Sprache (On the Way to Language, 1959, Heidegger)   119–20

Vagstein, Anne Marit   151

Valle Giulia   83, 84, 93
van Dijck, José   144
Varda, Agnés   42–4, 47, 90–1, 147–8
   Daguerréotypes (1976)   11, 42, 44
   The Gleaners and I (2000)   90–1, 147, 148
   My Shack of Cinema (1968–2013)   31, 43–4
Verga   85
Vesaas, Tarjei   115
Viaggio in Italia (Journey to Italy, 1954, Rossilini)   50
Vilain, Robert   128
Viterbo   13
vococentricm   23

walking   54
water   99, 100, 103–7
Wilken, Rowan   5–6, 92, 159
window
   as a frame for the human figure   121–2
   in Nordic countries   143
   of the train   59
The Window and I (2015, Andersen)   14, 137, 144, 146, 147
Windows: 'My Shack of Cinema' (2015, Andersen)   11, 31, 47
World War II   68–72, 75–9

X-ray   61–3, 142, 144, 147

Zürich   52, 69, 131

www.ingramcontent.com/pod-product-compliance
Lightning Source LLC
Chambersburg PA
CBHW070322230426
43663CB00011B/2195